D1531985

www.wadsworth.com

www.wadsworth.com is the World Wide Web
site for Thomson Wadsworth and is your direct
source to dozens of online resources.

At www.wadsworth.com you can find out
about supplements, demonstration software,
and student resources. You can also send email
to many of our authors and preview new
publications and exciting new technologies.

www.wadsworth.com
Changing the way the world learns®

Diversity Dynamics in the Workplace

Kecia M. Thomas
University of Georgia

THOMSON
TM
WADSWORTH

AUSTRALIA • CANADA • MEXICO • SINGAPORE • SPAIN • UNITED KINGDOM • UNITED STATES

THOMSON

★ ™

WADSWORTH

Acquisitions Editor: Michele Sordi
Editorial Assistant: Chelsea Junget
Technology Project Manager: Eric Fortier
Marketing Manager: Chris Caldeira
Marketing Assistant: Laurel Anderson
Advertising Project Manager: Tami Strang
Project Manager, Editorial Production:
 Candace Chen
Art Director: Vernon Boes
Print Buyer: Rebecca Cross

Permissions Editor: Stephanie Lee
Production Service: Vicki Moran,
 Publishing Support Services
Photo Researcher: Stephen Forsling
Copy Editor: Diane Ersepke
Cover Designer: Ross Carron
Cover Image: © Chad Baker/Ryan McVay;
 Getty Images
Cover/Text Printer: Webcom
Compositor: Stratford Publishing Services

For more information about our
products,
contact us at:
Thomson Learning Academic Resource
Center
1-800-423-0563
For permission to use material from this
text or product, submit a request online
at http://www.thomsonrights.com.
Any additional questions about
permissions can be submitted by email
to thomsonrights@thomson.com.

Thomson Wadsworth
10 Davis Drive
Belmont, CA 94002-3098
USA

Asia
Thomson Learning
5 Shenton Way #01-01
UIC Building
Singapore 068808

Australia/New Zealand
Thomson Learning
102 Dodds Street
Southbank, Victoria 3006
Australia

Canada
Nelson
1120 Birchmount Road
Toronto, Ontario M1K 5G4
Canada

Europe/Middle East/Africa
Thomson Learning
High Holborn House
50/51 Bedford Row
London WC1R 4LR

Library of Congress Control Number: 2004108374
ISBN 0-15-506920-9

This book is dedicated to Chad and Jordan so that they may each have fulfilling and challenging careers in healthy and inclusive workplaces.

Preface

Being a researcher and faculty member is not as easy as it may appear. As a faculty member you sometimes get used to negative feedback. Not everyone will agree with your teaching style or even the topics that you choose to teach (especially when they relate to diversity). Yet there are many successes as well. Students comment that your class was the best ever taken and at times manuscripts get published with little pain involved. Even a grant will get funded once in awhile. But of course, the negative feedback we receive always seems to outweigh all of the successes in life.

I frequently fall into that trap. I take my wins for granted and instead lament over my losses. Until I hear those words, "Dr. Thomas, your work gave me the motivation to pursue diversity as my program of research." I have heard this sentiment surprisingly often during the last 11 years yet it always catches me off guard. I am often overwhelmed by the extent to which a few journal articles or book chapters can speak to an anxious graduate student or young faculty member who is not yet sure whether it will be "okay" to engage in diversity research, and if this choice will have negative short- and long-term career consequences. My hope is that *Diversity Dynamics* will help support the interests of those students, and even faculty (and even mid- and late-career faculty), who just need a little motivation and encouragement to announce to their colleagues and to the world that they believe these issues are important and worthy of study if we truly want to have a world and workplaces that embrace fairness and excellence.

In addition to reviewing literature across disciplinary boundaries to help us better understand the experiences of minority workers (broadly defined),

I've offered Diversity Learning Points that expand a topic touched upon or focus our attention on narrow issues and topics that are emerging in the scholarly literature. Examples include, "Self-Fulfilling Prophecies in Job Interviews" (Chapter 6) and "Understanding Privilege" (Chapter 7). Diversity in Practice sections extend the conversation of each chapter to the real world and provide the student with examples of how organizations effectively manage diversity as a valuable resource. Examples of Diversity in Practice material include, "Can We Talk?" sessions at Kodak (Chapter 10) and an identification and description of professional associations, such as Catalyst and the Human Rights Campaign, that support the development of diverse workplaces (Chapter 5). Diversity Cases also provide the reader with descriptions of the diversity dynamics encountered by minority employees such as "Denice's Dilemma" (Chapter 5) and "Melanie: Not Par for the Course" (Chapter 4).

In *Diversity Dynamics* I do not intend nor do I try to cover all of the research in organizational behavior or industrial psychology. This is not an I/O text but rather an examination of the workplace from a diversity perspective. My goal is to open the reader to different avenues of thinking about important areas of organizational life. This book was written to express and value the perspectives and realities of women, people of color, and gay and lesbian workers so that their experiences are primary rather than an afterthought. Taking this unique perspective of organizational life will, I hope, encourage you to think differently about organizations and to ask new questions in your own research and practice.

ACKNOWLEDGMENTS

I am greatly indebted to the many friends, colleagues, students, and family members who supported my work on this effort. Lisa Hensley, my editor at the former Harcourt Brace College Publishing is the person who encouraged that this book be written. Michele Sordi, my incredible editor at Thomson Wadsworth (which acquired Harcourt) made sure it was completed. Thank you Lisa and Michele for your support and confidence in me during this process.

I would like to thank the following reviewers for providing feedback: Diana Stuber-McEwen, Friends University; Mark Frame, University of Texas, Arlington; Nancy Da Silva, San Jose State University; Todd Thorsteinson, University of Idaho; Bill Attenweiler, Northern Kentucky University; Michael Zickar, Bowling Green State University; Edward Levine, University of South Florida; and Lynn McFarland, George Mason University.

A number of my students assisted me directly and indirectly. The late Dr. Dan Mack cowrote Chapter 2, Dr. Kimberly Williams also helped to write Chapter 8, and finally soon-to-be Dr. Harriet Landau cowrote Chapters 3 and 6. I greatly appreciate your confidence in this project and your willingness to contribute to it. Drs. Douglas Johnson, Lesley Perkins, Amy Montagliani, and Donna Chrobot-Mason were always willing to offer feedback and encouragement. Jimmy Davis, Corey Munoz, and Wendy Reynolds Dobbs were also frequently waiting in the background willing to lend a helping hand.

Finally I am enormously grateful to my family. My husband Darren Rhym never wavered in his support of me taking on this challenge. He frequently made time for me to write without interruption while also knowing when it was time for all of us to escape from my work. Our young children, Chad and Jordan, consistently helped me to maintain perspective. Throughout this venture they also helped me to celebrate the completion of every chapter and the attainment of every goal along the way. It would have been impossible for me to finish this book without the love, support, and encouragement you three have provided. You are my best friends. Thank you.

Brief Contents

Contents

CHAPTER 7
Conflict, Perceptions of Justice, Privilege, and Diversity   111

CHAPTER 8
Stressors in a Diverse Workplace   129

CHAPTER 9

The Leadership–Diversity Dynamic: Breaking Barriers and Developing Multicultural Leaders   148

CHAPTER 10

Diversity Orientations: Organizations   165

CHAPTER **11**
Diversity Orientations: Individuals   180

CHAPTER **12**
Conclusion: Strategies for Success   195

About the Author

Kecia M. Thomas, Ph.D., is an associate professor at the University of Georgia where she has a joint appointment in the Departments of Psychology and African American Studies. She is also the coordinator for graduate education in the Department of Psychology. Her research on the psychology of workplace diversity spans the areas of recruitment, leadership, and career development. This work has been widely published in outlets such as the *Journal of Applied Psychology, Journal of Applied Social Psychology, Journal of Psychology and Marketing, Journal of Career Development, Journal of Black Psychology, Leadership Quarterly,* and *Journal of Business and Psychology* as well as in numerous edited volumes. She is an active member of both the Society for Industrial–Organizational Psychology and the Gender and Diversity in Organizations Division of the Academy of Management and has held positions of leadership in both organizations that advanced the importance of diversity. In addition Dr. Thomas is frequently called upon by companies such as BellSouth, the American Cancer Society, and Corning Glass to provide consulting services.

Diversity and the Workplace

CHAPTER 1

Dynamic Worlds

Diversity issues are everywhere; just look around. They are especially visible in our organizations. Just read the local headlines: "Hangmen nooses threaten climate for diversity at Southern Company," "Faking Diversity: Minority Students Airbrushed into U. of Idaho Photo," "Presidential Candidate Courts Americans with Disabilities," "Older Workers Fight for their Right to Work."

It is no wonder that diversity issues are constantly in the news. In the early 1990s researchers at the Hudson Institute published their "Workforce 2000" report (Johnston & Packer, 1987), which suggested that the U.S. population and subsequently the workforce would become increasingly more diverse. By the year 2000, demographers realized that the future was now. In fact, Offermann and Phan (2002) discuss how an organization near their home university employs over 800 employees who speak at least 36 languages and where 65% are foreign-born!

Current census projections for the year 2050 are that ethnic minorities will account for *at least* 47% of the U.S. population. Specifically it is expected that by 2013 Hispanics will surpass African Americans in order to become the second-largest U.S. racial group. In fact, as I write this chapter the current estimation is that Latinos are already the largest ethnic minority group in the United States. Asians and Pacific Islanders are actually the fastest-growing segment of the population. As "Workforce 2000" predicted, women, minorities and people with disabilities will account for the majority of the new entrants into the workforce. Writers refer to these changes as the "graying of the workforce," "the feminization of the workforce," and "the changing complexion of the workforce" (Sue, Parham, & Santiago, 1998).

Courtesy NASA

Diversity is a global issue

Organizations that want to remain competitive in today's environment must be knowledgeable about the diversity that is present in their workforce, in the overall labor force, and in the marketplace if they hope to have a viable business. Those leading modern organizations are facing many new challenges and opportunities that our growing national diversity presents. These new challenges include attempting to understand the differences between how work used to be done and how it will likely change in an increasingly diverse environment. Other challenges include attempting to understand the legal, ethical, and mundane issues that come with employing a more diverse workforce comprised of immigrants, racial and ethnic minorities, women, older workers, sexual minorities, and the disabled. Along with these challenges there are many opportunities as well, such as providing services, products, and information to a new segment of the market (see Diversity Learning Point 1.1). For example, by 2007 the buying power of African Americans, Asians, and Native Americans will be more than triple its level in 1990 and will total almost $1.4 trillion (Selig Center for Economic Growth, 2002). Multicultural workplaces can also offer the chance to incorporate new perspectives, ideas, and ways of working that employees from a variety of backgrounds may offer. Several studies have found a linkage between diversity in work teams and creativity and innovation (Cox & Beale, 1997). For example, McLeod, Lobel, and Cox (1996) examined the quantity and quality of marketing ideas generated by an ethnically diverse and an ethnically homogeneous team. Although no differences were found in the quantity of ideas generated, the diverse team's ideas were evaluated as 11%

Diversity Learning Point 1.1	**U.S. Buying Power Statistics by Race, 1990, 2000, 2002, 2007**			
	Buying Power (billions of dollars)			
	1990	**2000**	**2002**	**2007**
Total	4,277.2	7,025.3	7,632.6	9,870.1
White	3,738.6	5,800.0	6,252.5	7,910.3
Black	316.5	588.7	645.9	852.8
American Indian	19.3	36.4	40.8	57.3
Asian	117.6	254.6	296.4	454.9
Other	85.2	197.5	234.3	378.8
Multiracial	NA	148.1	162.8	216.0

Adapted from Table 1, "The Multicultural Economy 2002: Minority Buying Power in the New Century," *Georgia Business and Economic Conditions*, Vol. 62, No. 2 (2002): 10, Selig Center for Economic Growth, Terry College of Business, The University of Georgia, found at http://www.selig.uga.edu/forecast/GBEC/GBEC022Q.pdf. Reprinted by permission.

higher than the homogeneous teams on the feasibility and overall effectiveness of their ideas.

The goal, then, of organizational scholars, such as those who are trained in industrial/organizational psychology (I/O), human resource development (HRD), human resources (HR), and organizational development (OD), is to maximize the beneficial aspects of diversity for organizations and for individuals while minimizing and perhaps preventing any negative challenges of that same diversity. Researchers and practitioners trained in the organizational sciences have a unique background that provides them with the knowledge, skills, and abilities to accomplish this goal.

THE STUDY OF WORK AND ORGANIZATIONS

I/O psychologists, OD consultants, and those trained in HR work in a variety of settings such as large organizations, multinational and local consulting firms, colleges and universities, as well as for nonprofit agencies and local, state, and federal government. Regardless of where they work, they are generally charged with improving individual, group, and/or organizational functioning. They apply their knowledge of psychology and behavioral science to the problems and challenges that arise in organizations.

Just as these practitioners work in a variety of settings, they also specialize in a variety of areas, including selection and placement, training and development, organizational development, performance measurement, and quality of work life. If you think about this list closely, you'll recognize that issues surrounding diversity impact every area. Let's consider them one by one:

Figure 1.1 | Increasing Diversity

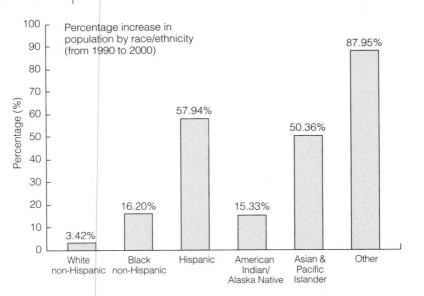

From Business–Higher Education Forum (2002), *Percentage increase in population by race/ethnicity.* Chart 1, "Investing in people: Developing all of America's talent on campus and in the workplace." Washington, DC: Business–Higher Education Forum. Reprinted by permission.

- **Selection and placement.** Those specializing in selection (a popular area of study for I/O and HR folks) are concerned with how to best select and place individuals into organizational positions. Often when we think of selection we think of testing, assessment centers, and interviewing. A major issue for these practitioners is the question of fairness. Much of their research and thought must go into selecting people for available jobs without introducing any sort of bias (e.g., due to issues such as race, gender, or age) into the selection and placement process. This is also the area of practice that is most tightly linked to our legal system. Decisions in high-profile court cases and government policy are in part shaped by the work of organizational researchers, especially those in I/O. However, the issues and questions studied in I/O are also in part shaped by the cases and public policy that comprise the legal landscape. That is, even though I/O can help guide the courts to ensure that organizations select and promote their personnel in the fairest manner possible, there are situations in which the recommendations that I/O practitioners offer to their clients will be influenced by court rulings.

- **Training and development.** Those working in training and development are concerned with preparing and developing worker talent as well as helping workers to plan careers. Training and development are important and popular areas of study for both those in I/O as well as those in HRD. From a diversity

Figure 1.2 | Numeric Growth in Labor Force by Race, Projected 2002–12

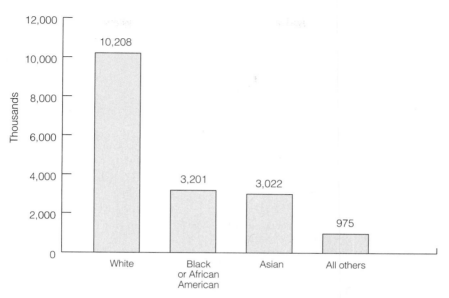

The Hispanic/Latino population is not taken into account in this figure examining *racial* projections. In regards to their ethnicity projections, numeric growh in labor force by ethnic origin for 2002–2012 is 5,843 for Hispanic/Latino and 11,562 for non-Hispanic/Latinos. Data and figure from the *Occupational Outlook Quarterly,* Winter 2003–2004.

perspective this area of study must consider differences in the opportunities for training and development that may exist for members of different demographic groups and the subsequent impact of the lack of developmental opportunities for career development. Other areas of concern include how best to train and prepare workers for jobs and careers given cultural, demographic, and developmental differences.

   • **Organizational development.** Those working in OD have the very broad task of improving an organization through understanding how its structure, technology, culture, and strategy can impede or facilitate its own success. Those working in OD can spend their time working at the individual, group, or organizational level. Their time and energy are spent on understanding and diagnosing organizational problems, developing a plan for resolving those problems, implementing plans that are based upon previously conducted and published research, and then evaluating the outcome. For the diversity scholar, the issue of diversity may actually be the focus of the diagnosis. Topics that those in this area would consider are: What is the climate for diversity in this organization? Does the climate for diversity hinder individual as well as organizational effectiveness? How can this climate be changed? Is the culture of the organization one that values its members' diversity?

Figure 1.3 | Labor Force Share by Race, Projected 2012

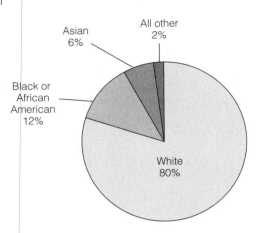

The Hispanic/Latino population is not taken into account in this figure examining *racial* projections. Labor force share by ethnic origin projected for 2012 is 15% for Hispanic/Latino and 85% for non-Hispanic/Latinos. Data and figure from the *Occupational Outlook Quarterly,* Winter 2003–2004.

- **Performance measurement.** Like selection and placement, those working in performance measurement at the individual level are largely concerned with fairness since promotions and future placements in the organization often depend in large part upon these ratings. Therefore those working in this field are also concerned with the extent to which personal beliefs and biases may contaminate the performance measurement process.

- **Quality of work life.** Simply put, those working in this area strive to make individuals' work lives more productive, more satisfying, and more meaningful. Issues surrounding diversity arise when work satisfaction is accomplished differently for different people. Consider the meaning of work satisfaction for a retiree working part-time, a young mother working full-time, a disabled worker who telecommutes to work, and a middle-aged male with a master's in business administration. It isn't unreasonable to assume that these four individuals may be working for different reasons and seeking different things in their work lives. Organizations and HR professionals then have the formidable task of satisfying and motivating different types of groups simultaneously.

Part of the excitement of working in fields such as HR, HRD, OD, and I/O has to do with the many changes that organizations undergo as a result of the larger environmental context. The diversity of this context helps to make organizations dynamic.

THE DYNAMIC WORLD OF WORK

A Dynamic Economy

One of the most pressing issues organizations are facing today is the shift in the products they provide. In fact, modern organizations are more likely to provide services or information than *products* per se. The U.S. economy has undergone a major shift from a manufacturing-based economy to one that is more focused on the provision of services and information (Sue et al., 1998). Figure 1.4 demonstrates that the service industry will expect among the largest amounts of growth. Therefore, questions to which many organizations have to respond, regardless of the services and information they provide include, Is the service/information/product we provide relevant to an increasingly diverse market? Is the marketing strategy upon which this organization has relied effective in minority and other emerging markets? To what extent does the

Figure 1.4 | Percent Change in Total Employment, Projected 2002–2012

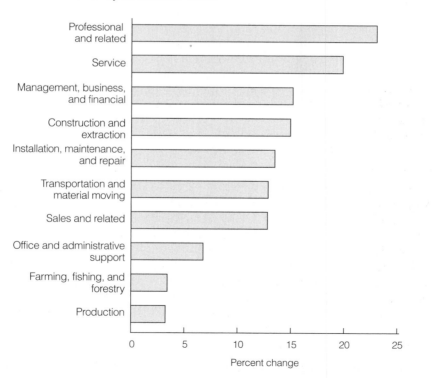

Adapted from the *Occupational Outlook Handbook 2004–2005* (http://www.bls.gov/oco/images/ocotjc06.gif).

growing minority consumer base present niche opportunities that this particular business is capable of capitalizing upon?

Dynamic Structures

Another dynamic issue related to the changing world of work has to do with organizational structure. When structure is discussed, it is normally thought of as how work gets done or how the organization is depicted in its organizational chart. The structure of an organization gives us insight into how the work gets divided, but it also reveals the relationships among people and the roles they occupy within the business. Structures within the American work context were previously and typically described as bureaucratic with many levels of management and a highly differentiated structure. That is, decisions were made by a select few people within the organization who occupied a great variety of roles, and the organization was highly complex in that there were many jobs that existed within a single organization.

The current trend for many organizations is to move toward a more decentralized, flat, and/or team-based structure (French & Bell, 1999). In these kinds of organizations workers become generalists rather than specialists. They work as a team rather than as individuals, thus eliminating the need for several hierarchies within a single organization. A new issue for organizations then becomes, with an increasingly diverse workforce, How can we ensure that people of a variety of different groups, cultures, and perspectives can in fact work effectively together? In addition, organizations must also be concerned with the extent to which working in a team or in other highly interdependent environments may not be an attractive work alternative for many workers due to their cultural norms.

Dynamic Contracts

Another issue facing many organizations, as well as the United States overall, is that of workers' expectations. Researchers studying the psychological contracts between workers and their employers investigate whether this contract is changing. Do workers who have been exposed to large-scale organizational changes (especially those who have been the *targets* of downsizing) have different expectations of their employers and subsequently their organizational lives?

The relationship between the workplace and worker has evolved. In the days of our parents and grandparents workers assumed that as long as they pulled their own weight and the organization prospered, worker effort and loyalty would be repaid with lifelong employment. However, the turbulent economy of the 1970s and the increase in organizational mergers and downsizings of the '80s and '90s resulted in unanticipated layoffs that subsequently changed the **psychological contract** (Rousseau, 1996) between workers and their employers. Psychological contracts are the "unwritten commitments made between workers an their employers" (p. 50). Through watching their family and friends lose jobs, many workers no longer expect their organization to be loyal to them and so worker loyalty has often been lessened in return. Today's workers are looking to an employer to provide them with résumé-building opportunities and skills that may be attractive to the *next* employer.

Furthermore, the terrorists' attacks of September 11, 2001, greatly impacted the economic market and thus the employment market as well. In booming economic times, jobs are plentiful, and job seekers have more opportunities to evaluate organizations in terms of their position and practices regarding diversity. However, in times of recession when jobs are scarce, job seekers may have greater tolerance for organizations whose diversity practices and policies are lacking. In fact, diversity itself may be perceived by organizations as less important when companies are merely fighting to stay viable. However, ignoring or mismanaging diversity may have an even greater negative impact on an organization's bottom line during times of economic struggle given workers' heightened sense of frustration and stress. In addition, workers are more likely to be "tuned in to" issues of equity and fairness during times in which companies are economically frustrated. Diversity therefore should *always* be high on any organization's strategic agenda.

Clearly the dynamic nature of organizations has implications for diverse workers. "Diversity" is likewise dynamic—it is discussed in different ways, it takes on different meanings in different arenas, it looks different from place to place, and it changes over time.

THE DYNAMIC NATURE OF DIVERSITY

Conceptual Ambiguity

The term *diversity* is used often and in many different ways (Dass & Parker, 1999). For most people the term is often used as a catchphrase to refer to a heterogeneous group or collective consisting of people who vary by gender, race, or age. Religion and sexuality also fall under the diversity umbrella. Others focus on diversity as a means of talking about membership characteristics of those in organizations, so that *diversity* encapsulates diversity in functional areas (e.g., sales, accounting, human resources), organizational levels (e.g., entry, middle management, top management), and work-related background variables (e.g., experience, type of education, degrees earned). Our diversity focus within this text will be those individual differences that are socially and historically significant and which have resulted in differences in power and privilege inside as well as outside of organizations; namely race, gender, and sexuality.

Shifting Metaphors

Our appreciation and understanding of *diversity* itself is dynamic. We can decipher the organic nature of diversity by simply identifying the shift in common metaphors to describe U.S. diversity. Whereas previous generations described the United States as a melting pot, today we talk about diversity as a stew, tossed salad, or mosaic. The evolution of these metaphors is significant in that this language reveals to us the change in how Americans are thinking, and perhaps dealing with, changing demographics.

The **melting pot metaphor** exemplifies past thinking that suggests those newly arrived immigrants and native-born people of color were expected to melt into a larger American identity. For many of these people, this metaphor came to symbolize societal pressure to assimilate to White American values, norms, and culture. The metaphor also symbolized the lack of American appreciation and value afforded to the native heritages of immigrants and people of color. The melting pot mindset came to symbolize Americans' perceptions and interpretations that (non-White) Americans were deficient, dysfunctional, and primitive especially when compared to (White) American culture.

Each of the new emerging metaphors depicts the country as being made of people who represent different racial groups, genders, and nationalities. Most importantly these metaphors also demonstrate that the diversity of the country's people is what makes it good! A salad of only lettuce is simply a bowl of lettuce. A mosaic of only one color is boring, and a stew with only potatoes really isn't a stew at all. These emerging metaphors signal that each of the unique heritages, backgrounds, cultures, and perspectives that we bring to our country, as well as our schools and workplaces, contribute to those institutions.

Regional Diversity

Diversity itself is also dynamic given that "diversity" is not the same everywhere, nor are the issues classified as diversity-related the same over time. That is, diversity is itself fluid. If we think about our entire country, we can easily see how diversity issues are not the same everywhere due to the different demographics of different regions. For example, in the Southeast, where I currently live, the diversity issues are mainly Black/White issues, although the growing influx of individuals of Mexican descent is changing this. Where I grew up in the Northeast, we see neighborhoods in cities that primarily represent ethnic groups. So that the Italian Americans live in one neighborhood, Black Americans in another, and Irish Americans in yet another. Diversity issues in the Southwest are primarily issues involving Whites and Latinos and to some extent those of Asian and Native American ancestry. Hawaii experiences diversity as issues between natives, Asian immigrants, and Whites.

Changing Times

Clearly, the diversity issues the United States dealt with during the post–Civil War Reconstruction are not the same as those we deal with today. In the times of Reconstruction the diversity issues mainly centered on the lack of free labor due to the emancipation of slaves, and the integration of these new slaves into the dwindling economy. Post–World War II issues included confronting the demands of women who were forced back into their traditional homemaker duties after having experienced the labor force during the war when their fathers, brothers, husbands, and sons were fighting it. In addition the passage of the Civil Rights, American with Disabilities, and Age Discrimination and Employment Acts has provided more opportunities for a diverse workforce although diversity resistance may persist. Today the diversity issues the country and organizations are facing reflect an increasingly diverse labor and consumer market, a turbulent economy and conflicting ideas about affirmative action, and increasing language diversity in and out of work. Pressures to accommodate the needs of sexual minorities are reflected in decisions regarding company benefit packages such as offering benefits to same sex partners.

INTRODUCTION TO DIVERSITY DYNAMICS

This book, unlike many others, is an examination of the workplace and organizations through the lens of a diversity scholar. Specifically, the goals of this text are to (1) help students understand the boundaries of current knowledge about organizations as it can be applied across various groups; (2) stimulate the development of new questions for research and practice related to diversity and organizational life; (3) help prepare students more fully for working in a world that is both diverse and dynamic. And so this book will not be a full coverage of the work and organization literature with a chapter on diversity stuck at the end of the book, or within a concluding chapter on "Emerging Issues in the Field." Instead, this text explores topics that cut across I/O, HR, OD, and HRD and which are also affected by diversity. My goal is to highlight issues and questions that are "ripe" for further thought and investigation by researchers, practitioners, and students who themselves are current and future workers.

Interdisciplinary Nature

Although the study of work and organizations has a lengthy history, relatively little attention has been paid to issues of race, gender, and sexuality within the world of work. Therefore, literature from areas such as women's studies, African American studies, international relations, and sociology is integrated into the discussions of each topic in order to enrich our knowledge of the relationships between diversity and organizational life.

Need for Greater Application

To assist with the learning of the material presented as well as to support an appreciation of how diversity dynamics occur in real life, each chapter contains supplemental material (e.g., cases, learning points, and examples of practice) in order to illustrate and expand upon the topic at hand. This material is drawn from a variety of sources. Some are descriptions of events that have taken place in organizations with which you are likely quite familiar, whereas others are accounts of a contributor's personal experiences. Again, the goal of these cases, learning points, and examples of practice is to make sure the reader understands that the issues presented in this text are neither superficial nor solely theoretical (although there is usually theoretical support for their existence). Real people within real organizations such as those for whom you or a relative may work, or even your university, encounter diversity-related dilemmas daily. Our best shot at resolving and preventing these dilemmas is to understand the dynamics that facilitate their occurrence. Therefore you'll find that this text values practitioner perspectives as much as those investigating diversity from the perspective of academe. Both perspectives are needed to more deeply comprehend the complex dynamics involved with diversity in the workplace.

OUTLINE OF THE TEXT

This text is organized in three parts that reflect individuals' experiences and relationships with organizations. The first section of the book pertains to the staffing environment and process. The chapters in this section underscore the point that organizations exist within a regulatory environment that they must navigate carefully. This regulatory environment shapes and impacts how companies address diversity issues. Likewise, individuals who are job seekers navigate through organizational environments throughout the recruitment process. Again, these individuals must be careful in how they interpret and respond to organizations during this period.

The second section of the text deals with issues faced by minority newcomers. Particular attention is paid to the experience of women, ethnic minorities, and gay men and lesbians in regard to their newcomer experience and career issues. The last section of the text revisits the issue of diversity intersections between organizations and their environments, and between people and organizations. The text concludes with recommendations based upon the lessons learned and successful strategies that are presented throughout the entire text. A chapter by chapter synopsis follows:

Chapter 2, Recruitment and Organizational Attraction, discusses how the growing diversity of the labor force challenges organizational scholars to reconsider how companies can best compete for and attract good workers. This is important since bringing in good workers is one way that organizations retain their competitive advantage. Organizational dynamics that interfere with diversity are outlined, as are strategies for overcoming those barriers.

Chapter 3, Diversity, Public Policy, and Organizational Decisions, covers legislation and court cases that are diversity related and which impact organizational efforts regarding diversity and decision making. Presentation of these laws and legal cases helps the reader to assess the evolving national climate for diversity. It also helps the reader to appreciate the challenges that diverse workers sometimes must confront.

Chapter 4, Socialization and the Newcomer Experience, covers the relationship between attempts to socialize and train new workers who as a group are increasingly diverse. This chapter covers contemporary theories of social-ization and training, and highlights those areas in which future research is needed to better engage in these functions with diverse employees.

Chapter 5, Career Development: Barriers and Strategies, discusses the unique issues that diverse workers encounter which can hinder their career de-velopment. Important topics such as mentoring and social networks are cov-ered to illustrate their importance to the career development of minority group members such as women and people of color.

Chapter 6, The Influence of Diversity on Group Dynamics and Outcomes, is important because, as previously mentioned, not only is the workforce more diverse but organizations are increasingly likely to use team-based structures inside the company. This means that people who belong to different groups and who are likely to have different expectations, backgrounds, and percep-tions will often work together. This chapter covers existing knowledge about how membership in a demographic group can influence work group dynamics as well as individual behavior and performance.

Chapter 7, Conflict, Perceptions of Justice, and Diversity, is a natural fol-low-up to chapter 6. Because of increasing diversity within work groups, con-flict may also escalate. This chapter discusses to what extent conflict can be constructive in an organization and how conflict can be managed to facilitate organizational effectiveness. A justice perspective is used to understand diver-sity-related conflict and to develop strategies for preventing and resolving such conflicts.

Chapter 8, Stressors in a Diverse Workplace, examines the extent to which stress, like conflict, can be either good or bad. In addition, the introduction of growing diversity in organizations may suggest that new sources of stress may emerge. For an increasingly diverse workforce, it may not be uncommon for sexual harassment, lack of mentoring and cultural role models, and affirmative action stigma to be stressors.

Chapter 9, The Leadership-Diversity Dynamic: Breaking Barriers and De-veloping Multicultural Leaders. Leadership is a popular area of study by orga-nizational researchers, and we have developed lots of propositions and theories about what leadership is and how to be effective at it. At times we have focused on the contingencies between leader behavior, the work being done, and the worker. We've also considered the influence of followers on the leaders who lead them, and leadership traits. This chapter takes a slightly different ap-proach to the topic of leadership. Primarily the goal of this chapter is to under-stand and prevent the glass ceiling as a barrier to leadership for ethnic minorities and women. Subsequently, a second focus of the chapter is to pre-sent different approaches for developing multicultural leaders who are able to help shatter the glass ceiling in their organization.

Chapter 10, Diversity Orientations—Organizations. This chapter high-lights different models of how organizations differ in regard to their diver-sity perspective and the impact of this perspective on the successes and failures of diversity initiatives. Lessons learned from these different models will be presented.

Diversity Case 1.1	A Case in the Dynamics of Diversity: Proctor and Gamble[1]

Diversity at Proctor and Gamble (P&G) has a long history of success. P&G's proactivity is largely responsible for its ability to respond to changes in the labor and consumer market, retain successful people of color throughout the organizational chart, and to be effective globally. Early diversity efforts at P&G date back to the 1960s when former CEO Howard Morgan initiated anti-discrimination efforts in the organization. In the late 1980s former president John Pepper initiated an organization-wide diversity task-force to create a diversity strategy. The late 1990s brought a global reorganization of the company, called the Organization 2005 strategy, in which the importance of diversity was emphasized (White, 1999).

A very successful diversity-related program within P&G is the Advancement of Women Initiative. The initiative has some key factors that are common components of other successful organizational diversity agendas. These include:

Action Planning Research based action plans related to the advancement of women, are developed and implemented yearly within P&G. Furthermore, senior line-managers are held accountable for the fulfillment of these plans.

Accountability The chief executive officer of P&G monitors the success of the initiative and further reports findings to an executive committee and P&G's board of directors. This accountability trickles down to general management who must demonstrate their ability to manage a diverse work force.

Communication P&G communicates its value of diversity regularly and this communication comes from the top leadership in the organization.

Evaluation Outcomes of P&G's diversity efforts are annually assessed against goals the company has set. This allows P&G to see where it has improved and areas where continual intervention is needed. Regular evaluation also provides P&G the opportunity to see which sectors or division of the company need additional attention related to diversity efforts.

An additional component of the Advancement of Women Initiative is the "Mentor Up" program. *Junior* women in the organization mentor senior level managers on issues affecting them as women in the company. This allows senior management the opportunity to gain knowledge and awareness of those issues, norms, and behaviors that may impede the upward mobility of women in the organization.

[1]More information on P&G's diversity strategy can be found in: White, M. B. (1999). Organization 2005: New strategies at P&G. *Diversity Factor, 18,* 16–20.

Chapter 11, Diversity Orientations—Individuals. Individuals likewise have different perspectives about diversity. This chapter highlights diversity-related identity development models which help illustrate that individuals themselves are at different levels of readiness for dealing with diversity. Again, strategies for encouraging diversity identity development are presented.

Chapter 12, Conclusion: Strategies for Success. This final chapter highlights the lessons regarding diversity (for individuals and organizations) that have been reviewed throughout the book. This chapter will be useful in helping both readers and their organizations engage in action planning regarding diversity in their future.

Discussion Items

1. In what ways have you noticed the dynamic nature of work?
2. What issues concern you most regarding the growth of ethnic minority populations in the United States?
3. Talk to someone who works or practices in the area of I/O, HR, OD, or HRD. What are the initiatives and strategies their field is engaging in to foster diversity and inclusiveness?
4. How would you describe the diversity perspective of an organization with which you are familiar? What practices, behaviors, or policies seem relevant to you in regard to diversity?

 InfoTrac College Edition

Be sure to log on to InfoTrac College Edition and search for additional readings on topics of interest to you.

2 CHAPTER | **Recruitment and Organizational Attraction**

Recruitment, from my perspective, is one of the most important functions organizations perform that affects their survival. At a minimum, effective recruitment helps organizations attract qualified pools of job applicants for current and future position openings. In a strong economy where the rates of joblessness are low, organizations engage in aggressive recruiting in order to reach out to a limited number of qualified job seekers. In a weaker economy where joblessness may be much higher, organizations are often overwhelmed with too many job seekers that may or may not be acceptable or desirable from the perspective of the organization. The task here for the organization is to restrict its recruitment message to a narrow and acceptable range of potential applicants. In addition to just the sheer number of available workers, organizations must pay attention to the skill levels of those potential workers and their education. Clearly, changing demographics of new entrants to the workforce now demand that organizations reconsider their recruitment strategies and ask, Will the ways in which we've recruited in the past be effective with these new job seekers?

Recruitment is also important for all job seekers. Recruitment messages distributed by organizations through television, radio, advertisements, and recruiters themselves provide valuable information to job seekers. Organizations use various forms of recruitment communication to shape their image for job seekers. However, job seekers must keep in mind that the image that organizations create of themselves through their recruitment efforts may not reflect the reality of the organizations.

Recruitment interview.

Attracting diverse workers to organizations is critical. This chapter examines two important theories of organizational behavior that illustrate the importance of effective recruitment of diversity to enhance organizational effectiveness. These theories include Kanter's model of homosocial reproduction and Schneider's attraction–selection–attrition (ASA) cycle.

Given the potential impact of recruitment on diversity and organizational effectiveness, we will take a novel view of recruitment by focusing on it as a strategy that organizations use to engage in impression management in order to market and sell themselves to attractive job seekers. That is, organizations attempt to attract potential job seekers through the image they project and in the ways in which they interact with potential job applicants as well as the public at large.

Organizations interact with job seekers through their formal representatives such as professional recruiters but also through interactions with job seekers and other organizational employees. Recruitment is a selling process in which the organization is selling itself as a potential employer and the potential applicant/employee is the consumer of the messages the organization delivers about itself.

The recruitment arena is a wonderful opportunity for interdisciplinary research. Research from industrial psychology, organizational behavior, advertising, social psychology, and consumer behavior is all useful in understanding

Diversity in Practice 2.1	Recruiting Strategies

A key theme of the American Management Association's meeting during the fall of 1997 was recruitment and retention. At that meeting a number of scholars and practitioners addressed the issue of strategically recruiting for diversity (Capowski, 1997). Themes from that meeting included:

- **Tap into foreign markets**. Given the level of globalization organizations now face, those hiring must take advantage of the global perspective potential workers from outside of the United States offer. The Internet and foreign offices and agencies are all sources of globalizing an applicant pool.
- **Take the offensive**. Organizations that complain that diverse job seekers do not apply for jobs with their organizations are reactionary and defensive. To recruit a diverse workforce organizations must take the offense and cultivate relationships with communities of color and other organizations in order to develop a diverse pipeline of job seekers. In addition, organizations need to realize that recruits who are in demand will command high salaries, counteroffers, bonuses, and the like.
- **Take a Marketing Perspective**. Organizations need to view themselves as selling a product to a consumer who is the potential applicant. Specifically, organizations must learn to target their market of job seekers, make learning about the organization and employment opportunities convenient for these job seekers through direct mailing, and create a positive recruitment image tailored to this market of job seekers.
- **Explore alternative staffing**. Organizations must broaden what they view as an appropriate or attractive recruit. For example, many boards of education throughout the country have been able to address a shortage of elementary, middle school, and high school teachers by recruiting retired professionals and workers in transition. For example, the College of Education at my university has a "Business to Teaching" program which allows those interested in a teaching career but who are not yet certified to teach to earn their teaching credentials in an alternative and flexible arrangement.

how organizations construct images of themselves, successfully market themselves (Mauer, Howe, & Lee, 1992), and sell themselves to potential applicants. This chapter focuses on what organizations can do to most effectively recruit a diverse workforce.

DEFINING AND APPRECIATING RECRUITMENT

Barber (1998) defines **recruitment** as, "those practices and activities carried on by the organization with the primary purpose of identifying and attracting potential employees . . . the primary objective of recruitment is to attract future employees. To do this, an appropriate pool of potential applicants must first be identified. Recruitment activities, then, are intended to help locate potential applicants and persuade them to pursue, and ultimately accept, employment with the organization" (p. 5).

The immediate outcome of effective recruitment is attraction; however, what are the longer-term implications of recruitment for both the individuals recruited as well as the organization overall? For the individual applicants, recruitment has consequences for their post-hire attitudes (e.g., satisfaction, commitment) and behaviors (e.g., turnover). Likewise, recruitment affects the same attitudes and behaviors of existing employees as well as customers and suppliers given their necessary interactions with newly hired recruits (Barber, 1998). "All of these outcomes are relevant to understanding the effect that recruitment might have on organizations. Taken in aggregate, they can have an effect on higher-level organizational outcomes such as productivity, profitability, or other measures of firm performance" (Barber, 1998, p. 11).

Delaney and Huselid (1996) also found that **recruitment intensity**; that is, the ratio of applicants to job openings was positively related to perceived market performance, suggesting a relationship between how organizations are perceived to perform competitively and their ability to attract job seekers. Likewise, Turban, Forret, & Hendrickson (1998) similarly found that an organization's reputation (which may or may not be related to its performance) influenced job applicants as well.

RECRUITMENT AND ORGANIZATIONAL EFFECTIVENESS

The goal of recruitment efforts by organizations is to attract job applicants. There are a number of interesting theories and proposals regarding this attraction process that have special importance to the examination of diversity and its ultimate impact on organizational effectiveness. Kanter's homosocial reproduction system and Schneider's attraction–selection–attrition process are two such models.

Kanter's Homosocial Reproduction

Kanter introduces the term **homosocial reproduction system** in her important 1977 text, *Men and Women of the Corporation*. In this book, Kanter provides the reader with a guide to the inner workings of a single organization. She highlights the ways in which organizational members (both men and women) sustain gender roles and restrictions. This work clearly exemplifies the subtle pressures within organizations that limit women's mobility and create **glass ceilings**. By *glass ceiling*, I mean those invisible but real barriers that seem to impede the career progression of women and people of color and other minority group members within organizations.

One of the issues she discusses in relation to women's barriers to managerial positions reflects male managers' needs to reproduce themselves in order to reduce the uncertainty that is naturally inherent in managerial jobs. That is, decision makers within this organization (and likely many others) base personnel decisions on the extent to which a recruit's personality and values fit with their own attitudes, values, and beliefs. In many ways, reproducing oneself within organizations provides managers and other top-level officials with **consensual validation.** That is, by surrounding themselves with others who are like them and who are likely to conform to the status quo, these managers limit the extent to which their ideas, beliefs, and attitudes are challenged by dissimilar others—instead they are affirmed and validated. Unfortunately, a system of homosocial reproduction within organizations also limits diversity.

The need for managers and other decisions makers to reduce uncertainty through homosocial reproduction clearly limited the career mobility opportunities for women within the organization studied. Kanter writes,

> Management becomes a closed circle in the absence of better, less exclusionary responses to uncertainty and communication pressures. Forces stemming from organizational situations help foster social homogeneity as a selection criterion for managers and promote social conformity as a standard for conduct. Concerned about giving up control and broadening discretion in the organization, managers choose others that can be "trusted." And thus they reproduce themselves in kind. Women are occasionally included in the inner circle when they are part of an organization's ruling family, but more usually this system leaves women out, along with a range of other people with discrepant social characteristics. . . . There is a self-fulfilling prophecy in all of this. The more closed the circle, the more difficult it is for "outsiders" to break in. Their very difficulty in entering may be taken as a sign of incompetence, a sign that the insiders were right to close their ranks. The more closed the circle, the more difficult it is to share power when the time comes, as it inevitably must, that others challenge the control by just one kind. And the greater the tendency for a group of people to try to reproduce themselves, the most constraining becomes the emphasis on conformity. (Kanter, 1993, p. 68)

What lessons does Kanter's work hold for recruitment and diversity? This work exemplifies how individuals within organizations are motivated to reproduce themselves in the workplace. The easiest way in which to do this is to recruit individuals who resemble themselves and others who are already organizational members. By targeting recruitment to those individuals who resemble existing organizational members, organizations restrict opportunities for a diverse pool of job applicants. If diversity does not exist within the applicant pool, it will certainly not exist among the organization's new hires that come from that pool.

Kanter's work also demonstrates that homosocial reproduction systems that influence how organizations recruit and select employees limit opportunities for women and other individuals with discrepant characteristics. For those dissimilar individuals who may persist at joining the organization, current organization members resist their inclusion and attribute their subsequent inability to successfully become a part of the group as evidence of continued need to exclude these non-right types in the future. Schneider's work on the ASA cycle illustrates these issues more directly than can I.

ASA Cycle

Schneider's 1987 article, "The People Make the Place," introduced the **attraction–selection–attrition**" (ASA) cycle of organizational behavior. The ASA framework outlines the interactions among the attraction, selection, and attrition processes within organizations and their subsequent influence on creating organizational homogeneity and limiting behavior.

At the basis of this model is the organizational founder. It is the founder who establishes organizational goals and who puts in place human resource policies, practices, and procedures that reflect those goals (Schneider, Goldstein, & Smith, 1995). The goals and the policies, practices, and procedures that result are believed to be reflective of the personal values and vision of the founder and his top management team.

Job seekers are then attracted to the organization based upon their perceived similarity and compatibility to it given recruitment messages sent by the organization. "The attraction process concerns the fact that people's preferences for particular organizations are based upon an implicit estimate of the congruence of their own personal characteristics and the attributes of the potential work organizations. That is, people find organizations differentially attractive as a function of their implicit judgments of the congruence between

Figure 2.1 | Schneider's Interactionist Model of Attraction–Selection–Attrition

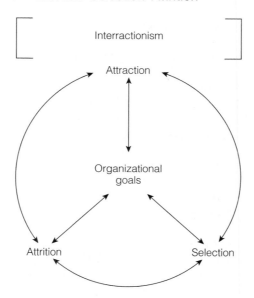

From B. Schneider, "An Interactionist Perspective on Organizational Effectiveness," in K. S. Cameron and D. A. Whetten (eds.), *Organizational Effectiveness: A Comparison of Multiple Models* (San Diego, CA: Academic Press, Inc., 1983), p. 35. Reprinted by permission.

those organizations' goals (and structures, processes, and culture as manifestations of those goals) and their own personalities" (Schneider et al., 1995, p. 749).

Selection refers to the formal and informal selection used by the organization at both the recruitment and the hiring stages. Organizations seek out individuals who resemble the backgrounds of those individuals who currently succeed in the organization and avoid those about whom little is known (Schneider, 1983). For example, if an organization has found success in recruiting top performers from State University it is likely to return to that university for subsequent recruiting. Likewise, decision makers responsible for the actual selection function within organizations inherently evaluate the viability of job candidates by evaluating them relative to themselves and to current job holders (Kanter, 1993).

Attrition refers to the behaviors of newcomers rather than organizations. Just as organizations avoid and distance themselves from job seekers not believed to fit within the organization, discrepant new hires will leave organizations where they do not feel comfortable or valued (Scheider et al., 1995).

Organizations are therefore a result of a process that produces and reinforces similarity and homogeneity. For example, Schneider, Smith, Taylor, and Fleenor (1998) examined the personality characteristics of 13,000 managers from over 100 organizations and found that organizations were relatively homogeneous in regards to the personalities of their managers. Likewise, the industries in which these organizations operated also demonstrated homogeneous personality profiles.

At first glance, this may seem like a good process; after all, don't organizations desire cohesion and feelings of unity? It could be argued that early in an organization's life cycle homogeneity actually facilitates functioning. If everyone is in agreement about the organization's values and strategy, then the organization will be likely to function more effectively in the early years. However, Schneider et al. (1995) caution that, "Over time, the tendency for organizations to become homogeneous with regard to person types can be dangerous for long-term organizational effectiveness. . . . ASA proposes that homogeneity is always potentially dangerous" (p. 768). Organizations that are too homogenous fail to capitalize on the diversity of educational backgrounds, experience, and knowledge that exists among the labor force. Without this diversity among organizational members, organizations leave themselves vulnerable to unexpected changes within its environment that may challenge its future effectiveness. That is, organizations must capitalize upon a variety of interpretations of the environment to prepare for future changes in the market. Without this diversity of interpretation and the preparation that can result, organizations may be unable to deal with the future challenges that will confront them. Schneider (1983) argues,

I believe that people, not organizations, make decisions, that people *are* organizations; that organizations are differentially activated, directed, and maintained as a function of the nature of the people they attract, select, and retain; and, that over time organizations have a tendency to become internally homogeneous and externally inflexible unless steps are taken to create the kind of tension necessary for appropriate decision making." (p. 51)

The strategic recruitment of diversity is one initial means of ensuring that an organization is itself diverse in the talent and expertise necessary to be a forward-looking and effective organization. However, the strategic recruitment of diversity cannot be the sole means of achieving diversity unless the organization itself is open to selecting diverse job seekers and supporting them once they are there.

RECRUITING DIVERSE WORKERS

The work of Kanter and that of Schneider provides evidence that organizations inherently value homogeneity, but that too much of it can lead to glass ceilings for underrepresented groups as well as organizational decline and decay The strategic recruitment of a diverse workforce is an initial method for organizations to challenge the cycle of homogeneity.

In regard to the strategic recruitment of a diverse workplace, two areas of the recruitment research seem most salient. The research on responses of job applicants to formal recruitment messages such as recruitment advertisements provides clear and convincing evidence that minority job seekers pay attention to how organizations choose to portray themselves in the media. The literature on the effects of recruiters—namely, their demographic characteristics, their behavior, and their knowledge—may also shed light on how to strategically use recruiters in the marketing of organizations to potential employees.

Like individuals, organizations engage in **impression management** (Perkins, Thomas, & Taylor, 2000). Impression management, also known as self-presentation, addresses how we manage our verbal and nonverbal behavior to convey a positive image to others (Rahim & Buntzman, 1991). That is, in order to attract future employees, organizations attempt to shape a positive **organizational image** of themselves, explicitly and implicitly, in order to be perceived positively by future job seekers. Organizational image influences those early opinions, beliefs, and feelings about an organization—how the organization is perceived (Tom, 1971).

An important issue then for organizations to identify and understand is the extent to which certain organizational messages are found attractive and for whom. One of the ways in which organizations engage in impression management and construct images for the job-seeking population is through recruitment advertisements. Recruitment advertisements are an important tool in recruiting for diversity, specifically because minority job seekers are more likely to use formal sources of job information and recruitment than are nonminority job seekers (Caldwell & Spivey, 1983; Powell-Kiran, Farley, & Geisinger, 1989).

A common recruitment advertisement.

Constructing the Organizational Image: Recruitment Advertisements

Perkins et al. (2000) examined the extent to which the demographic makeup of actors in a recruitment advertisement would influence future job seekers' feelings of organizational attraction, their perceived compatibility with the organization, and their overall assessment of organizational image. In addition, these authors also examined the extent to which these potential relationships would be moderated by either the race or the gender of the research participant. It was confirmed that attraction, feelings of compatibility, and assessments of organizational image were positively affected by the demographic compositions of the actors portrayed in the recruitment advertisement. Specifically, attraction, compatibility, and image assessments increased as the composition of the actors in the advertisements were portrayed as more diverse (the highest level of diversity portrayed was 50% Black and 50% White). In addition, participant race moderated each of the previous effects found. The pattern of results indicated that Blacks were differentially impacted by the diversity portrayed in the recruitment ad in regard to their attraction and compatibility to the organization as well as their assessment of image. White participants, on the other hand, appeared relatively unaffected by the diversity of the recruitment advertisements either way. That is, attraction, compatibility, and assessments of image by Whites for the organization changed very little regardless of the level of diversity portrayed in the recruitment advertisement. These findings were interesting in that they suggested that organizations could aggressively recruit diverse workers through the manipulation of recruitment advertisements with very little cost to their overall recruitment effort. Specifically, there was no evidence of a negative backlash by White job seekers when confronted with diverse images of potential employers.

In a follow-up to the study by Perkins et al. (2000), Avery, Hernandez, and Hebl (2004) examined the extent to which the impact of race in recruitment advertising would influence applicant attraction in White, Black, and Hispanic participants. Their results replicated the overall findings of Perkins et al. They found that Black and Hispanic participants were more attracted to organizations when recruitment advertisements depicted minority representatives; White participants were relatively unaffected by representative race. Furthermore, Avery et al. (2004) also found that the extent to which participants believed themselves to be similar to the representative depicted fully mediated the effect for minority participants. That is, the influence of diversity in the recruitment advertisement on minority attraction to organizations operates through its influence on minority job seekers' sense of compatibility with the organization. Avery (2003) also suggests that responses to recruitment advertisements may be shaped not only by race but also by individual difference characteristics such as one's openness to diversity.

In addition to paying attention to the demographic composition of actors in recruitment advertisements as a means of attracting diverse job seekers, researchers have also attended to the text included in those advertisements. Williams and Bauer (1994) examined the extent to which diversity messages in recruitment brochures influenced potential job applicants' attraction. Specifically, these researchers developed two brochures. Each brochure indicated that the organization was an affirmative action employer. However, one of the brochures also indicated that that organization had a diversity management policy. The organization with the diversity policy was seen as more attractive than the organization only mentioning an affirmative action policy. In a similar study examining responses to family-friendly human resource policies, Honeycutt & Rosen (1997) found that flexible career paths were associated with greater attraction to the organization for their sample of executive MBA students and MBA program alumni. This effect was most strong among individuals for whom it was most salient—those individuals with family responsibilities.

Highhouse, Steirewat, Bachiochi, Elder, and Fisher (1999) examined the reactions of Black engineering students and engineers to a hypothetical job advertisement. In addition to manipulating the staffing policy of the organization (identity-blind vs. identity-conscious), they also manipulated the compensation system of the organization (individual vs. team-based) and the work characteristics (individual vs. team-based). All engineers in the sample were more attracted to the organization that employed an identity-conscious staffing policy. The respondents differed by work status in regard to their preference for individual and group-based work yet agreed in their negative reactions to the

Who is the target of this recruitment advertisement?

| Diversity in Practice 2.2 | **Diversity on the World Wide Web** |

Fannie Mae, a diversity leader, has its diversity philosophy on the World Wide Web.

From Fannie Mae, "Philosophy on Diversity," found at http://www.fanniemae.com/careers/diversity/index.jhtml. Reprinted with permission from Fannie Mae.

combination of group performance–based pay for individually based work. Again, this study demonstrates that potential job seekers pay attention to the information provided in recruitment advertisements or brochures and that they are differentially impacted by that information (especially when it is diversity sensitive) due to their own characteristics.

Recruitment advertisements can be powerful tools for attracting attention to your organization. Increasingly diverse advertisements are appearing in the mainstream media such as *Business Week, Fast Company,* and *Newsweek* as well as those outlets targeted to specific groups such as *Working Woman,* or *Black Enterprise.* Another trend in diversity recruitment and the media involves the increasing presence of ethnically diverse images in recruitment advertising on the World Wide Web. In addition, some diversity recruitment advertisements are not ads at all. Thaler-Carter (2001) discusses how Microsoft Corporation has broadened their diversity recruitment strategy to the opinion-editorial pages of respected newspapers around the country. These "advertorials" are short essays published in the op-ed sections of newspapers in order to convey to the public (both job-seeking and non-job-seeking) the organization's needs and commitment to diversity. If perceived as legitimate by job seekers, the news-story format of these advertorials may give extra credibility to diversity recruitment efforts (Thaler-Carter, 2001).

Recruitment ads are only one way in which organizations engage in impression management in order to construct attractive organizational images and market themselves to potential job seekers. Those who represent the organization, such as its recruiters, also assist in the impression management function. The recruiter as an organizational representative not only provides job seekers with information regarding position openings and starting salaries, the recruiter also gives job seekers their first look at the type of person the organization will hire. Doverspike, Taylor, Shultz, & McKay (2000) recommend the strategic use of minority job incumbents to help in this effort,

> To increase the recruitment of minorities by public employers, successful minority job incumbents should be used in advertising (e.g., commercials, pamphlets, Web sites) and in recruitment efforts. When feasible, organizations should deploy minorities as recruiters, particularly in settings where minorities are prevalent (e.g., historically Black colleges or universities, majority-Black or Hispanic geographic areas, etc.). The presence of successful minority employees sends a signal to applicants that the organization is committed to diversifying its workforce, that potential role models exist within the organization, and that minorities have a strong likelihood of success. These actions have the powerful impact of enhancing the company image as an ardent employer of minorities. (p. 452)

Therefore, understanding how recruiters' characteristics, behavior, and knowledge impact job seekers is also important in respect to our discussion of diversity recruiting.

Recruiter Effects

Recruiter Demographic Membership   Recruiters may play a key role in recruiting minority professionals (Thomas & Wise, 1999). In their study of MBA candidates' recruitment experience preferences, Thomas & Wise found that recruiter characteristics like race, gender, personality, and knowledge were more important to minority job seekers than to nonminorities. Yet, the overall evidence suggests inconsistency in regard to the impact of recruiter characteristics on recruitment outcomes. The empirical research on this topic is inconsistent and the effect sizes have been relatively small. Furthermore, these studies are most likely to find significant proximate effects of recruiter demographics on applicants' job attitudes, rather than more distal effects such as applicants' decisions to apply for a position (Barber, 1998).

Liden and Parsons (1986) found that applicants evaluated female recruiters as more personable and knowledgeable than male recruiters. However, applicants interviewed by female recruiters were less attracted to the job. In addition to recruiter gender, Taylor and Bergmann's (1987) longitudinal study examined recruiter age, race, experience, tenure, education and training on applicants' attraction to the job and the probability of accepting a job. Together this group of demographic characteristics did significantly contribute to both organizational attractiveness and the probability of job acceptance. Interestingly, this study also demonstrated that recruiter gender played a positive and significant role in female applicants' job acceptance but not that of men, indicating that perhaps demographic similarity of recruiters and applicants may be useful in the recruitment of women (and perhaps other minority groups) but not in the recruitment of men (and members of majority groups). In contrast, Turban and Dougherty (1992) found only a gender similarity effect on organizational attraction for *men* and not women! Mauer et al.'s (1992) study of engineering students found that recruiter–applicant match with respect to gender was not important to either general impressions of the recruitment process or intentions to accept a job offer. In fact this study found that gender dissimilarity between women and male recruiters resulted in more positive reactions to the recruitment process.

> In general, then, support for the argument that recruiter demographics influence applicant reactions is fairly weak. There is some evidence that recruiter demographics influence overall evaluations of organizations or jobs, but effects are not often replicated across studies. Further, there is little evidence that recruiter demographics influence intentions to pursue jobs. Finally, there is limited evidence of similarity effects, and what evidence exists does not often match the anticipated pattern—similarity does not necessarily lead to more favorable applicant attraction. (Barber, 1998, p. 62)

Recruiter Behavior   The literature regarding the effects of recruiter behavior is much more positive and straightforward. Generally, applicants respond more favorably during the recruitment process when recruiters' behaviors are evaluated positively—applicants are more attracted, more likely to apply for a job with the organization, and more likely to accept an offer. Specifically, applicants are more likely to develop attraction to jobs and organizations when recruiters are perceived as warm or personable (Harris & Fink, 1987; Liden & Parsons, 1986; Powell, 1984; Rynes & Miller, 1983; Taylor & Bergmann, 1987), interested in the applicant (Turban & Dougherty, 1992) and enthusiastic (Mauer et al., 1992).

Recruiter Knowledge   Like recruiter behavior, recruiter knowledge is consistently found to result in positive recruitment outcomes. Generally, recent reviews of the literature demonstrate that applicants respond favorably to jobs and organizations when they perceive recruiters as being knowledgeable and informative (Barber, 1998; Breaugh & Starke, 2000). The specificity and credibility of recruiters' knowledge and the information provided likely have significant effects on applicants' satisfaction with the recruitment experience and on their impressions of the organization (Breaugh & Starke, 2000). Given the importance of job information specificity and recruiter credibility, prospective supervisors or coworkers are generally perceived as more effective in regard to recruiter knowledge than recruiters outside of the applicants' job function area such as human resources or personnel (Breaugh & Starke, 2000).

CONCLUSION

This chapter argues for the importance of strategic diversity recruitment in order to dismantle the glass ceiling but also to ensure continued organizational viability. In addition, this chapter reviewed the literature on the influence of recruitment advertisements and recruiter characteristics in attracting diverse job seekers. For those responsible for attracting more diverse job seekers to an organization, there is good news. Organizations can aggressively recruit minority job seekers through manipulating the messages sent through recruitment advertisements. In addition, the literature also seems to suggest that organizations can effectively target specific types of applicants by addressing those issues that concern them most in these advertisements. Of importance are the findings of Perkins et al. (2000) and Avery et al. (2004), which appear to suggest that engaging in targeted recruitment via recruitment advertisements does not produce negative backlash on the parts of those individuals not directly targeted by the recruitment strategy. Perkins and Thomas (2002) also report data suggesting that ethnic minority job seekers pay attention to a variety of diversity cues that will become increasingly important in future diversity recruitment efforts. Specifically, their study indicates that diversity cues present in an organization's environment spill over into the recruitment process. Therefore, organization must attend to the messages they deliberately send out to job seekers through advertisements and choice of recruiters. However, they must also be aware of what job seekers see when they first visit the organization and whether the demographic composition of the workforce is congruent with the image that the organization has constructed. It seems quite possible that minority job seekers may be repelled by organizations that create quite diverse images of themselves through recruitment advertisements, but who in reality employ very few people of color or women. Organizations must also consider where diversity is found in the organization. Having diversity in the executive boardroom sends a very different message to diverse job seekers as compared to the message sent when the diversity is found only within the secretarial pool.

Diversity in Practice 2.3 | **University Advertisements**

One of the ways in which many organizations choose to attract diversity is through recruitment advertisements. The research of Thomas & Wise (1999), Perkins et al. (2000), and Avery (2003) indicates that ethnic minority applicants value diversity and that portraying diverse employees in recruitment advertisements is an effective method of developing attraction to the organization without infringing upon nonminority attraction. Yet at times some institutions have gone too far in their efforts to attract diversity through the use of recruitment advertisements. Consider the following examples:

- A writer for the student newspaper at the University of Wisconsin notices that the sun was shining only on a single student's face in the university's newly released undergraduate admissions booklet (Ernst & Degroat, 2000; Jacobson, 2001). With further investigation by the school newspaper staff it was discovered that the face of this African American student, Diallo Shabazz, was superimposed onto another student's body in the photograph in order to make the university appear more diverse. Officials apologized to Mr. Shabazz. He insightfully commented, however, that the doctoring of the picture was not the issue: "It's much easier to falsely portray diversity instead of creating policies and programs—and backing them up with budgets—to actually create diversity on your campus" (Jacobson, 2001, p. A41).
- Admissions brochures are not the only places were diversity is constructed. Web sites for the University of Idaho and the State University of New York at Binghamton were both found to contain doctored photographs where the faces of minority students were superimposed on white students or where the universities assembled a diverse group of students in order to make the campus appear diverse and welcoming (Jacobson, 2001).

Although these institutions were attempting to embrace diversity by portraying it in the recruitment efforts, news of these untruths likely impeded the recruitment efforts of both minority and nonminority students. The University of Wisonsin's Diallo Shabazz helped to facilitate the recruitment of diverse students by traveling to Chicago and meeting with high school students; he discovered, however, that they had decided not to apply to Wisconsin given the university's false portrayal of diversity (Jacobson, 2001).

In addition to attracting diversity and avoiding backlash, one's diversity recruitment strategy may reach the broader consumer audience and inform that audience of the organization's value of diversity. Monica Reed, the manager of image and proactive sourcing at Prudential in Newark, New Jersey, commented, "Our corporate culture is diverse, so we want recruiting to be diverse, because that brings a variety of new ideas and perspectives into the company. We also want to sell to a diverse audience, and someone who sees a recruitment ad that focuses on diversity may also become a customer" (Thaler-Carter, 2001, p. 95). Organizations can develop their own future applicant and consumer pools through engaging in outreach with local community organizations, especially educational institutions (Doverspike et al., 2000). Through community and organizational partnerships, organizations can not only facilitate the training of the next generation of workers but can also help construct positive images of themselves as potential employers.

Image, and subsequently attraction, may also be shaped by the organization's reputation as a business, as part of the community, as well as its overall social performance (Luce, Barber, & Hillman, 2001). Backhaus, Stone, and Heiner (2002) investigated the role of an organization's social performance on job seekers. These researchers identified five dimensions of social performance (e.g., environment, community relations, employee relations, diversity, and product issues) important to job seekers' perceptions of organizations. Furthermore, environment, community relations, and diversity also affected job seekers' attraction to organizations. This emerging literature suggests to me that organizations can strategically engage in diversity recruiting, but they must also pay attention to how they treat current workers and the communities that support them in order to be successful at their recruitment goals.

Discussion Items

1. Review Schneider's ASA cycle. Now think back to your college search process. In what ways does the ASA cycle explain your attraction to your university? Does it explain the turnover of students who have decided to transfer to another university?
2. Have you ever purchased a product that did not live up to its claims? How did you respond? Did you tell others? Now review Diversity in Practice 2.3. Think about this issue of strategic recruitment in light of the practices employed by the University of Idaho and the University of Wisconsin. How would you respond to these organizations as a potential student given your knowledge of their problematic efforts to recruit diversity? Why?
3. Place yourself in the role of consultant to the personnel office at an organization. In what ways would you advise this office to honestly but aggressively recruit underrepresented students to your company? Discuss.
4. Review a popular business magazine such as *Business Week* or *Fast Company*. Critique the recruitment advertisements. What images are these organizations trying to project and what mechanisms do they use to convey their message?

 InfoTrac College Edition

Be sure to log on to InfoTrac College Edition and search for additional readings on topics of interest to you.

Diversity, Public Policy, and Organizational Decisions[1]

CHAPTER 3

With the increasing globalization of business and the presence of tight labor markets, in addition to the increase in the number of minorities and women available in the workforce, the selection of more diverse individuals must become an important aspect of an organization's business strategy. Gatewood and Feild (2001, p. 3) define **selection** as "the process of collecting and evaluating information about an individual in order to extend an offer of employment." The employment can "be either a first position for a new employee or a different position for a current employee," as may be the case with a promotion or lateral job move. Moreover, the selection process is conducted within legal and political environmental constraints that affect those seeking positions as well as the employers. Similarly, the selection process has been referred to as "identifying the best candidate or candidates for jobs from the pool of qualified applicants developed during the recruitment process" (Sims, 2002, p. 141).

THE REGULATORY ENVIRONMENT

A key ingredient of human resource selection is the regulatory environment. In particular, several amendments, laws, court cases, and other governmental regulations and guidelines exist for the purpose of ensuring equal employment opportunity. Given the history of unfair treatment and discrimination toward various classes of individuals (e.g., Blacks, women) in the United States, the

---

[1]The late Dr. Dan A. Mack and Ms. Harriet Landau, J.D., served as co-authors on this chapter.

Discrimination is costly for organizations.

enforcement of equal employment opportunity serves to reduce the incidence of discriminatory practices and allow the increasingly diverse labor market an equal opportunity for employment. The Equal Employment Opportunity Commission (EEOC) enforces all of the federal equal employment opportunity laws and provides oversight and coordination of all federal equal employment opportunity regulations, practices, and policies (www.eeoc.gov).

This chapter summarizes the key legislation, constitutional amendments, and Supreme Court cases associated with equal employment opportunity in selection. The chapter includes brief discussions of court cases that reflect the regulatory environment. The chapter concludes with a recent and interesting court case that challenges organizations to achieve their diversity goals in fair and equitable ways.

Title VII of the Civil Rights Act of 1964

The most important legislative act affecting selection is **Title VII of the Civil Rights Act of 1964** (Gomez-Mejia, Balkin, & Cardy, 1994; Sims, 2002). The original intent of Title VII was to prohibit discrimination on the basis of race, color, religion, and national origin. Near to the time in which the act was passed, opponenets of the Civil Rights Act proposed adding sex with the belief that the addition of sex would cause a loss of support, thus killing the act. Title VII was subsequently enacted, though, with sex included (Gutman, 2000; Twomey, 2002). The covered entities under Title VII were private employers with 25 or more employees, employment agencies, unions, and joint labor-

Figure 3.1 | Charge Statistics, 1999–2003

	FY 1999	FY 2000	FY 2001	FY 2002	FY 2003
Total Charges	77,444	79,896	80,840	84,442	81,293
Race	28,819	28,945	28,912	29,910	28,526
	37.3%	36.2%	35.8%	35.4%	35.1%
Sex	23,907	25,194	25,140	25,536	24,362
	30.9%	31.5%	31.1%	30.2%	30.0%
National Origin	7,108	7,792	8,025	9,046	8,450
	9.2%	9.8%	9.9%	10.7%	10.4%
Religion	1,811	1,939	2,127	2,572	2,532
	2.3%	2.4%	2.6%	3.0%	3.1%

Based on "Charge Statistics FY 1992 Through FY 2003," found at http://www.eeoc.gov/stats/charges.html.

management committees that direct apprenticeships and training programs (Gatewood & Feild, 2001). The **Equal Employment Act of 1972** strengthened Title VII by modifying the coverage to include private employers with 15 or more employees (Cascio, 2003; Gatewood & Feild), expanding coverage to government and educational system employees and strengthening exemptions for religious-affiliated institutions (Gutman). A 1978 amendment further expanded the coverage of Title VII to prohibit discrimination based on pregnancy, childbirth, or related conditions (Gatewood & Feild; Sims, 2000).

While the nature of selection practices is to discriminate or distinguish between individuals, what Title VII prohibits is the discrimination between individuals based on their race, sex, color, religion, or national origin. The term *discrimination* as used in Title VII and other legislation and court cases refers to two types or theories of discrimination: **disparate treatment** and **adverse impact** (sometimes referred to as disparate impact).

The first type, disparate treatment, occurs when individuals are treated differently due to their membership in a particular racial, gender, religious, or ethnic group (Gold, 2001; Twomey, 2002). Thus different standards are applied to specific groups (e.g., racial) of individuals. This type of discrimination is what most individuals think of when discrimination is discussed (Gomez-Mejia et al., 1994). Disparate treatment involves direct and intentional discrimination, unequal treatment, and the use of decision rules based on characteristics such as race or sex. An example of such practices might include hiring men with children while not hiring women with children. Although disparate treatment may itself be unfair, it is not illegal if it can be proven that the selection procedure is valid. Organizations should therefore strive to identify and use selection procedures that are valid and low in their probability of producing disparate treatment.

| Diversity in Practice 3.1 | Discrimination Around the Globe |

Cases involving employment discrimination occur throughout the world; not only in the United States. Consider the complaints of London citizen Indrajeet Lalbeharry, who was born in Guyana. Lalbeharry has worked for the Lloyd Register for over 23 years. During that time there has never been a person of color in the top management ranks.

He has filed a lawsuit with the employment tribunal (the court that hears employment-related cases in the United Kingdom) arguing that he has been overlooked for promotion to a more senior rank on nine different occasions without being informed about the vacancies. He argues that information and other work-related information has been withheld because he is prohibited from eating in a dining room that exists for the exclusive use of senior management (again, none of whom are ethnic minorities). The company is arguing vehemently that they do not discriminate, especially given the fact that they are a multinational organization that employs people of different nationalities worldwide (*The Guardian*, Oct. 10, 2000).

The second type of discrimination is called adverse (or disparate) impact. Adverse impact occurs when organizations engage in practices that *unintentionally* have negative consequences for employees who belong to a protected group. Adverse impact is a unique aspect of Title VII (Gutman, 2000) and occurs when the same standards are applied to all applicants or employees but the standard differentially affects a particular group (Gold, 2001; Sims, 2002). Although the selection procedure may be used uniformly with all individuals, the net result is that members of a specific group are adversely affected. Thus, in the case of adverse impact, the discrimination is indirect or unintentional, involves facially neutral actions, and results in unequal consequences. One classic example of adverse impact is the use of cognitive ability tests for selection, which adversely impacts Black and Latino workers by resulting in their being less likely to be hired. Another example would be the use of a height requirement for selection of police officers or firefighters, which has an adverse impact on women (it is the "more is better" assumption of this requirement that makes it problematic).

Title VII of the Civil Rights Act of 1964 has had a significant influence on how individuals are selected into organizations, and even within organizations (e.g., selection to training programs and promotions). Issues involving which types of questions can be asked during pre-employment screening (e.g., asking for religion on application blanks) and interviewing (e.g., inquiring about marriage or children) are often based on Title VII. Certainly, the area of employment testing has been greatly affected by Title VII. The controversy surrounding the use of cognitive ability tests for selection, which often results in adverse impact for Blacks and Hispanics, is grounded in the interpretation of Title VII. Thus the Civil Rights Act of 1964 provides the basis for the majority of equal employment opportunities in selection, but other laws have provided supplemental protections as well.

Diversity Learning Point 3.1	Reverse Discrimination?

It is not uncommon to hear arguments that affirmative action efforts in employment selection and admissions are unfair and that these efforts *discriminate* against Whites; especially White males. This line of reasoning typically continues and suggests that people of color and women are taking away the opportunities that White males deserve. Roy Jacques has an interesting reaction to these complaints that he discusses in his book chapter titled, "The Whiteness of Being: Reflections of a Pale, Stale, Male." Specifically Jacques identifies this sentiment as one of five myths often expressed by angry White males:

> *Qualified White Males Are Being Passed Over for Unqualified Others.* Do you have solid evidence that the women and minorities selected are unqualified? This question boils down once again to the logic that there should be a place guaranteed in society for every qualified white man, but others can compete for what's left. When an individual loses credibility, he or she must win it back over time; this is equally true of societies. The evidence prior to the 1970s suggests that when the only criterion for jobs was merit, those seen to have merit were overwhelmingly straight (or closeted), white, and male. To accept this as an adequate explanation is no less an act of white male supremacy than is joining a skinhead group. Classism gives this form of hate-group behavior a veneer of respectability, but to accept the perpetuation of structural violence is not ethically superior to skull cracking. At least, Aryan Nation provides a concrete enemy to honestly oppose. (1997, p. 90)

Executive Order 11246

An **executive order** is a policy implemented by the president covering the federal government and organizations that contract with the government. **Executive Order 11246 (EO 11246)** was issued by President Johnson in 1965 and covers all employees and contractors of the federal government with at least $10,000 in procurement or construction. EO 11246, as originally issued, prohibits discrimination based on many of the same characteristics covered in Title VII (i.e., race, color, religion, and national origin). In 1967, a Johnson amendment (EO 11375) expanded the protection to include sex, and EO 11478, issued by President Nixon in 1969, added age and disability to Part I of EO 11246, which prohibits discrimination by federal employment organizations (Gutman, 2000).

In addition to prohibiting discrimination, EO 11246 adds an **affirmative action** requirement. Entities covered by EO 11246 (government contracts in excess of $50,000 and at least 50 employees) are required to establish an affirmative action plan to promote the employment of individuals in the protected classes (e.g., race, sex) (Sims, 2002). This affirmative action is based on under-utilization of members of the protected classes in the organization and focuses on using increased recruitment, training, and promotion of these individuals.

Organizations are expected to put forth a "good faith" effort to ensure equal opportunities exist for the protected classes. As such, the typical affirmative action plan involves calculating statistics based on several factors to determine whether affirmative action is needed. For instance, factors such as the minority population of the relevant (typically local) labor market and their percentage of the total population in the area, the number of employed and unemployed minorities, the amount of training the employer can reasonably undertake, and the availability of other minorities in the organization who can be promoted or transferred are considered in an investigation of the need for affirmative action. Similar criteria are used for identifying affirmative action needs for members of other protected groups. If affirmative action is necessary, the organization develops timelines to increase, through recruitment and selection, the representation of the underutilized individuals (Gutman, 2000).

Age Discrimination in Employment Act

The **Age Discrimination in Employment Act (ADEA)** was enacted in 1967 and was created to prohibit discrimination of individuals from 40 to 65 years of age. An amendment in 1978 increased the ceiling age to 70, which was then eliminated entirely in 1987 (Gutman, 2000). The ADEA, as amended, was designed to promote employment of older individuals based on their abilities rather than their age. The ADEA covers private organizations, federal and state governments, employment agencies, and labor organizations. One exception to the ADEA involves high-level members of organizations who exercise substantial executive authority over a significant number of employees and a large volume of business. These individuals may be subject to compulsory retirement at the age of 65, provided specific criteria are met and certain benefits are provided (Gutman, 2000; Moran, 1998). Thus a younger executive could be selected to replace an executive who is subject to compulsory retirement.

Diversity in Practice 3.2	**Age Discrimination at Allstate?**

Seventy employees of Allstate have recently filed a complaint with the EEOC alleging the large company, typically hailed for its diversity efforts, had committed age discrimination. In November 1999 Allstate converted 6,000 of its permanent full-time sales force to contractual workers. Most of these employees were over the age of 45. Those who did not accept the offer to convert to contractual worker status were offered severance packages. Furthermore, Allstate asked these employees to sign waivers upon accepting these offers that they would not sue the company at a later date. The EEOC has already responded that Allstate acted unlawfully in converting workers to contract employees without benefits. More information about this case can be found at http://www.eeoc.gov/press/4-2-04a.html.

Americans With Disabilities Act of 1990

In 1973, Congress passed the **Rehabilitation Act**, which prohibited discrimination against individuals with disabilities. The Rehabilitation Act was similar to an Executive Order in that it applied only to the federal government and contractors of the federal government and included a requirement of affirmative action. In 1990, Congress passed the **American with Disabilities Act (ADA)**, which greatly expanded the extent of coverage and protection of the disabled. Title I of the ADA, which contains the employment provisions, applies to all employers with 15 or more employees (Cascio, 2003; Sims, 2002; Twomey 2002). Title I of the ADA prohibits employment discrimination against individuals with disabilities who can perform the essential functions of the job with or without reasonable accommodation. The three essential components of the ADA requirement of nondiscrimination are individuals with disabilities, essential functions of the job, and reasonable accommodation (Cascio, 2003; Gutman, 2000). Each is defined and discussed in the following text.

Under ADA, individuals with a disability are those who have a physical or mental impairment that substantially limits one or more major life activities, who have a record of such impairment, or who are perceived as having such an impairment. *Physical impairment* is defined as any physiological disorder or condition, cosmetic disfigurement, or anatomical loss affecting any of the following systems: neurological, musculoskeletal, respiratory, cardiovascular, reproductive, digestive, genitourinary, hemic, lymphatic, and endocrine as well as the skin and special sense organs. *Mental impairment* is defined as any mental or psychological disorder, such as mental retardation, organic brain syndrome, emotional or mental illness, and specific learning disabilities. *Major life activities* may include speaking, breathing, walking, sitting, lifting, seeing, hearing, learning, working, reading, caring for oneself, and performing manual tasks. *Substantially limit* is defined as significantly restricting an individual's ability to perform an entire class of jobs or a broad range of jobs in various classes, as compared to the average person with similar training, skills, and abilities (Gatewood & Feild, 2001; Gomez-Mejia et al., 1994; Twomey, 2002).

The impairment must be physical or mental, as previously defined, and not due to environmental, cultural, or economic disadvantages. However, the ADA does not cover sexual behavior disorders, compulsive gamblers, kleptomaniacs, pyromaniacs, or active alcoholics unable to perform their job duties or who present a danger to the safety or property of others (Gatewood & Feild, 2001; Twomey, 2002). The ADA does cover rehabilitated alcoholics or drug users (Gatewood & Feild, 2001; Twomey, 2002).

The inclusion of protection for a history or perception of a disability means that individuals with a history of back problems or heart troubles, for instance, cannot be discriminated against because of the potential for the reoccurrence of the problems, provided the individual can perform the essential functions of the job with or without reasonable accommodation. Essential functions are the job duties that every employee must do or be able to do to be an effective employee. Reasonable accommodation includes action taken to

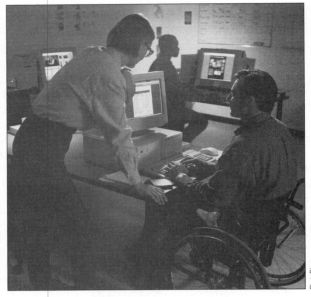

One dimension of diversity is physical ability.

accommodate the known disabilities of applicants or employees to provide the individual with a disability an equal employment opportunity. Employment cannot be denied to a disabled individual to avoid providing an accommodation unless the accommodation creates an undue hardship on the organization. Whether an accommodation is considered an undue hardship depends on the cost of the accommodation and the organization's resources. The individual with the disability is typically the one obligated to request the accommodation and if the accommodation creates an undue hardship on the employer, the disabled individual should be allowed the option of providing the accommodation. Finally, no accommodation is required if the individual is not qualified for the position (Cascio, 2003; Gatewood & Feild, 2001; Gomez-Mejia et al., 1994).

The ADA has had a significant effect on pre-employment inquiries and interview questions. Application blanks and interviews should not directly ask whether an individual has a disability. Applicants should be told what tasks are necessary for the job and asked if they are able to perform these tasks with or without reasonable accommodation. In addition, the ADA prohibits the use of employment tests, selection criteria, and other qualification standards that screen out individuals with disabilities unless they are job-related and considered a business necessity.

Civil Rights Act of 1991

The **Civil Rights Act of 1991** includes a comprehensive set of amendments designed to strengthen the Civil Rights Act of 1964. Several key important as-

Diversity in Practice 3.3	**Northwest Discriminates Against Diabetics?**

The EEOC has filed a discrimination lawsuit against Northwest Airlines Corporation on behalf of plaintiff Kevin Armstrong. The suit alleges that the airline withdrew an offer of employment to Armstrong after learning that he was a diabetic.

Armstrong was originally offered a position as an equipment service employee for the airline during January 1998. Employment was contingent upon passing a physical examination. The physical revealed his dependency on insulin to control his diabetes. After the revelation of his disease Armstrong was asked by Northwest to fill out an accommodation request form and to comply with employment restrictions that prohibited him from driving heavy equipment and vehicles and working at unprotected heights. Northwest's reasoning for the restrictions was that Armstrong could experience sudden loss of consciousness or incapacitation. Armstrong's response was that the restrictions were unnecessary since he had a valid driver's license and had worked in a comparable position with another airline without any conditions or restrictions. After receiving Armstrong's response, Northwest withdrew its offer of employment according to the suit against the airline. More information about this case can be found at http://www.eeoc.gov/press/10-31-02.html.

pects of the Civil Rights Act of 1991 are a prohibition against quotas and race-norming, clarification of the burden of proof, expansion of the damages recoverable by the plaintiff, and the creation of the Glass Ceiling Commission. Each is described following here.

In an attempt to avoid adverse impact suits, many organizations were using score adjustment techniques on selection tests to increase the representation of minorities hired. This practice came under fire as a result of a challenge of reverse discrimination against the U.S. Employment Service (USES), within the Department of Labor, when they decided to promote the use of its **General Aptitude Test Battery (GATB)** to state employment services. The GATB, a general cognitive ability test, was considered a valid selection tool but resulted in adverse impact against minorities, particularly Blacks and Hispanics. To rectify the adverse impact, USES began using **race-norming**, a form of score adjustment in which individuals are ranked by test score within their respective racial group and then the top scorers are selected from each group. With a public outcry against this policy, Congress passed an amendment as part of the Civil Rights Act of 1991 that explicitly forbids quotas, any type of score adjustment, establishment of different cutoff scores, or other alteration of scores on employment-related tests for a particular race, sex, religion, color, or national origin (Cascio, 2003; Gatewood & Feild, 2001; Gomez-Mejia et al., 1994).

A second important aspect of the Civil Rights Act of 1991 involves the burden of proof in discrimination cases. In essence, the burden of proof lies with the employer once the employee files a complaint and shows justification for it (prima facie evidence). According to the decision in **Griggs v. Duke Power** (1971), discussed later, the organization must then prove that it had a

| Diversity in Practice 3.4 | **Racism and Sexism at Microsoft?** |

Microsoft is being sued for both racial and gender discrimination in promotion and wages due to what the suit refers to as a subjective employee evaluation system.

The employee evaluation system at the center of this lawsuit is used by a predominantly. White male management corporation responsible for evaluating employees. The plaintiffs argues that the evaluation system is susceptible to the personal biases of these managers, which have resulted in the poor evaluations of African American and female employees that subsequently have hindered both the career and wage growth of these groups. The suit against Microsoft further alleges that the company assigned low performance evaluations or fired employees who complained about discriminatory behavior in the past.

---

job-related reason for its decisions. In the 1989 ***Wards Cove v. Atonio*** decision, also discussed later, the Supreme Court shifted most of the burden of proof back to the plaintiff, resulting in an increase in the cost and difficulty for the plaintiff to bring a successful lawsuit. The Civil Rights Act of 1991 reestablished the standard set in *Griggs* (Cascio, 2003; Gomez-Mejia et al., 1994).

Prior to the Civil Rights Act of 1991, successful plaintiffs could only collect back pay awards for Title VII claims. The Civil Rights Act of 1991 allowed for the collection of both punitive and compensatory damages. Punitive damages are awarded to the plaintiff as a form of punishment of the defendant and require a demonstration of malice or "reckless indifference" on the part of the defendant. Compensatory damages are awarded to the plaintiff as compensation for financial and psychological harm suffered by the plaintiff and are capped at $50,000 to $300,000 depending on the size of the employer (Cascio, 2003; Gomez-Mejia et al., 1994; Sims, 2002).

Also, the Civil Rights Act of 1991 permitted the use of jury trials if requested by the plaintiff. Previously, Title VII cases were decided by a single judge. The use of a jury is thought to increase the plaintiff's chances for success because juries are primarily other workers who can sympathize with the plaintiff (Cascio, 2003; Gatewood & Feild, 2001; Gomez-Mejia et al., 1994).

Finally, Congress found that, although there was an increase in women and minorities in the workforce, they were still underrepresented in higher-level, decision-making positions, an effect known as the glass ceiling. Thus the Civil Rights Act of 1991 established the **Glass Ceiling Commission** to investigate how businesses fill these high-level positions, how prepared minorities and women are to fill these positions, and what developmental and skill enhancing practices are needed to increase the qualifications of minorities and women. Also, the Glass Ceiling Commission was charged with studying the reward and compensation systems in the workforce and making comparisons with businesses that actively promote minorities and women and the reasons for their success (Gatewood & Feild, 2001; Twomey, 2002).

OTHER LEGISLATION AND DOCUMENTS AFFECTING SELECTION

In addition to the laws already described, two other laws affect the selection of individuals through protection of certain classes of individuals from discrimination. The **Vietnam Veterans Reform Act of 1974**, which applies to the federal government and its contractors, prohibits discrimination against Vietnam-era veterans and disabled veterans, and includes a form of affirmative action for veterans as well (Sims, 2000). The **Immigration and Reform Control Act of 1986** prohibits discrimination based on citizenship or national origin by government employers and private employers with four or more employees (Gold, 2001) and makes it illegal to hire unauthorized aliens (Sims, 2002).

Uniform Guidelines on Employee Selection Procedures

The **Uniform Guidelines on Employee Selection Procedures** (Guidelines) is a document issued in 1978 that provides the characteristics of acceptable selection procedures as agreed upon by the EEOC, the Departments of Labor and Justice, and the Civil Service Commission. While the Guidelines do not carry the force of law, the courts give them "great deference" (Zimmer, Sullivan, Richards, & Calloway, 1997). The underlying principle of the Guidelines is that any selection procedure that has adverse impact against members of any race, sex, or ethnic group, is illegal under Title VII unless justified by business necessity.

The Guidelines delineate a practical determination of adverse impact through the use of the four-fifths rule. The four-fifths rule states that if the percentage of a particular protected group chosen by a specific selection method is less than four-fifths of the percentage of the majority group chosen, adverse impact is indicated. While some exceptions exist (e.g., small samples, small number of individuals affected), this rule is the guiding principle organizations should use in determining the adverse impact of their selection procedures (Gatewood & Feild, 2001).

According to the Guidelines, any selection method that results in an employment decision is covered; not just scored or formal selection methods. Unscored or informal methods of selection, such as interviews, that result in adverse impact should be eliminated or modified to a formal, scored selection procedure that does not result in adverse impact. For any selection procedure that results in adverse impact, the procedure should be discontinued and the use of an alternate selection procedure with less adverse impact should be adopted or the organization must defend the use of the selection procedure that results in adverse impact (Gatewood & Feild, 2001).

The defense of the selection procedure typically includes a statistical validation study of the relationship of the selection procedure to successful performance on the job. The Guidelines provide detailed steps that should be followed when attempting to validate the selection procedure. The Guidelines also discuss cutoff scores, appropriate job performance measures, and types and manner of record keeping, as well as issues that are appropriate as a selection requirement, such as representativeness of the validation sample and test fairness. In addition to the validation of the selection procedure, the organization must also show that there are no other selection methods that are both valid and result in less adverse impact (Gatewood & Feild, 2001).

Constitutional Amendments and Other Legislative Acts   Several amendments to the Constitution and older civil rights acts have become important as either a supplement to recent equal employment opportunity statutes, such as those discussed above, or as the primary basis for a discrimination complaint when other equal employment opportunity statutes are not applicable. They include the **5th, 13th, and 14th Amendments** and the **Civil Rights Acts of 1866 and 1871**.

The 5th and 14th Amendments are parallel in prohibiting the deprivation of employment rights without Due Process, with the 5th Amendment applicable to the federal government and the 14th to state and local government entities. Both amendments apply to all citizens, not just certain classes of individuals, and thus allow discrimination claims not covered by Title VII, such as discrimination based on sexual orientation. The 13th Amendment differs from the 5th and 14th in that it applies only to discrimination based on race and ethnicity and covers only private entities. All three amendments require a showing of intentional discrimination, thus one cannot charge adverse impact under these amendments. Moreover, there is no employee minimum, hence employers with less than the 15 employees required under Title VII are covered by the amendments. Another key advantage to a constitutional claim is uncapped damages, both punitive and compensatory, recoverable for a successful plaintiff (Gutman, 2000).

The Civil Rights Act of 1866, based on the 13th Amendment, protects against discrimination based on race, ethnicity, and, to some extent, national background by private employers, unions, and employment agencies. As opposed to Title VII claims, which apply to employers with a minimum of 15 employees, the Civil Rights Act of 1866 has no limitation or minimum number of employees. The Civil Rights Act of 1871, based on the 14th Amendment, prohibits discrimination based on just about any attribute, including those covered by Title VII and others not covered by Title VII (e.g., sexual orientation, physical attributes) and there is no employee minimum requirement. However, both of these Civil Rights Acts require a finding of intentional discrimination (Gutman, 2000).

MAJOR SUPREME COURT CASES

Griggs v. Duke Power Company (1971)

The first major Title VII case decided by the Supreme Court (and according to some, the most significant equal employment opportunity case ever) was *Griggs v. Duke Power* (Cascio, 2003). This case involved a class action suit by 13 Blacks workers at Duke Power Company. Undisputed facts of the case include the finding that prior to the Civil Rights Act of 1964, the company actively discriminated on the basis of race in hiring and assigning its employees. Of the five operations departments, Blacks were confined to the lowest-paying labor department. Following the passing of the Civil Rights Act of 1964, the company discontinued its policy of restricting racial minorities to the labor department. Subsequently, three requirements for obtaining positions in the other four operating departments were initiated. These requirements included a high school diploma and passing two professionally developed tests: The Wonderlic Personnel Test, purported to measure general mental ability, and the Bennett Mechanical Comprehension Test. At the time of the initiation of the requirements, current White employees who did not possess a high school diploma continued to perform satisfactorily on the job. Moreover, the requirements of a high school diploma and the two aptitude tests were not intended to measure ability to learn or particular job skills or abilities, but were initiated because the company thought it might improve the overall quality of the workforce. The two requirements were not instituted to measure a person for the job, but rather a person in the abstract, in hopes of having a higher quality workforce (Twomey, 2002; Zimmer et al., 1997)

The District Court found, and the Court of Appeals agreed, that the company had ceased its discriminatory practices and that there was no evidence showing that the initiation of the diploma and aptitude tests was for a discriminatory purpose. Of particular importance was the finding that, because the requirements were applied to all persons equally, the fact that a disproportionate number of racial minorities were disqualified by the requirements did not mean they were unlawful under Title VII (Zimmer et al., 1997).

The Supreme Court, in a unanimous decision, reversed the decisions of the District and Appeals Courts. The Supreme Court found that the objective of Title VII was to achieve equal employment opportunity and the removal of barriers that favor White employees over other employees. Thus practices that are facially neutral but result in preservation of the status quo are illegal under Title VII (Cascio, 2003; Gatewood & Feild, 2001). Given that at the time only 12% of Blacks had received a high school diploma as opposed to 34% of Whites, the high school diploma requirement had an adverse impact on Blacks (Zimmer et al., 1997).

Regarding the aptitude tests, Duke Power argued that section 703(h) of the Civil Rights Act of 1964 allows the use of a professionally developed test if it is not designed, intended, or used to discriminate because of characteristics such as race. The Supreme Court suggested that the professionally developed tests were allowed but they must be job-related. In fact, Duke Power had not shown that either the diploma or the aptitude tests had any relationship to job performance. The Court noted that many employees who had not completed high school or taken the aptitude tests were performing satisfactorily (Gatewood & Feild, 2001; Twomey, 2002). Thus, the two precedents set by the *Griggs* case were that the plaintiff bears the burden of proving the adverse impact of a selection device and then the employer has the burden of proving that the selection device is valid, or job-related.

McDonnell Douglas Corp. v. Green (1973)

While *Griggs v. Duke Power* dealt with the issue of adverse impact, **McDonnell Douglas v. Green** involved disparate treatment. The plaintiff, who was Black, was employed as a mechanic and laboratory technician from 1956 to 1964. In 1964, he was laid off as part of a general reduction of force. The plaintiff, who was a long-time activist in the civil rights movement, argued that the discharge and the hiring process at McDonnell Douglas was racially motivated. In 1965, the plaintiff engaged in an illegal protest, along with the Congress of Racial Equality, by stalling his car in front of an entrance to the plant. Three weeks after the "stall-in," McDonnell Douglas advertised for qualified mechanics, the plaintiff applied, and was denied employment. The plaintiff then filed a formal complaint with the EEOC, claiming he was denied employment due to his race and involvement in the civil rights protests, both of which are illegal under the Civil Rights Act of 1964 (Zimmer et al., 1997).

Although the EEOC determined that there was reasonable cause to pursue the discrimination complaint due to retaliation, they did not believe the plaintiff had a case in regard to his discrimination due to race complaint (Gutman, 2000). The District Court dismissed the racism charge without trial given the EEOC ruling and tried and dismissed the retaliation charge. The Court of Appeals agreed with the District Court regarding the unlawful protest but reversed the dismissal of the claim of racially motivated hiring practices and indicated that Green did not require a ruling of reasonable cause by the EEOC to pursue the racism charge. The 8th Circuit tried the racism charge and subsequently ruled in Green's favor (Gutman, 2000). However, the company was also charged with showing the business necessity of not rehiring Green. The company also demonstrated that all employees who engaged in demonstrations against the company were treated the same regardless of race. Ultimately, Green lost his suit.

The Supreme Court agreed with the lower courts regarding the right of the employer to not hire individuals who engaged in unlawful protest, but that the employer may still have engaged in discriminatory practices if the denial of employment due to the protest was a pretext for discrimination. Thus, at issue for the Supreme Court was the proper order and burden of proof in actions involving Title VII. The Supreme Court found that the establishment of a prima facie case of discrimination involves the plaintiff showing that he or she (a) belongs to a protected group, (b) applied for and was qualified for the job, and (c) despite qualifications, was denied employment, and (d) after rejection, the position remained open and the employer continued to seek applicants from persons with the complainant's qualifications. The burden of proof then shifts to the employer to provide a legitimate, nondiscriminatory reason for the denial of employment. The complainant should then be given the opportunity to provide evidence that the legitimate, nondiscriminatory reason is simply a pretext for discrimination (Twomey, 2002; Zimmer et al., 1997). Thus the *McDonnell Douglas v. Green* decision provided the structure for litigating inferential cases of disparate treatment.

Connecticut v. Teal (2001)

In **Connecticut v. Teal,** the question before the Supreme Court was whether an employer was liable for racial discrimination if part of the employer's selection process resulted in adverse impact, but the "bottom line," or final selection results, did not result in adverse impact (Gatewood & Feild, 2001). Four Black employees for the State of Connecticut were promoted provisionally to a supervisory position for a period of two years. To attain the supervisory position permanently, they had to participate in a selection process, which included a written examination. Of the 329 candidates who took the exam, only 54% of Blacks passed the exam, which was 68% of the passing rate for Whites. The four Black employees were among those who failed the exam. After several other stages in the selection process, including some use of affirmative action, the state made its promotions. The final selection resulted in a greater percentage of Blacks promoted than Whites (Zimmer et al., 1997). Thus, even though the end result of the selection process did not appear to result in adverse impact, did adverse impact occur during the selection process given the results of the examination?

The Supreme Court found that Title VII prohibits employment practices that deprive any individual of employment opportunities. As a result, the focus is on the individual, not the group. In essence, individual members of a minority group cannot be told that they have not been discriminated against because others in their group were hired. As such, the decision suggests that each part of a selection process should be free of adverse impact (Gatewood & Feild, 2001).

Watson v. Ft. Worth Bank & Trust (1988)

The issue in **Watson v. Ft. Worth Bank and Trust** was whether adverse impact analysis can be applied to subjective selection procedures, such as interviews. Watson, a Black woman, was hired in 1973 as a proof operator and was promoted to teller in 1976. Between February 1980 and February 1981, Watson applied for, and was denied, four promotions, which were subsequently given to Whites. The bank had no formal process or criteria for evaluating candidates and relied on the subjective judgment of supervisors acquainted with the candidates and with the nature of the job to be filled. All of the supervisors who denied Watson the promotions were White (Gatewood & Feild, 2001; Zimmer et al., 1997).

Watson sued the bank claiming racial discrimination. The District Court, using the standards for disparate treatment as set forth in *McDonnell Douglas v. Green,* found that Watson had established a prima facie case of discrimination but the bank had provided a legitimate and nondiscriminatory reason for denying her employment. Watson appealed stating that the District Court erred by not using the adverse impact standards rather than disparate treatment. Under the adverse impact analysis, the bank would have to provide validity evidence for its selection process, which given the subjectivity of the process, would be difficult to establish. The Court of Appeals found that the

Diversity Learning Point 3.2

U.S. Laws and Supreme Court Cases Having Implications for Recruiting and Selecting Employees

Civil Rights Act of 1964   Federal law that declared many forms of racial and sexual discrimination illegal. Title VII of this act made it illegal to fail or refuse to hire or to discharge any individual, or otherwise to discriminate against any individual with respect to his compensation, terms, conditions, or privileges of employment because of such individual's race, color, religion, sex, or national origin. A federal agency, the Equal Employment Opportunity Commission (EEOC), was created to administer the law.

Executive Order 11246 (1965)   President Lyndon Johnson issued an executive order in which all employers having contracts with the federal government in excess of a specified were prohibited from discrimination on the basis of race, religion, color, sex, or national origin. This order also requires employers to take *affirmative action* to ensure that women and minorities are hired. Employers were required to file timetables and goals in which they report areas of underutilization of protected groups and steps they will take to remedy these deficiencies. The Department of Labor was given authority to investigate and monitor compliance with the order.

The EEOC Uniform Guidelines (1978)   Rules set down by a panel of experts from industry, government, and education for fair employment practices. The guidelines called for systematic record keeping on employment decisions (e.g. tabulation of who is and isn't hired, validity studies). According to the *four-fifths* rule, a hiring procedure has "adverse impact" against a group when the selection rate for the group is less than 80 percent of the group with the highest rate of selection. If there is adverse impact, the employer must show that the hiring procedures are valid.

Age Discrimination in Employment Act (ADEA)   The original act was passed in 1967 and later amended in 1978 and protects employees between the ages of 40 and 70 from discrimination on the basis of age. Employers may use age as a qualification but only if it is a legitimate and necessary qualification (also called a bona fide occupation qualification or BFOQ).

***Griggs v. Duke Power* (1971)**   The Duke Power Co. in North Carolina had a policy of only promoting employees out of the labor pool to higher skill jobs if they had a high school degree and passing scores on two aptitude tests. Black applicants tended to score lower on the two tests and were less likely to have a high school de-

continued

---

adverse impact analysis was inappropriate and that use of the disparate treatment standards was correct when subjective selection procedures, such as interviews, were used. The Supreme Court disagreed, stating that subjective selection procedures can be challenged with adverse impact analysis, and that otherwise, employers would simply use only subjective procedures as they would be easier to defend (Zimmer et al., 1997).

**Diversity
Learning Point 3.2**   Continued

gree. Consequently, they were more likely to be passed over for promotion. The Supreme Court ruled that if selection procedures have an inverse impact on the hiring of a protected group, the employer must show that the procedures are valid even if the discrimination was unintentional.

Albermarle Paper Company v. Moody (1975)   As in Duke Power, the company's use of tests led to discrimination against Black employees in hiring and promotion. Unlike Duke power, the company in this case presented evidence for the validity of the selection procedures. The Supreme Court ruled against the employer largely on the basis of the poor technical quality of the validation research. Employers were expected to adhere to the technical quidelines set forth in the Uniform Guidelines of the EEOC.

Americans with Disability Act (1990)   This act makes it unlawful to discriminate against a qualified person with a disability. Disability is defined broadly as including a physical or mental impairment that substantially limits one or more of the major life activities, a record of such an impairment, or being regarded as having such as impairment. The act states that employers may not discriminate against a qualified individual in employment decisions, including selection, promotion, and placement. A qualified individual with a disability is defined as an individual with a disability who, with or without reasonable accommodation, can perform the essential functions of the employment position. This act has yet to be interpreted in the courts.

Civil Rights Act of 1991   During the 1980s the U.S. Supreme Court in several court decisions made it much harder for a person filing a suit (the plaintiff) to prove discrimination. *Griggs v. Duke Power* made it clear that if there is adverse impact against a protected group, the burden would be on the employer to show that selection procedures are valid. In *Wards Cove Co., Inc. v. Atonio et al* (1989), however, the U.S. Supreme Court placed much more of a burden on the plaintiff. In the Civil Rights Act of 1991 Congress stated that the decision of the Supreme Court in *Wards Cove Packing Co. v. Atonio*, 490 U.S. 642 (1989) has weakened the scope and effectiveness of federal civil rights protections. Consequently, the act made into law the concepts set forth in *Griggs v. Duke Power* (1971) and also extended the Civil Rights Act of 1964 by allowing the plaintiff to have a jury trial and to claim punitive damages.

From R. L. Dipboye, C. S. Smith, and W. C. Howell, *Understanding Industrial and Organizational Psychology: An Integrated Approach* (Fort Worth, TX: Harcourt Brace and Company, 1994), pp. 457–458. Reprinted by permission of Wadsworth, a division of Thomson Learning, Inc.

Wards Cove Packing Co. v. Atonio (1989)

The **Wards Cove v. Atonio** case involved a salmon packing company made up of two groups of jobs, cannery and noncannery jobs. The cannery jobs were unskilled, low paying, and seasonal, and were filled predominantly by non-Whites, primarily Filipinos and Alaskan Natives. The noncannery jobs were skilled, higher-paying jobs filled by Whites. The cannery workers filed suit alleging that the hiring and promotional practices, which involved a lack of objective hiring criteria, separate hiring channels, and nepotism, created the racial imbalance in the workforce (Gatewood & Feild, 2001).

The Supreme Court decision had several key parts. First, the Supreme Court stated that the lower courts erred in accepting the statistics showing the high percentage of non-Whites in cannery jobs and a high percentage of Whites in noncannery jobs. Instead, the comparison should have been between qualified job applicants or the qualified population on the labor force and the skilled, noncannery positions (Gatewood & Feild, 2001).

Second, the Court stated that the plaintiff's burden of establishing a prima facie case goes beyond simply showing a statistical imbalance. Plaintiffs must demonstrate that the racial disparity is a result of one or more of the employment practices they are challenging by showing that each challenged practice has a significantly adverse impact on the employment opportunities for Whites and non-Whites. If this burden is met, the company must show a legitimate business justification, but they are not required to show that the practice is essential or indispensable, thus the company has only a burden of production (of employment practice legitimacy). The burden of persuasion always remains with the plaintiff. The plaintiff must then show that other tests or devices would serve the employer's purpose with less adverse impact. The alternative practices, though, must be equally as effective as the company's chosen procedures in achieving its goals (Zimmer et al., 1997).

Regents of the University of California v. Bakke (1978)

The medical school at the University of California (Davis campus) set a goal of having 16% of its admissions reserved for minority applicants. To accomplish this goal, the admissions office kept two lists of applicants: one list of White applicants and another list of minority applicants. For two years in a row, some minority applicants were admitted to the medical school although their ratings were lower than those of White applicants who were rejected. Allan Bakke was one of these White students.

Bakke sued the university and argued that the university violated the equal protection clause of the Constitutions's 14th Amendment, Title VI of the Civil Rights Act of 1964, and the state constitution of California. Ultimately the U.S. Supreme Court ruled in Bakke's favor. The U.S. Supreme Court indicated that "set-asides" and "quotas" are not permissible practices for bringing about a diverse student body. However, their decision also indicated that schools were allowed to treat characteristics "acquired at birth" such as one's sex or skin color as "plus factors" when making selections among *qualified* applicants (Crosby, Iyer, Clayton, & Downing, 2003).

Where Are We Now? The Cases Involving the University of Michigan

In the early 1990s three White applicants (Jennifer Gratz and Patrick Hamacher who both applied for undergraduate admission and Barbara Grutter who ap-

| Diversity Case 3.1 | The ADA Protects Everyone |

The protection provided under the various federal employment discrimination statutes reviewed in this chapter are also applicable to actions that occur prior to actual employment. Therefore, job applicants who are in the midst of the recruitment process (such as attending on-campus informational interviews or job fairs) are covered under these statutes as are applicants being interviewed or merely filling out an application form. Comments made by organizational representatives during the application, recruitment, and selection processes can all be held as potential sources of liability for companies that attempt to hire (Zachary, 1999). Consider the case of *Griffin v. Steeltek, Incorporated*[1]:

Griffin, a nondisabled individual, applied for a grinder position at Steeltek, Inc. In the application form he was asked if he had received workers' compensation or disability income. To this he responded that he had received unspecified disability income payments. The application form also inquired as to whether he suffered from any physical problems that would prevent him from performing certain duties. To this item he offered no response. Although Griffin was informed that he was the most qualified applicant for the job, and he was never told that experience was a requirement, he did not receive the position. He then brought an ADA case against Steeltek.

Initially a district court ruled in favor of the employer on the grounds that Griffin was not disabled or perceived to be disabled and thus lacked any standing to sue under the statute. However, on appeal this decision was reversed. "The court of appeals held the ADA created a cause of action for all job applicants, not just those disabled or perceived as being disabled, who suffer an injury because of an illegal disability-related question. Thus, the applicant did not have to prove he was disabled or perceived as being disabled in order to sue under the ADA" (Zachary, 1999, p. 21). Thus the court determined that the purpose of the ADA, in order to prevent discrimination based upon disability, was to allow *anyone* who is subjected to illegal questioning, and injured by the items, to sue.

[1]Other similar cases that illustrate federal statutes' impact on pre-hires can be found in: Zachary, M. K. (1999). Discrimination laws provide protection to job applicants. *Supervision, 60* (8), 21–23.

plied to the law school) sued the University of Michigan after having been denied admission while ethnic minority candidates with "lesser paper credentials" were admitted (Crosby et al., 2003). The undergraduate admissions procedures were point based and assigned additional points to students who were minority status. The law school admissions procedure in contrast sought to achieve a critical mass of minority students through considering race in their vaguer and less structured admissions system (www.msnbc.com, accessed June 23, 2003). The law school plan combines both objective variables like grade point average with more subjective criteria such as letters of recommendation, unique talents, and overcoming a disadvantaged background (Gutman, 2003).

Not only did the institution encounter two cases simultaneously being directed at two different divisions, but these cases are unique in that over 100 "friends of the court" briefs were filed. Most voiced the opinion of big business that support the University of Michigan's goal of educating a diverse student body that would eventually become the workforce.

Both cases moved throughout the judicial system. Finally on June 23, 2003, the U.S. Supreme Court upheld the law school admissions policy and overturned the undergraduate admission policy that relied upon a point system. The court indicated that diversity presents a compelling interest and that the law school's narrowly tailored use of race in admissions decisions was warranted (Gutman, 2003). In contrast, the use of a point system in which the same number of points was assigned to all minority applicants, as was the case in the admissions procedures, was perceived by the court as a veiled quota and an unconstitutional attempt at achieving diversity.

CONCLUSION

Organizations and the mechanisms they use to accomplish their goals (such as the selection system) exist within a larger, and very complex, environment. When it comes to selection, organizations are continually influenced by changes in public policy and rulings from local, state, and federal courts. Likewise, research conducted by organizational researchers such as industrial/organizational psychologists can also have an impact on court rulings. The regulatory is constantly changing. Therefore those responsible for selection and promotion within organizations must keep up with these changes in order to engage in fair human resource practices.

Discussion Items

1. Which body of legislation reviewed in this chapter are you most aware of? How has it affected your life or someone close to you?
2. Review the Americans with Disabilities Act (www.usdoj.gov/crt/ada/pubs/ada.txt). Now consider the job of your department's secretary. Imagine that your department had a secretarial position open and that an experienced applicant with a hearing disability was being considered for the position. What kinds of accommodation might you consider adopting in order to hire this person?
3. Review the information provided on the uniform guidelines on employee selection procedures. How do these guidelines impact the use of applicant interviews for selection purposes?
4. Compare and contrast popular notions of affirmative action with Executive Order 11246.

InfoTrac College Edition

Be sure to log on to InfoTrac College Edition and search for additional readings on topics of interest to you.

Socialization and the Newcomer Experience

For any newcomer to an organization, it is a time of pride, excitement, and concern. Newcomers experience pride in their ability to secure admission or a new position with the organization and experience excitement in the adventure before them. Newcomers also experience some fear and trepidation over all there is to learn. Not only must newcomers learn to do their job (regardless of previous education and training), but they must also learn their new role and place in the organization, as well as who's who and how things really get done in the new company.

Organizations understand that for newcomers things are difficult. To help with newcomer adjustment and transitions, many companies, both formally and informally, provide opportunities for organizational socialization. Training is one organizational tool for socialization. In addition, the socialization process is not simply something "done" to the newcomer. Newcomers themselves may proactively engage in their own socialization.

Although socialization is important for all newcomers, it may be especially important, and at times difficult, for newcomers who are "different" from organizational old-timers and insiders (Jackson, Stone, & Alvarez, 1993). This chapter discusses organizational socialization from the perspective of the "distinctly different" newcomer. We'll review why socialization is important and how organizations may go about accomplishing it. We discuss training as an important socialization tool and how this tool can also convey the organization's value for diversity. Lastly, we'll talk about newcomers as more than just passive entities that get socialized, but also as individuals who can actively participate in their own socialization.

Job incumbents are important resources for newcomer socialization.

WHAT IS SOCIALIZATION?

Socialization involves attempts made by the organization to impart its values, goals, and perspectives to individuals that make it up, especially newcomers. Socialization is also described as being "concerned with the learning content and process by which an individual adjusts to a specific role in an organization" (Chao, O'Leary-Kelly, Wolf, Klein, & Gardner, 1994, p. 730). The socialization process may be described as simply as learning the ropes or it may be perceived as more complex and involving the entire process by which individuals come to know not only their job but also the values, expectations, and history of the employer (Chao et al., 1994). According to Cascio (2003) socialization is a joint activity in which both the individual newcomer and the organization are getting to know one another.

Clearly this process of learning is critical for a newcomer to the organization who must learn how to execute the duties of the new position, determine who are superiors and who are peers, and learn the unwritten expectations and rules of survival in the company. Effective socialization can also enhance a newcomer's commitment, job satisfaction, and job performance (Cascio, 2003). The socialization process is usually discussed as comprising four tasks: task mastery, role clarification, acculturation, and social integration (see Diversity Learning Point 4.1).

Demographic diversity of the organization may present several interesting dynamics given the goals of socialization. The achievement of **task mastery** is likely to be the same regardless of one's demographic membership or similarity/dissimilarity to organizational insiders. Still, insider stereotypes and misconceptions regarding a minority newcomer's intelligence, ability, and or competence

Diversity Learning Point 4.1	**Primary Tasks of the Socialization Process**[1]

Task	Description
Task mastery	Learning how to perform the components of one's job
Role clarification	Developing an understanding of one's role in the organization
Acculturation	Learning about and adjusting to the organization's culture
Social integration	Developing relationships with coworkers

[1]Morrison, E.W. (1993). Longitudinal study of the effects of information seeking on newcomer socialization. *Journal of Applied Psychology, 78*(2), 173–183.

may influence how task mastery is achieved. Goldstein and Gilliam (1990) in their review of the training literature found that there are many training programs designed to help female and minority newcomers make the transition to their organizations and do their jobs when deficits have never been found to suggest such training is even necessary. Clearly an insider that questions a newcomer's competence is likely to "water down" training activities and other tasks used to help the newcomer achieve task mastery. Furthermore, the skeptical insider may decide that the time investment in training and mentoring a minority newcomer is just not worthwhile, thus further threatening the effective socialization of the new hire.

Some Whites may feel that sponsoring or supporting a minority subordinate is riskier than sponsoring Whites because of the closer scrutiny given to minorities. Yet many minority executives have attributed much of their success to developmental relationships with superiors and peers (Thomas & Gabarro, 1999). Trust between the various parties must also be established if a successful socialization is to occur, yet this may be a difficult task, especially for those of dominant groups who lack experience with diversity (Moreland & Levine, 2002). Dissimilarity may pose additional challenges to a demographically different newcomer's ability to gain role clarification, acculturation, and, especially, social integration.

Role clarification involves newcomers' ability to gain information about their role in the organization. In trying to acquire role clarification the newcomer must ask, What is my position and status in the organization? Where does my role take me as I progress in my duties? How insiders such as peers and supervisors respond to the newcomer (formally as well as informally) may be shaped in part by the insiders' reactions to the demographic membership(s) of the newcomer.

The **acculturation task** involved in socialization involves learning about the company's culture and adjusting to it (Harquil & Cox, 1994). A lone Black woman manager reflected on her experience as a manager in a manufacturing plant of a *Fortune 500* company: "I had never felt so disadvantaged as a black woman. . . . It was very difficult. I entered a company where the whole world was the world of men. Everything was male culture. . . . They used different language, had different mores. I had to learn white male culture. I had to learn the culture of baseball and football. None of my analogies, none of my metaphors were appropriate. They didn't understand what I said . . ." (Bell & Nkomo, 2001, pp. 122–123).

A barrier to minority socialization may involve the extent to which company culture reflects the dominant group culture (likely a White or Eurocentric culture). In other words the question to be asked is, Are the organizational culture and White American culture distinguishable? If so, then it seems likely that a minority newcomer will have the opportunity to learn about the culture and embrace it. If the company culture is not distinguishable from White culture, then this overlap may pose a problem for socialization if minority newcomers feel the organization's values put them at a cultural disadvantage. Consider the case of Melanie (Diversity Case 4.1).

The final goal of newcomers is **social integration** into their new organization. This task is one that may present the most obvious barrier to minority socialization. Supervisors' and coworkers' stereotypes are clear barriers to a

| Diversity Case 4.1 | Melanie: Not Par for the Course |

Melanie was a new corporate lawyer fresh out of law school. She is a Latina from a working class background and attended college and law school in an urban setting. As a child she did what other kids in her neighborhood did during the summer. She played kickball and stickball, went to movies and bowling, and took dance classes at the local youth center. The backgrounds of other students at her college and law school were not very different from that of Melanie. Yet, when Melanie joined the law firm, she found that her background and youth experiences were quite dissimilar to others in the firm and to her clients. Melanie's employer expected her to not only be a good lawyer but to also "court" potential clients by joining them on golf and tennis outings. Furthermore, Melanie's employer frequently used phrases such as "par for the course" and "on the green," phrases she didn't quite understand. Melanie had never touched a golf club or a tennis racket in her life. She began to tire of being left out of the loop of conversations because she didn't speak the "lingo." Furthermore, she also started to resent the perception that her background was unusual (and that to some people in the firm it was perceived as deprived) because she didn't grow up playing golf and tennis. She also resisted her coworkers' subtle suggestions that she take up these games to be more of a team member. Eventually Melanie tired of being the "outsider" and eventually left the firm to take a position in the district attorney's office in her home city.

minority group member's social integration. Because of the sense of discomfort that often comes with mingling with members of minority groups, dominant-group members may hesitate to include minorities in social activities or in informational networks (Thomas & Gabarro, 1999). Additionally, Pettigrew & Martin (1987) discuss how one's position as a **solo** or **token** may interfere with integration into an organization. They define solos as individuals who are one of a kind in their organizational setting. Tokens on the other hand also are one of a kind, but they are believed to be in their position due to affirmative action. Furthermore, this belief is tied to the misconception that minority newcomers are less qualified than nonminority newcomers and unlikely to be able to pull their weight and contribute to the organization. Of course, racism, sexism, **ableism** (prejudice against the disabled), and the like may also interfere with minority newcomers' ability to socially integrate into their work setting and subsequently gain effective socialization.

WAYS OF THINKING ABOUT SOCIALIZATION

Researchers who study the process and content of organizational socialization all agree that it is an important process needed to achieve individual, and subsequently, organizational success. New hires cannot succeed in their job, despite the best credentials, if they are not knowledgeable about the inner workings of the company as well as where it has been and where it hopes to go.

Despite the perceived value of socialization, those who study it examine the issues in different ways. Saks and Ashforth (1997) identify the four dominant theoretical perspectives that drive this work: Van Maanen and Schein's model of people processing through socialization tactics, uncertainty reduction theory, social cognitive theory, and sense-making theory.

People Processing   Van Maanen and Schein (1979) proposed that organizational tactics to provide socialization experiences to newcomers fall along six bipolar dimensions (see Diversity Learning Point 4.2). They argue that the choice of tactics used by an organization subsequently influences the roles that newcomers adopt and their adjustment to the organization.

Uncertainty Reduction Theory   This perspective asserts that newcomers experience uncertainty. This uncertainty motivates them to reduce this uncertainty (and likely anxiety) so that the workplace becomes "more predictable, understandable, and ultimately controllable" (Saks & Ashforth, 1997, p. 236). This uncertainty ultimately gets reduced through organizational orientation and training programs, through other formal information provided through the employer, as well as through the relationships that form between newcomers and their peers and supervisors.

Social Cognitive Theory   Research on socialization conducted from this perspective typically argues that newcomers are socialized through their at-

Diversity Learning Point 4.2	**People Processing Socialization Tactics**[1]

Socialization Tactic Dimensions	Organizational Decision
Collective vs. Individual	• How will socialization be delivered to newcomers? • Will socialization be provided to groups or to individuals?
Formal vs. Informal	• Is the newcomers' status as such made public? • Are newcomers segregated from insiders?
Sequential vs. Random	• What is the process by which we will socialize newcomers? • Must newcomers jump over a series of hurdles in order to become full members (insiders) of the organization?
Fixed vs. Variable	• Do newcomers know when their status as such ends? • Is there a known period of probation?
Tournament vs. Contest	• Do we identify newcomers in terms of their potential? • Are some newcomers identified as being on the "fast track"?
Serial vs. Disjunctive	• How will newcomers be trained and socialized? • Will training and socialization be provided by their predecessor or someone from a training and development unit?
Investiture vs. Divestiture	• What is the role of training and socialization? • Is our training and socialization program an opportunity to build newcomers' efficacy for their new job or is it to remind them of how much they do not know?

[1]See Feldman, D. C. (1991). Socialization, resocialization, and training: Reframing the research agenda. In I. L. Goldstein & Associates (Eds.). *Training and development in organizations* (pp. 376–416). San Francisco: Jossey-Bass.

tempts to gain information from role models around them, such as supervisors and peers, and through goal setting and attempts to master one's new position and role. Acquiring information through role models and gaining mastery over one's job subsequently increases self-efficacy for one's new role. Bandura (1982) describes self-efficacy as the belief that one can accomplish a particular task or goal.

Diversity Learning Point 4.3	**Louis's Five Forms of Surprise During Organizational Entry**	

Surprises	Louis's Surprise Definition	Newcomer Experience
Surprise #1	When conscious expectations of the job are not met during early newcomer experience	"I thought I would find my new job more challenging intellectually."
Surprise #2	When expectations about oneself are unmet	"I thought I would be happier if I made more money, but I'm not."
Surprise # 3	When unconscious expectations of the job are unmet or features are unanticipated	"I knew it would be difficult to start over with a new organization; however, I had no idea how important it was to me to work around people my own age."
Surprise #4	Difficulties in accurately anticipating reactions to a new experience during the entry period	"I knew it would be difficult starting a new job with a new company; however, I underestimated how isolated and lonely I would feel."
Surprise # 5	When faulty cultural assumptions are made based upon one's previous organizational experience	"I thought casual Fridays meant that employees could wear jeans; it did at my previous employer."

Sense Making   Louis (1980) asserts that socialization occurs as newcomers attempt to make sense of the new world around them, especially those events that "surprise" the newcomer (see Diversity Learning Point 4.3). Through interactions with insiders, newcomers learn to effectively interpret and anticipate those events formerly classified as surprises.

If you examine closely the four perspectives described above, there are several opportunities where racial, cultural, or even gender differences may influence the effective socialization of a newcomer. For example, in both the social cognitive and uncertainty reduction models, newcomers are highly dependant upon the people around them to assist in their socialization. In the case of the social cognitive theory, newcomers rely upon role models through whom they can interpret the beliefs, appropriate behaviors, and actions in the organization. Yet the self-regulation literature also suggests that as individuals we are more likely to value and seek models like ourselves; this may also extend to demographic similarity. If the only similarities are organizational membership or

| Diversity in Practice 4.1 | **Top 10 Worst Diversity Practices**[1] |

1. **Having a diversity focus that is too broad.** By training to address all forms of diversity simultaneously, diversity efforts sometimes fail. Early data driven assessments and diversity needs analyses help inform decision makers of the most pressing diversity issues upon which to initially focus.
2. **Using code words rather than direct language.** For example, using the term *lifestyle* when you mean *sexual orientation*. Code language often masks our discomfort with issues around diversity.
3. **Continually researching and arguing the case for the diversity.** There is no lack of information about changing demographics or the growing minority market. Don't wait for a crisis to hit; start taking action.
4. **Avoiding the collection or use of data.** Data provide opportunities for learning about diversity-related needs and triggers for resistance (see point #2).
5. **Delegating the work for creating an inclusive climate to people in staff positions.** Top management must be involved in all diversity efforts, including training, in order for it to be successful.
6. **Focusing efforts on members of the nontraditional or excluded groups.** Diversity efforts should focus on inclusion rather than exclusion. Efforts therefore should be taken on by a diverse team of leaders who are able to articulate how diversity benefits *everyone*.
7. **Using a series of activities that appear to have no link to business success.** Diversity efforts gain credibility when organizational leaders and members see their impact on the bottom line, money.
8. **Developing a plan to create an inclusive climate with the belief that everyone will be happy.** This is simply unrealistic. Resistance occurs with any organizational change and is intensified when "touchy" subjects like diversity are targeted. Communication, training, and involvement are key mechanisms for reducing diversity resistance.
9. **Assuming that training is all that is needed.** Training should be partnered with action. Organizations have to both "talk the talk" and "walk the walk."
10. **Focusing the diversity efforts on customers and external public relationships.** Diversity is as much an internal organizational issue as it is an external issue. Organizations that fail to create inclusive organizational climates risk losing diverse talent that promotes diversity learning, and which could help institutions to deal with external pressures and diversity issues.

[1]From D. D. Frost, "Review Worst Diversity Practices to Learn From Others' Mistakes," *HR Focus* 76(4): 11–12. Reprinted by permission.

job classification, it may become difficult for the newcomer to ascertain if insider beliefs, actions, and goals are those that represent the employer or those that actually represent the insider's social identity group (e.g., their ethnic group).

Likewise, uncertainty reduction theory focuses upon the newcomer's ability to forge social relationships with peers and supervisors in order to learn the appropriate "way to be" in the organization. Yet difficulties may arise in forging these relationships if they occur across demographic memberships.

Louis's sense-making model suggests that newcomers are motivated to make sense of their new organization as they encounter surprises that are in large part based upon previous experiences. Again, the effective socialization of "different" newcomers may be threatened if their previous employment or membership did not demographically resemble the new organization. For example, consider the arguments against same gender or same race colleges. Some argue that these colleges do their students a disservice given that the world at large is not of a single gender or race. Upon graduation new professionals are not only faced with learning the ins and outs of their new employer (or graduate school), they must also make the transition from being with others who are mostly like themselves to being with others who are demographically different, or even to being the numerical minority. Jackson et al.'s (1993) review of the socialization and diversity literature suggests that women and members of ethnic groups who are organizational newcomers and dissimilar from insiders experience significant tension as they attempt to deal with their multiple group memberships. This scenario may present an additional socialization burden in that there is additional learning that needs to take place, but it also may be a threat to a newcomer's sense of efficacy for adjusting.

HOW IS SOCIALIZATION ACCOMPLISHED?

As mentioned previously, socialization can occur formally or informally. Formal mechanisms for socialization include new employee orientation programs, training, employee handbooks, and company-sponsored mentoring programs. Often, there is some type of formal recognition that this person is a newcomer (Wanberg & Kammeyer-Mueller, 2000). Informal mechanisms for socialization, which are more likely used (Morrison, 1993), include conversations with peers and supervisors, lunches with coworkers, and company parties and cookouts.

Training

For many organizational newcomers training programs are the main vehicle or tool by which they get socialized (Feldman, 1991). **Training programs** deliver information about the mechanics of doing one's job, but they also help establish employee expectations of their new role and organization. Feldman states:

> Over the past fifteen years, training has been used as a means of converting employees to the corporation's ideology (for example, "positive personnel practices," training in "union prevention"), as a reward for past good performance (as opposed to training for remediation), as a career development tool, as a test for promotion, and as an outplacement device. (p. 378)

Training then assists in the accomplishment of many of the tasks and goals of socialization that were stated earlier. Most obvious is the ability of training to help accomplish the task mastery goal of socialization. The function of teaching newcomers how to accomplish their jobs is what most of us typically perceive to be the role of training. Training also aids in accomplishing role clarification and acculturation through the delivery of information about the organization's structure (i.e., who reports to whom and how different individuals and departments are connected) as well as its history (e.g., who was its founder and what were that person's goals). In addition, training can help in the newcomer's social integration, especially if it is done in groups where newcomers themselves start to form bonds. Social integration can also be assisted by training if it is delivered by predecessors or peers thus providing another opportunity to establish relationships with organizational insiders. It is clear that many of the learning processes involved in socialization start with newcomer training programs (Goldstein & Ford, 2002).

Training can facilitate or hinder effective socialization of minority newcomers depending on whether the training is responsive to their unique needs (Ferdman, 1995). Training for the sake of learning mastery is unlikely to differ with respect to minority participants unless some portion of the training population has a particular educational or skill need that has to be remedied. Training to establish role definition is not likely to hinder the socialization of a diverse workforce unless such training reinforces the status quo of the organization. In fact, training for role definition can facilitate minority socialization when it reinforces to trainees that a variety of people can hold a position as long as they have the requisite knowledge, skills, and abilities (KSAs).

Training that assists in the socialization tasks of acculturation and social integration are those areas that must be examined most closely in terms of their diversity dynamic. Yet many working in management and supervision believe that in a multicultural organization, training should be used to eradicate barriers to minority success and must therefore focus on fulfilling the "special" needs of nontraditional groups. In their analysis of this philosophy, Goldstein and Gilliam (1990) suggest:

> Training issues are more complex than can be addressed by simply asking what training the individual requires. Rather, the organization needs to provide the training necessary for helping individuals at work to accept persons first entering the organization. In the case of women entering new careers, that point cannot be emphasized enough. The issue is the same for minorities. There is no evidence that the task requirement for the job of a manager for a female or minority male are any different than for a White male. Also, there is no evidence from person analysis that females need special training on particular KSAs that is not required by males. Thus, it is not presently possible to support the need for special training programs for women. However, that has not prevented the development of thousands of such specialized training programs for women, even though data supporting accomplishments of these programs is virtually nonexistent. . . . However, it is clear that individuals already in the organization often need training on how to provide a supportive climate for individuals just entering the workplace. This is especially true when individuals entering the workplace are from populations that have in the past been nontraditional in that work setting. (p. 140)

Training therefore can promote the effective socialization of nontraditional newcomers through promoting diversity and the values that will sustain it to all employees—regardless of racial and gender group membership. Diversity training is an industry that has grown exponentially over the past 20 years. Although there are many practitioners offering these types of training and development programs, organizations are rightly becoming more picky about the programs that they offer to their employees. The following section of this chapter will review what we know about this industry, provide examples of the types of programs being offered, and present information about the factors that are believed to lead to their success in promoting a supportive climate for the socialization of nontraditional newcomers.

Training as a Tool for Imparting Diversity Values   Just as there is conceptual ambiguity associated with the term *diversity*, there is similar ambiguity associated with the concept of **diversity training** (Ferdman, 1995). Diversity training is used to refer to programs providing information and enhanced awareness of women and racial minorities, programs that challenge employees' feelings of self and identity (e.g., Kirkland & Regan, 1997), sensitivity training, anti-bias training, values training, interpersonal skills training (Rynes & Rosen, 1995), increasing awareness, knowledge and understanding, attitude change, skill enhancement, and raising leader awareness of diversity issues (Goldstein & Ford, 2002). Ferdman and Brody (1996) further argue that the term *diversity training* does not refer to any one particular activity and that it is broadly used to refer to one-hour briefings as well as long-term organizational change efforts. See Diversity in Practice 4.2 for examples of diversity training programs in different types of organizations.

Ferdman and Brody's (1996) review of diversity training covers the why, what, and how of this growing industry. The authors argue that many organizations provide some sort of training programs to their employees for three potential reasons (the why). Organizations are increasingly facing social and legal pressure to do so. As companies observe others in their industry as well as their competitors providing this form of training, they feel the pressure to do likewise. Furthermore, employees also come to expect that training will be offered. In addition, some organizational leaders may believe that the provision of diversity training may help protect the organization from having to pay fines associated with discrimination claims if they use diversity training to at least appear to be a culturally fair and progressively minded company. Organizations also provide diversity training because leadership believes it is the fair and moral thing to do. Others provide diversity training because they believe that it will aid in their overall business success. Perhaps such training can enable a workforce to deal more effectively with an increasingly multicultural marketplace, or aid a multicultural workforce to work together more effectively (at least avoid the costs of conflict related to diversity).

Ferdman and Brody (1996) describe the "what" of diversity training as dealing with four issues: level of change, orientation, objectives/targets, and positioning. When deciding about the level of change, organizations and those

Diversity in Practice 4.2

Examples of Diversity Training

Organization	Goals	Practices
Wisconsin Power and Light[1]	• Understand, respect, and value the differences among employees in order to fully utilize human resources for a competitive advantage in the marketplace • Foster a work environment that encourages mutual respect. Expectations about diversity are: — There will be an appreciation of diversity at all organizational levels. — Employees will respect one another's differences. — The company will provide an environment supportive of diversity. — Employees will seek and nurture different perspectives. — Employees throughout the company must not tolerate behaviors that violate these objectives.	• Diversity steering committee formed a diversity training team to ensure all employees received training. • Training content based upon the results of a survey of all employees. • One of the vice presidents or managers opens each training session to ensure employees understand the commitment of the company to diversity issues. • Workshop facilitators explain the benefits of diversity for the company, the company's expectations of employees, and helps trainees to recognize organizational behaviors that support and that hinder diversity. • Trainees are given workbooks that include the training agenda as well as other support materials and company policies regarding selection and promotion. • Trainees also develop specific action plans that will assist in achieving the company's goals. They also develop work group norms to meet company objectives.

Mercedes Benz-USA[2]

- Improve diversity awareness.
- Encourage employee ownership of the diversity effort.
- Provides company's Diversity Awareness Training program to 1,600 employees.
- Uses interactive workshops of 14–20 employees that discuss diversity as a business issue.
- Ideas generated are shared with the executive management team and subsequently impact the company's diversity strategy.

The Seattle Times Co.[3]

- Makes efforts to embrace pluralism which they define as the existence and preservation of various groups within society. Their stated objectives are to:
  — Communicate diversity commitment to all employees.
  — Establish department/employment goals, timetables, and action plans.
  — Develop company-wide assessment and evaluation systems to monitor progress.
  — Development a review and feedback system of diversity progress.
  — Develop an ongoing system of communication to create and reinforce employee awareness.
- Two-day training program called Exploration into Diversity held 10 times per year.
- Training is mandatory for managers and voluntary for other employees.
- The only training available to everyone in the company.
- Each training program begins with a review of the philosophy and terminology related to diversity such as pluralism and multicultur-alism. Other activities include discussing reasons for why the company embraces diversity, brainstorming barriers to diversity, and action planning.
- Supplemental activities include two-hour follow-up sessions, a diversity newsletter, and the establishment of a diversity council.

Continued

Diversity in Practice 4.2 | Continued

Organization	Goals	Practices
Coca-Cola Co.[4]	• Convey that diversity is a keystone to the company's future success. • Create an employee population with advanced diversity skills, understanding, and awareness.	• Two-day training program held annually over a four-year period. • All U.S. employees will undergo training beginning with the top management team. • Training program takes a unique cumulative approach so that each year's training will build upon that delivered the previous year.

[1]Mueller, N. L. (1996). Wisconsin Power and Light's model diversity program. *Training and Development, 50*(3), 57–60.
[2]Francois, V. G. (March 20, 2000). Employee input key to Mercedes-Benz diversity training. www.DiversityInc.com.
[3]Anfuso, D. (1995). Diversity keeps newspaper up with the times. *Personnel Journal, 74*(7), 30–41.
[4]Stavraka, C. (Oct. 11, 2000). Coke mandates diversity training for all U.S. workers. www.DiversityInc.com.

Figure 4.1 | Diversity Training: The Why, What, and How

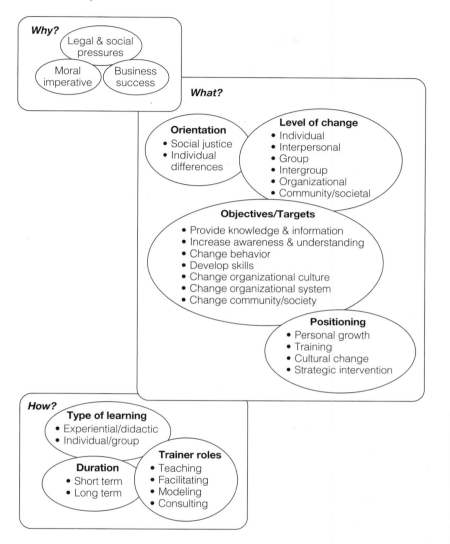

From B. M. Ferdman and S. E. Brody, "Models of Diversity Training," in D. Landis and R. S. Bhagat (eds.), *Handbook of Intercultural Training* (Thousand Oaks, CA: Sage Publishing, 1996), p. 283. Reprinted by permission.

responsible for the delivery of diversity training must decide if the training is intended for the individual, interpersonal, group, intergroup, organizational, or community/societal levels.

The orientation question deals with the perspective of the training. Should the training take on a social justice perspective, which is righting wrongs and working against discrimination and oppression, or an individual differences perspective, which encourages trainees to value all differences?

Potential objectives/targets of diversity training include providing information, increasing awareness, changing behavior, developing skills, changing organizational culture, changing the organizational system, and changing the community or society. The objective/target chosen likely reflects the level of change intended.

The "how" of diversity training involves making decisions regarding the type of learning that will occur (experiential vs. didactic, individual vs. group), the duration of the training (short vs. long term) and the role of the trainer. That is, is the trainer a teacher, facilitator, model, or consultant?

Perceived Success of Diversity Training   Rynes and Rosen (1995) found that the perceived success of diversity training was in large part related to the support that top management offered to the training. Their study of over 700 human resource professionals further suggested that perceived training success was also related to the mandatory attendance of all managers in the training, the long-term evaluation of training results, awards offered to managers for increasing diversity, and a broad and inclusive definition of diversity existing within the organization. Roberson, Kulik, and Pepper (2001) have further demonstrated that the perceived effectiveness of diversity training can be influenced by the context of the training, specifically the racial composition of the training group. Their field study of graduate students' (teaching assistants) responses to diversity training revealed that trainees with prior diversity training experience respond favorably to the training when learning within racially homogeneous groups. For those trainees without prior diversity training experience, the homogeneity or heterogeneity of the training experience did not seem to matter in regard to their evaluations of the training. Perhaps training should occur across stages so that broad lessons about diversity can be offered in heterogeneous groups. Later sessions can follow up with deeper-level conversations about race, gender, sexuality, power, and privilege within one's workplace.

DESPERATELY SEEKING SOCIALIZATION: PROACTIVE SOCIALIZATION

Organizational newcomers are not simply empty vessels into which organizations and their members pour in information in order to achieve socialization. Newcomers are also active socializers; that is, they engage in proactive socialization (Crant, 2000; Morrison, 2002). **Proactive socialization** can involve behaviors such as information seeking and feedback seeking (both of which are classified as sense-making behavior), relationship building, job change negotiation, and positive framing (Ashford & Black, 1996). Diversity Learning Point 4.4 expands upon these behaviors.

Diversity Learning Point 4.4 | Proactive Socialization Behaviors

Behavior	Description
Information seeking	Reflects newcomers' search for information about the job and about the organization. Likely reflects a desire to reduce uncertainty. Information may be acquired through those around them or from formal documents.
Feedback seeking	Reflects newcomers' search for information regarding how they are doing.
Relationship building	Reflects newcomers' attempts to establishing relationships and social interactions with those around them.
Job change negotiation	Reflects newcomers' attempts to change their jobs in order to further reduce uncertainty and fulfill a need for control.
Positive framing	Reflects newcomers' attempts to alter their initial impressions of their new experiences by looking on the positive side or putting a positive spin on things. Described by Ashford and Black (1996) as a self-management technique.

(Ashford & Black, 1996)

Proactive socialization attempts by newcomers who are members of the dominant organizational group often lead to positive results (Crant, 2000; Morrison, 2002). On the other hand, proactive socialization attempts by women, people of color, or other nontraditional newcomers may impair their ability to be effectively socialized. For example, information seeking and job change negotiation by a nontraditional newcomer may both be perceived by an organizational insider as asking for "special favors" or preferential treatment.

Insiders may further be reluctant to provide honest feedback to proactive newcomers for fears of being perceived as biased; especially if the feedback is negative (Cox, 1994; Rynes & Rosen, 1995). Insiders are also believed to be reluctant to form relationships with newcomers who are underrepresented in their work environment for fear that such newcomers will fail in their job duties and thus reflect negatively upon the insiders themselves.

Lastly, positive framing may prevent the nontraditional newcomer from developing an accurate "read" of the organization, especially in terms of the climate for diversity and the potential biases of peers and supervisors that can threaten subsequent performance and performance evaluation. If newcomers do not have a clear and accurate vision of where they stand, then how can they prevent or resolve biased reactions and evaluations of their job performance?

Berry's (1984) work on the **socialization orientation** of cultural newcomers also has implications for how newcomers affect their own socialization. This concept of how a newcomer frames his or her experience is interesting since it suggests that how newcomers perceive or think about their organizational experiences can influence if and how they are socialized. When discussing the experiences of immigrants or expatriates to new countries and cultures, Berry (1984) suggests that these cross-cultural newcomers impact their adjustment and socialization through how they attempt to negotiate their memberships in their own (home) culture with that of their new membership in the "donor" culture. I believe, as do others (Jackson et al., 1993), that this cross-cultural research has implications for understanding minority newcomers' experiences in socialization within new organizational settings.

Berry's framework suggests that cross-cultural newcomers use one of four different orientations in dealing with their newcomer experience: Assimilation, integration, marginalization, and separation. Those who **assimilate** to the donor culture totally replace their home culture with that of the donor's. Other immigrants or sojourners may instead attempt to **integrate**, become a part of, their home and donor cultures. Those newcomers who have a **separation** orientation reject the culture of the donor country while adhering to the norms and values of their home culture. Those who are **marginalized** do not immerse themselves in either the donor or the home culture (Berry, 1984).

What are the implications of this work for understanding a minority newcomer's experience in an organization? Well, clearly from the vantage point of the organization, socialization appears easiest for those who choose assimilation. Yet assimilation may result in an individual's anxiety and stress related to the rejection of that person's ethnic and/or gender group membership; both of which are very important components of one's sense of self. Integration also appears beneficial, although likely difficult, especially if the new organization is not very tolerant of diversity or its members hold on to negative stereotypes of a newcomer's group. Separation may threaten minority newcomers' ability to gain the information needed from insiders to effectively do their job as well as eventually become a full and bona fide insider. Additionally, marginalization may make minority newcomers feel as though they lack any type of identity and further exacerbate typical feelings of isolation and uncertainty that accompany this stage of organizational life.

CONCLUSION

Socialization is an important facet of organizational life. This chapter has focused on the socialization process of newcomers. However, many argue (e.g., Saks & Ashforth, 1997) that socialization is a continual process as organizations (and their leadership) change and evolve. Furthermore, insiders are socialized into new positions and roles as they get promoted within the organization. New socialization may also occur as the organization experiences transformation as in the case of a merger or downsizing.

The presence of a demographically diverse cohort of newcomers into an organization poses many opportunities and challenges for the organization and those individuals. There are many possible barriers to the effective socialization of minority newcomers such as strong, albeit ethnocentric (Triandis, 1995), organizational cultures that favor the ethnicities and cultures of existing insiders. Given that the socialization process is so dependent upon the relationships newcomers build with insiders, insiders' stereotypes and biases may impact the ability of the newcomers to form productive relationships with these organizational members. Training is a formal socialization opportunity used by many organizations to impart an organization's value of diversity to all of its members. However, training that reinforces stereotypes, that is nonresponsive to trainee needs, or that is designed to compensate for presumed minority and female deficits (even when they are not proven to exist) may further threaten effective socialization. Lastly, we discussed the proactive strategies that some newcomers use to acquire effective socialization as well as how the orientation or mindset of newcomers poses additional socialization opportunities and challenges.

Discussion Items

1. Describe the process by which you were socialized at your institution. In what ways did this process (explicitly or implicitly) inform you about diversity at your university?
2. Compare and contrast a successful socialization experience versus one that is less successful. What are the outcomes of unsuccessful socialization for the newcomer and for the organization?
3. Think of a time in which you experienced being a member of a minority group. What issues affected your ability to form relationships with majority group members?
4. Review the examples of diversity training efforts provided in Diversity in Practice 4.2. Analyze an organization's diversity effort from the perspective of Ferdman and Brody (1996) (see Diversity Figure 4.1).

 InfoTrac College Edition

Be sure to log on to InfoTrac College Edition and search for additional readings on topics of interest to you.

5 CHAPTER | Career Development

Barriers and Strategies

Read Case 5.1 on page 73. What could have happened in between Denice's graduate school years and her start as a new executive? Most likely, the disconnect between Denice's school days and her professional life could have been avoided with more effective career development, especially through the building of developmental relationships. Career development is an important process for any employee, but it seems especially critical for employees who are somehow different in their workplace. Women, racial minorities, and gay and lesbian employees who work in nontraditional career paths are at risk for lacking effective career development, which can subsequently impair their opportunities for **career mobility**; that is, their chances for promotion and career movement.

This chapter will examine the ways in which difference due to demographic characteristics can interfere with the ability to establish much needed **developmental relationships** that are critical for career development. Developmental relationships include relationships with mentors and with a workplace network that provide individuals with information, support, and feedback among other benefits. The chapter concludes by offering suggestions for both individuals and organizations that want to ensure that *all* employees have an equal opportunity to develop their careers.

Career development is a lifelong process that encompasses three sets of activities. Career development includes understanding one's own career interests and preferences; that is, developing self-awareness and knowledge. Career development also includes identifying, obtaining, and developing the needed skills and education for a career. Third, career development involves the con-

Career development is a continuous workplace challenge.

Diversity Case 5.1	# Denice's Dilemma

Denice W. was a young executive with a new MBA who was on the fast track in one of the big eight accounting firms. Denice was able to secure this highly prized position in large part due to her success as a graduate student.

During her graduate program, Denice displayed admirable leadership skills that propelled her to the position of president of the Business Graduate Student Association. As a new graduate student, Denice had an effective mentor in Dr. Stahl. Dr. Stahl introduced her to several important people within the business school as well as in the university administration. Dr. Stahl provided substantial feedback and guidance to Denice regarding school-related matters like choosing courses but she also provided significant support in encouraging Denice to think about her future goals and career. With Dr. Stahl's support, Denice was able to effectively network with her peers, and gain important positions of influence and visibility.

Given Denice's incredible success in graduate school, she simply could not understand why she seemed to have so much difficulty in exhibiting the same level of leadership in her new job. She was working with the same kind of people with whom she had studied in graduate school, yet she felt disconnected and very much alone in the workplace. She did her job well, but lacked motivation to improve her performance or to find new ways to contribute to the organization. Even worse, no one else seemed to care that she just simply did her job. Her position on the fast track seemed to be taking her nowhere.

Diversity Learning Point 5.1 | **Career Development Initiatives**

Giscombe and Mattis (2002) examined the results of the diversity programs of 15 *Fortune* 500 companies. One of the areas typically covered by these programs is career development. These programs typically include succession planning, high potential identification, mentoring, network groups, and individual development planning or career pathing.

Frequent Diversity-Focused Career Development Initiatives in the *Fortune* 500

Career Development Initiative	Activity
Succession Planning	Succession planning efforts range from informal discussions about minority group members assuming new and higher-level roles to more formal plans that include timelines and plans for which supervisors are held accountable.
Identification of high potentials	Identifying high potentials is tightly linked with succession planning given that development of any employee only pays off for the individual and for the organizations when opportunities for advancement are available.
Network groups	Sometimes called affinity groups, formal network groups allow members of minority groups to gain social and professional support, professional development, and access to role models.

tinual assessment of your career interests and your skills in order to determine if they are meeting your needs as well as those of your employer (Zunker, 1990). Career development is an important activity no matter where you are in your career. It is as important at the beginning of your career as it may be at the end of your career.

At the beginning of one's career we are attempting to assess person–job fit, and gather feedback as to how we are actually performing in our jobs. At the early career stages we are also looking for opportunities to figure out our career path, our job, and our organizations and what we need to do and learn in order to reach our career goals. Career development is even important at the "end" of one's career given that the "no-work" retirement is quickly becoming a thing of the past; retirees are interested in how to use the huge amount of education, skills, and experiences they have acquired in new, creative, and helpful ways.

Figure 5.1 | The Spectrum of Career Development Activities

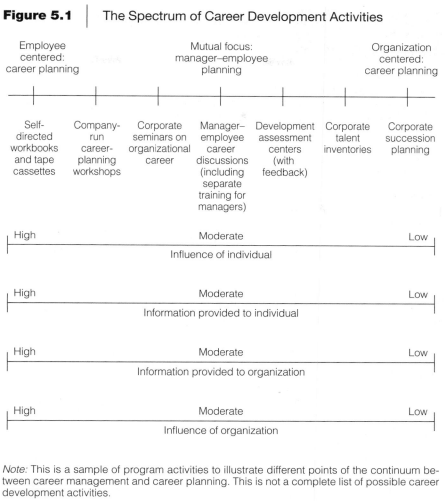

Note: This is a sample of program activities to illustrate different points of the continuum between career management and career planning. This is not a complete list of possible career development activities.

From D. T. Hall, "Individual and Organizational Career Development in Changing Times," in D. T. Hall (ed.), *Career Development in Organizations* (San Francisco: Jossey-Bass, 1986), p. 4. Reprinted by permission.

CAREER DEVELOPMENT AS AN OPPORTUNITY FOR INDIVIDUAL VITALITY

Career development is a multifaceted activity (see Figure 5.1). Through career development activities, workers are able to gain new insight about their organization and its future, as well as learn and develop new skills. I believe most importantly, effective career development facilitates personal introspection. It gives individuals the opportunity to reflect upon their strengths, weaknesses, interests, and needs—both personal and professional. Furthermore, effective career development allows workers the opportunities to set goals and develop plans for their professional futures.

CAREER DEVELOPMENT FOR ORGANIZATIONAL VITALITY

The activities that encompass career development can also be a source of organizational vitality. As employees develop new career interests, knowledge, and strengths, they bring these competencies to the workplace. Organizations benefit from retaining employees who are constantly developing and helping the organization to be competitive in new and different ways. Employees who have opportunities for continuous learning and development also help make the organization an attractive employer for job seekers who are looking for the same type of work environment. Thus effective career development can create a cycle of employee recruitment–development that facilitates organizational effectiveness.

There are two important facets of career development. **Career planning** reflects the career-related activities of an individual employee who is attempting to plan a satisfying and successful career. The process of career planning can include becoming self-aware of one's strengths, weaknesses, and interests as well as one's goals and developing a plan for one's education, work, and development related to one's goals. **Career management** reflects those activities of an organization to select, evaluate, assign, and develop employees so that they can meet future workforce needs. Career management is a process focused on preparing, implementing, and monitoring plans acquired by individual employees or developed in conjunction with the organization's career system (Hall, 1986). These activities are rarely done in isolation from one another but instead often reflect a range of activities that are ongoing to assist in career development.

This chapter examines both aspects of career development, with specific focus on the barriers to career development that stem from prejudices and biases that exist in society and which spill over into the workplace. We will also examine unique organizational situations and circumstances that may prevent the effective career planning of minority workers. The chapter concludes with suggestions for both individuals and organizations to facilitate the effective career development of minority workers.

BARRIERS TO THE CAREER DEVELOPMENT OF NONTRADITIONAL EMPLOYEES

There are many barriers to the career development of groups that are underrepresented within an organization. Prejudices and biases that exist outside of the organization spill over into the workplace and interfere with the ability of

Diversity Case 5.2	Two Successful Career Development Efforts

Hewitt Associates, a Chicago-based international human resources consulting firm, recently conducted a study of 240 of the worlds top multinational companies. Hewitt ranked these organizations on their ability to develop executives and found that companies most effective at career development engaged in three key efforts: consistent development, improving core skills and coaching from top management. Those organizations most successful at developing their executives had nontrendy career development plans that were consistently applied throughout a person's career. Furthermore, these career development plans were consistent across departments and divisions so that executives used the same language and principles in their development efforts. These companies also found opportunities for their employees to develop in areas of weakness and to exhibit areas of strength. Coaching from high-level leaders was also a bonus for employees working at these organizations. Two of the companies listed in the top five were IBM and General Electric (GE).

IBM's career development program includes training, professional development opportunities, and e-learning. In addition they have two mentoring programs. One is a 6- to 12-month skill mentoring program that provides employees with a mentor in order to develop a skill critical to their particular business unit. IBM also has a new employee mentoring program that assists employees in developing a comprehension of the organization and its culture as well as new skills.

Visit www-8.ibm.com/employment/sg/graduates/cd.html for more information on IBM's career development efforts.

Like IBM, GE encourages mentoring through informal methods. GE encourages its employees to take the initiative in developing mentoring partnerships through talking with peers and managers and other people with experiences to learn from. Networking is also important at GE and they describe their organization as having a "boundaryless environment" that supports "horizontal learning," suggesting their organization does not have rigid barriers and that learning and development in GE can occur throughout the organization, not simply from the top down. GE supports professional communities and networking forums. GE networks include an African American Forum, an Asian Pacific American Forum, a Hispanic Forum, and a Women's Network. More information about GE's career development efforts can be found at www.gecareers.com/Career/management.cfm.

More information on the Hewitt Associates study can be found at Hewitt's Web site, http://was4.hewitt.com/hewitt/resource/newsroom/pressrl/2003/09-30-03.htm and at the site of their research partner *Chief Executive* at http://www.chiefexecutive.net/mag/192/index.html.

---

minority employees to form constructive and healthy workplace relationships that are critical for career development. Pharr (1988) identified several common elements of oppression that impact minority group members outside of the organization, but which may also impair the ability to develop diverse workplace relationships.

External Barriers That Spill Over into the Workplace

Pharr (1988) identified several common elements of oppression that can undermine equality outside of the workplace and impair career development inside of organizations. Among these elements of oppression are a defined norm/other, lack of prior claim, and stereotyping. These elements of oppression reflect subtle biases that impede the ability of women, ethnic minorities, or gay/lesbian individual to have equal access to developmental relationships and the career opportunities that they deserve.

Our societal **defined norm** establishes what is perceived as normal—the status quo. This norm is never questioned (Pharr, 1988). For example, White men may be more identified as "high potentials" in their workplace because they make up the defined norm for those who hold leadership positions. It seems almost "normal" that they would be on the fast track and no one questions if their mere race, gender, sexuality, or class affords them preferential treatment in their workplace.

Just as there is a defined norm, those who are different from that norm are defined as the **other**. "Others" are always evaluated in reference to the defined norm and are thus marginalized because of their differences, which may be due to race, gender, sexuality, or all of the above (Pharr, 1988). Women, people of color, and gay men and lesbians may experience more difficulty in being identified as "high potentials" because they belong to groups identified as the defined others. Others who are underrepresented within an organization or a career path may experience difficulty in "breaking through" to more desirable positions held by the defined norm because they don't fit the image of what a leader or manager is supposed to look or be like.

Those individuals who belong to groups that lacked power at times in which institutions were being established often lack claim to those same institutions in more contemporary times. **Lack of prior claim** is an argument used by "the defined norm" to maintain their own base of power and to refuse access to that power for "the defined other" (Pharr, 1988). For example, women have had to fight consistently for access to country clubs that extend memberships only to men. The refusal to admit women and other minority groups is often based upon the sentiment that "this is the way it has always been done" or "you should have been involved at the beginning." Yet at the time many of these organizations were founded it was legal to lock certain groups out of membership. Having access to these clubs, groups, or forums is important because they often provide informal but important opportunities for networking and deal making that facilitate career development.

Stereotypes are (often negative) generalizations that are based upon group membership. Stereotypes are power impediments to the upward mobility of members of minority groups in organizations. If we consider the stereotypes of women as weak and ethnic minorities as lazy, it is easy to see how these stereotypes can affect managerial attitudes and behaviors that subsequently deny women and minorities opportunities for career development and upward movement in organizations. Yet even presumably positive stereotypes can deny someone career development opportunities. For example, Asians and Asian Americans are stereotyped as smart and especially gifted in the areas of mathematics and sciences. Although these talents are highly revered in our society, the stereotype of Asians as a "model minority" can impair their ability to acquire positions of leadership, given that those who are oriented toward the math and sciences are rarely presumed to have a comparably high level of people skills and leadership potential. A presumed language barrier, again another stereotype, may interfere with the ability of organizations to evaluate Asians and Asian Americans for positions of leadership. Cox (1994) also has discussed how the lack of a presumed "payback potential" limits the career development (and perhaps the promotion) of women and older workers. Women are presumed to have less opportunity to pay back their employer in years served due to the presumption that they will eventually leave their careers to take care of families. Older workers are simply presumed to be too close to retirement to be able to pay back the organization with a significant number of years of service.

Barriers That Exist Inside Organizations

Many of the barriers facing minority group members in organizations are a result of difficulties in the **structural integration** of diverse groups throughout the organization (Giscombe & Mattis, 2002). For example, when women and ethnic minorities are disproportionately represented at the lowest levels of the organizations rather than being represented across levels, divisions, and departments, there is a lack of their structural integration. Even in industries that may have a majority of minority employees, oftentimes dominant group members hold the power in those workplaces. For example, Maume (1999) found evidence of **occupational segregation** in female-dominated industries such as banking. In many banking organizations the majority of the employees are women, such as bank tellers, but the executive levels of those organizations are composed mainly of men. Many of the elements of oppression articulated by Pharr (1988) might be responsible for the occupational segregation that frequently limits opportunities for ethnic minorities and women and likely of gay men and lesbians.

Furthermore, minority group members may also lack **social integration**, that is, they may lack access to important workplace relationships that are important in developing one's career (Giscombe & Mattis, 2002). Thus minority group members are often locked out of opportunities for relationships with co-workers and more senior employees due to the difficulty they experience in forming workplace relationships across demographic differences. In many ways lack of diversity throughout the organization creates barriers for diverse newcomers to establish these relationships with similar others in positions of power and authority (Giscombe & Mattis, 2002). Access to relationships with mentors and access to informal workplace networks are key to successful career development.

LACK OF OPPORTUNITIES FOR MENTORING

Mentoring provides important career-building opportunities. Mentoring is typically identified as a relationship between a junior employee (the protégé) and a more senior adviser (mentor) in order to develop the protégé's career. Career outcomes related to effective mentoring include career satisfaction and career success (Collins, Kamya, & Tourse, 1997).

Mentoring serves both **instrumental functions** as well as **psychosocial functions** for employees (Kram, 1985). The instrumental function of mentoring reflects the career information and workplace advocacy that mentoring can offer. In addition, the psychosocial functions include the social and emotional support that effective mentoring can offer (Kram, 1985).

Lack of structural integration limits opportunities for diverse mentoring (Giscombe & Mattis, 2002). For example, Korn/Ferry International and the Columbia Business School (cited in Cole, 2002) report that 80% of their sample of high-level professionals of color and women lacked **formal mentors**. A third reported not having **informal mentors** too. Formal mentors are assigned through formal mentoring programs established by the organization. These programs are usually responsible for matching mentors and protégés, providing them with training as to how to establish a successful mentoring relationship, and at times providing oversight and evaluation of the program. Informal mentoring relationships develop more naturally and occur when relationships form between a junior and a senior colleague.

Ragins (1997) mentions that "mentoring relationships involving minority members differ from their majority counterparts in the development processes, and outcomes associated with the relationship" (p. 513). For example, women and ethnic minorities appear to have different mentoring experiences as compared to their male and White counterparts. At times there are differences in regard to mentoring access and at other times the type of mentoring provided appears to be different for different types of protégés.

Thomas (1990) found no gender differences in mentoring access but he did find racial differences in access to mentoring relationships. Cox and Nkomo (1991) found similar results. Dreher and Ash (1990) found no differences in mentoring access across gender.

Although women appear to have mentors as often as do men, women do appear to encounter more difficulties in establishing mentoring relationships. The lack of structural integration of women throughout the highest levels of organizations clearly creates a barrier for upwardly mobile women to be mentored by more senior women. There are also barriers for women who must therefore seek to be mentored by more senior men. For example, Ragins and Cotton (1991) found that women, as compared to men, report greater barriers to mentors. Barriers to cross-gendered mentoring relationships include (1) the potential that male mentors may mistake female protégés' attempts at forming a mentoring relationship as an attempt to initiate a romantic relationship, (2) prevalent sex roles that encourage women to adopt a more passive position in relationships and that may make it difficult for women to be proactive in developing mentoring relationships, especially with men, and (3) women may lack access to the same informal opportunities that male protégés may have to initiate mentoring relationships with male mentors (Ragins & Cotton, 1991).

Why are there barriers to mentoring relationships for minority group members? As was the case with women, the lack of structural integration of minority group members in many organizations limits their career development opportunities. Minority group members are almost forced to form mentoring relationships across groups and this issue itself serves as a barrier to acquiring a mentor (Ragins & Cotton, 1991).

Similarly, some dominant members may resist forming mentoring relationships with women, ethnic minorities, or sexual minorities simply out of prejudice. "Specifically, negative stereotypes, attributions, and perceptions of competence, combined with increased visibility and negative work group reactions, restrict minority members' access to mentoring relationships and the outcomes associated with the relationship" (Ragins, 1997, p. 513). Mentoring is an asset and an advantage for any employee, including mentors. The career success of protégés often reflects positively on the leadership and the development offered by mentors, thus increasing career opportunities for the mentors themselves. Mentors who believe that minority groups members are less likely to be successful at their jobs will avoid mentoring relationships with these employees out of the fear that minority employees' ultimate failure will reflect negatively upon them.

Women and employees who are openly gay encounter an additional barrier to mentoring—employee perceptions. As is the case for women and people of color, openly gay and lesbian employees may encounter **interpersonal discrimination** in the workplace. Interpersonal discrimination, at times referred to as **distancing**, reflects face-to-face discrimination in which individuals avoid, exclude, and distance themselves from others based upon some characteristic (Lott & Maluso, 1995). Race, gender, and sexuality have all been identified as cues for distancing behavior. Fernald's (1995) review of literature on interpersonal heterosexism revealed that heterosexuals distance themselves from *labeled* homosexuals through a variety of ways. Heterosexuals physically place themselves farther away from individuals they perceive to be gay, they report having less in common with someone they believe is gay, and they overall report feeling less attracted to individuals labeled as gay and see less potential for friendship with gay individuals.

The prevalence of interpersonal heterosexism has very negative consequences for gay workers who attempt to form developmental relationships, like mentoring relationships, at work. As was the case for female protégés, gay and lesbian protégés encounter some of the same barriers to mentoring that reflect the perceived importance of managing the **external relationship** of the mentoring relationship. In other words, both protégés and mentors involved in these forms of diverse mentoring relationships are concerned with how the relationship is perceived or evaluated by people outside of the mentoring relationship. For example, for men who are potential mentors, there may be an avoidance of developing relationships with women out of fear that the relationship may be perceived as romantic (or that the protégé herself may start to view the relationship as romantic). Likewise, heterosexual mentors may avoid forming relationships with openly gay or lesbian employees out of fear that other employees may perceive that the mentor is also gay. There is also a likely suspicion of same sex mentors, that their gay protégé will be attracted to them and attempt to initiate a romantic relationship.

Even if a minority group member is able to acquire a mentor, the mentoring delivered may be different from the mentoring offered to majority group member colleagues. McGuire (1999) found neither race nor gender differences in mentoring access yet found that the mentoring received was qualitatively different for men and women, as well as that provided to Whites and Blacks. In their survey of professionals, Whites and men were more likely to receive the instrumental functions of mentoring whereas women and Blacks received mainly social support. Furthermore, there was clear evidence in this study that mentoring relationships often occurred within demographic groups; that is, men mentored other men, and Blacks were more likely to be mentored by other Blacks. In fact, the results summarized may be more a reflection of the mentor more than the identity of the protégé.

Male mentors were more likely to provide instrumental support to their protégés (regardless of protégé gender) as compared to female mentors. Female mentors were more likely to provide more socioemotional support, especially to the female protégés. White mentors provided more instrumental support (especially to White protégés) as compared to Black mentors, who provided more socioemotional support (particularly to Black protégés). In many ways it is difficult to disentangle whether the type of mentoring provided is a function of the protégé or of the mentor. However, both types of support are necessary for reaching your career potential.

Thomas (2001) conducted a longitudinal study of ethnic minority and White managers and found that professionals of color that only received instrumental support from their mentors were likely to plateau in their careers. Minority executives who had fuller developmental relationships with their mentors were more likely to be successful. The social support and closeness they experienced in their mentoring relationships helped these executives build confidence, credibility, and competence (Thomas, 2001).

LACK OF OPPORTUNITIES FOR NETWORKING

The lack of structural and social integration of minority group members in many organizations can create barriers for these individuals when they attempt to gain access to mentors as well as access to informal networks in the workplace as well. **Networking** involves attempts at making contacts with other people with the purpose of sharing information, thoughts, and experiences. "A network can provide visibility, information, solutions to problems, opportunity, encouragement, and support" (Reid, 1994, p. 123). Peer networks can provide both instrumental and social support as well as enhance opportunities for developing one's professional identity and growing in self-esteem and acceptance (Knouse & Webb, 2001), and they play a critical role in the career development of all managers and executives (Pittenger, 1996). Therefore, lacking access to these networks due to demographic dissimilarity reduces minority group members' abilities to acquire informal information that may assist in their career development.

Ibarra (1992) demonstrated that there is a **homophily bias** in regard to networking relationships. This bias refers to people's preference to affiliate with others they perceive to be of similar characteristics such as race, socioeconomic status, or gender. The presence of this bias in the workplace is significant for minority group members who are underrepresented in their organizations. Members of these groups experience difficulty in developing informal networks (and mentors) with same group peers, and minority group members have little choice but to develop multiple networking relationships to gain access to many of the benefits networking can offer. Networks with dominant group peers are used to provide instrumental support, whereas those relationships with minority peers are used for social support.

Bell's (1990) study of Black professional women revealed an interesting pattern for these individuals that sheds light on how minority group members cope with their lack of social integration and the potential negative career outcomes that could result. Black female professionals in Bell's study were likely to have significant relationships both in and outside of the workplace that supported their careers. These women reported that relationships established with coworkers and peers in professional organizations provided them with job-relevant information, but that they turned to their Black community relationships and networks (e.g., family members, fraternities/sororities, church groups) in order to acquire the social support needed to persevere toward their career-related goals.

Veronica Chamber's (2003) *Having It All? Black Women and Success* provides several stories and interviews of how professionally accomplished Black women negotiate multiple networks. At times Chamber's respondents traveled between two networks—one workplace network composed of White peers and the other workplace network predominantly Black and often composed of subordinates (assistants, receptionists, and even maintenance people). Bell (1990) uses the term **bicultural boundary spanning** to reflect the journey cultural minority professionals, especially women, face as they attempt to acquire the networking resources needed to develop their careers.

Although minority group members are often forced to form several networks in order to gain both instrumental and social support, the picture is not all bleak. Ibarra (1995) found that successful "high potential" minority managers were well connected to both a minority and to a predominantly white network. However, high potential whites and average (those not on the fast track) minority employees were rarely tied to networks of ethnic minorities. The high potential ethnic minorities found having multiple networks useful in that they gained both instrumental and social support. Furthermore, White networks could provide job-related information and advice, but this support was often limited in its applicability to the often race-related career challenges

| Diversity in Practice 5.1 | **Assessing the Organizational Culture for Mentoring and Development**[1] |

Some organizations are better than others in creating opportunities for their employees to develop constructive workplace relationships that facilitate career development. In order for informal mentoring relationships and networks to develop, organizations have to create environments that are conducive to building these relationships. Stacey Blake-Beard suggests that organizational leaders should ask themselves the following questions; however, they seem important for job seekers to ask as well.

Are there opportunities for communication and interaction across organizational levels?
If as an employee you never have access to employees in other functions or divisions, or employees who work at higher levels than your own, how do you meet potential mentors or form networks?

Is the development of employees a valued function?
Organizations demonstrate value for the development of their employees through the time, effort, and financial and human resources that they dedicate to this effort. How are employees rewarded for their continued learning and development?

Do the reward and evaluation systems reflect the importance of mentoring and developmental support for all employees?
Good mentors should be rewarded and recognized for their efforts. Is mentoring taken into account in managers' and supervisors' own performance evaluations? Also, are managers rewarded for the effective development of a diverse workforce?

[1]Adapted from Blake-Beard, S. D. (2001). Mentoring relationships through the lens of race and gender. *Center for Gender and Organizational Effectiveness Insights, Briefing note 10.*

and obstacles that employees of color may face. In addition, the opportunity to have solely an ethnic minority network was limited for these high potential ethnic minorities since there were rarely enough people of color working above them in the organization to construct a network.

STRATEGIES FOR BUILDING DEVELOPMENTAL RELATIONSHIPS FOR CAREER DEVELOPMENT

In identifying some of the barriers that minority group members encounter in developing their careers, we have also highlighted some strategies. Clearly, forming healthy and constructive relationships at work, either through mentoring or through networking (try both!), is essential for career development.

Establishing diverse networks and mentoring relationships is important for both minority and dominant group employees.

Collins et al. (1997) suggest that diverse mentoring relationships can help improve race relations to the extent that these relationships challenge stereotypes and help combat the misconceptions held by either protégés or mentors. McGuire (1999), for example, found that racial minority protégés felt closer to same group mentors than to White mentors. Blake's (1999) study of Black professional women revealed that one barrier to cross-racial mentoring among women is Black women's distrust of White women. Likewise Bell and Nkomo's (2001) study of Black and White professional women revealed that both groups have very strong negative stereotypes of the other group that limit their ability to develop effective relationships with one another. Diverse mentoring may be an opportunity to simply help employees develop better relationships across difference.

Individual minority employees may attempt to acquire mentors or networks through a dual approach. That is, based upon our review, they may form instrumental relationships with dominant group members and relationships that provide social support with members of their own minority group. Although this approach may help to close the resource gap these employees may encounter in their workplace, it takes energy and time to balance all of these relationships.

Individual employees and the organizations that employ them must both take responsibility for the career development of a diverse workforce. Diversity itself may create pressures that limit opportunities for building developmental relationships in the workplace; however, these relationships are necessary. In closing, suggestions for individual employees and employers are offered to facilitate diversity in these relationships and in career development.

SUGGESTIONS FOR INDIVIDUALS

- As individuals, employees must be proactive in evaluating the career development opportunities that exist at potential employers. Diversity in Practice 5.1 provides some assistance in assessing an organization's culture for mentoring and networking.
- Take full advantage of the many resources (like networks and mentors) that professional organizations may offer (see Diversity in Practice 5.2). Mentors outside of your organization can provide both instrumental and social support without being too entangled in the politics of your specific organization. Networks and mentors who share your professional identity but who work outside of your organization can provide you with fresh perspectives about the challenges and opportunities you may encounter at your job.
- Engage in **peer mentoring/networking**. Peers can be an effective source of support and information. Developing relationships with peers enhances opportunities for engaging in a developmental relationship with someone

| Diversity in Practice 5.2 | **Organizations That Facilitate the Development of a Diverse Workforce** |

In addition to affinity groups and informal networks within organizations, there are also professional organizations that assist individuals and organizations in enhancing the opportunities for career development for a diverse workforce.

The **Catalyst Organization** is the most well-known nonprofit organization that promotes the development of women in corporate America. Catalyst was founded in 1962 by Felice Schwartz to help women enter the workforce. Based in New York City, Catalyst has become an international organization that helps companies recruit, retain, and advance top female talent and provides information to individual women who want to develop their careers. Catalyst conducts research on women's work issues, provides advising for corporate board placements, and gives annual awards to recognize companies who succeed in their diversity efforts. Several influential reports have been published by Catalyst that have shaped organizations' and researchers' perspectives on gender diversity. Included among these reports are *The Census of Women Board Directors*; *Women in Corporate Leadership: Progress and Prospects*; and *Women of Color in Corporate Management: Opportunities and Barriers*. More information on Catalyst can be found at www.catalystwomen.org.

The **Executive Leadership Council (ELC)** is a professional organization, based in Washington, D.C., that comprises 250 upper-level Black executives from *Fortune* 500 companies. The goal of the ELC is to "build a reservoir of African American executive leadership."

Professional organizations like the ELC help hiring organizations in a number of ways. ELC, and similar professional organizations, create a network of minority professionals that can be tapped for a hiring organization's recruitment purposes. One of the missions of ELC is to provide a mechanism for major organizations to diversify their corporate boards. ELC members reap benefits of their association with the organization through the enhanced opportunities that ELC offers members for creating networks based upon similarities among their geographic locations or work functions. More information on the ELC can be found at www.elcinfo.com.

The **Human Rights Campaign (HRC),** also located in Washington, D.C., is a gay, lesbian, bisexual, and transgendered (GLBT) advocacy group that monitors both government and corporate organizations. HRC provides gay workers and their allies with resources on how to obtain domestic partner benefits in organizations, how to establish a GLBT network in the workplace, and how to address discrimination based upon sexuality. In addition, like Catalyst, HRC evaluates major organizations in regard to sexual diversity through producing a corporate equality index that job seekers and consumers can use to evaluate organizations based upon their treatment of the GLBT workforce. The corporate equality index evaluates organizations based upon the extent to which an organization has an inclusive nondiscrimination policy, offers domestic partner benefits, supports GLBT employee networks, provides inclusive diversity training, markets products/services to the GLBT community, and does not engage in action that would undermine the goal of equal rights for the GLBT community. More information on the HRC can be found at www.hrc.org.

from your own or another group since diverse workers are most likely to be found at lower levels of the organizational ladder. Peer relationships are important in that they can serve as a source of information and validation, especially for individuals experiencing discrimination (Tatum, 1999).

- Virtual networking through Web pages, chat rooms, and electronic mail may be the future of enhancing diverse mentoring and networking (Knouse & Webb, 2001). Certainly the World Wide Web opens the possibility of connecting with similar others.

Some organizations have instituted diversity efforts that assist minority employees in developing healthy workplace relationships so that they can gain both the instrumental and social support resources good mentoring and networks can provide. Affinity groups and mentoring circles are two efforts that can be effective in ensuring that minority group members have equal opportunity to develop their careers successfully. Creating a positive climate for diversity is also key to fostering an environment that is conducive to diverse developmental relationships.

RECOMMENDATIONS FOR ORGANIZATIONS

- **Affinity groups** are formal "same group" networks established by employees or the organization to facilitate the networking and subsequently the career development of a specific group. For example, both Xerox and AT&T developed Black manager networks in the 1970s in order to help retain these workers (Knouse & Webb, 2001). These groups initially were met with some resistance on the part of nonminority workers, but they have become more accepted with time. Affinity networks have been evaluated as facilitating the sharing of career information and enhancing employee optimism, but they are unlikely to also provide specific job performance feedback or even employees' perceptions of discrimination (Knouse & Webb, 2001). Mentoring and networking among similar employees is also important in that it can be helpful in assisting minority group employees in integrating their professional and minority group identities (Collins et al., 1997). Button (2001) and Ragins & Cornwell (2001) also both report that having affinity groups for gay employees and supportive policies may assist in creating a climate that deters discrimination based upon sexuality.
- **Core groups** and **mentoring circles** are another option (Kram & Hall, 1996). Core groups allow individuals from diverse backgrounds the opportunity to engage in collective learning about how to have effective relationships across difference. Mentoring circles bring together one or several high-level executives and senior managers with junior colleagues for the purpose of developing the junior colleagues' careers (Kram & Hall, 1996). Higgins and Kram (2001) and Thomas (2001) view mentoring as not simply a one-on-one relationship. But instead effective mentoring, especially

for career success, is provided through a network of supporters, including friends and family (Blake, 1999).

- Ragins (1997) recommends that organizations must address the lack of access minority group members encounter in regard to developmental relationships. Organizations must attempt to create a climate for informal mentoring (and networks too). Methods of establishing an organizational climate conducive to diverse mentoring and networking have been identified by Ragins (1997). Her recommendations to organizations include:
  - — Identifying pools of potential mentors and protégés rather than attempting to force matches
  - — Providing training for potential mentors and protégés regarding the development of effective mentoring relationships and paying special attention to diversity issues
  - — Providing information opportunities for the development of informal mentoring relationships
  - — Structuring diverse work teams that span departments and levels within the organization in order to increase informal opportunities for building diverse networks (Ragins, 1997)
  - — The effective development of minority group members should be important to all organizations, therefore organizations should recognize manager success in developing these employees in performance appraisals and in salary decisions (Ragins, 1997).
- Thomas (2001) also suggests that executives can help create the organizational conditions that foster the career development and upward mobility of people of color. Among his recommendations are that organizations should support in-house minority associations and networking groups. Companies should also challenge stereotypes when they are visible, especially during discussions of individuals' promotion and payback potential. Executives must also educate mentors and potential mentors about diversity issues, especially as they relate to mentoring. Finally organizations should ensure that the pool of people being considered for promotions and key assignments reflect the diversity of the organization.

CONCLUSION

Developmental relationships within the workplace are a critical tool for career success. Yet barriers to networking and mentoring persist in a diverse workplace. There are a variety of strategies that individuals and organizations can adopt to facilitate developmental relationships in the workplace. The literature reviewed in this chapter indicates that diverse developmental relationships benefit everyone, mentors and protégés alike, through breaking stereotypes and prejudice and enhancing opportunities for learning and success.

Discussion Items

1. Visit the Web sites for several professional organizations in your major or career (e.g., Academy of Management). How do these organizations address diversity? In what ways do they support mentoring and networking?
2. Use the assessment issues identified in Diversity in Practice 5.1 to assess the culture for mentoring and networking within an organization with which you are familiar. What can this organization do differently to enhance opportunities for mentoring and networking, especially given a diverse workforce?
3. As a class discuss how stereotypes of different minority groups spill over into the workplace. How do these stereotypes decrease opportunities for career development?

 InfoTrac College Edition

Be sure to log on to InfoTrac College Edition and search for additional readings on topics of interest to you.

6

CHAPTER

The Influence of Diversity on Group Dynamics and Outcomes[1]

GROUPS AND THE NATURE OF ORGANIZATIONS

A **group** is an aggregation of individuals. With respect to the workplace, a group may be defined "as two or more individuals, interacting and interdependent, who have come together to achieve particular outcomes" (Robbins, 1998, p. 240). Organizations can be viewed as "macro-groups within which many micro-groups operate" (Cox, 1994, p. 139). There are many types of groups operating within the structure of organizations: departments, divisions, business units, committees, task forces, work units, project teams, focus groups, cross-functional work teams, quality circles, and so forth. Although there are several distinctions between work groups and work teams, for purposes of this chapter we will consider them both under the umbrella of work groups.

Groups differ in terms of size, formal leadership, role structure, norms and values, expected duration, status, autonomy, cohesiveness, type of task, and composition. Of particular interest in this chapter is composition. Work groups are often composed of many different types of individuals, creating diversity. The amount and type of diversity in work groups influence internal group dynamics as well as group and individual outcomes (Jackson & Ruderman, 1995). Groups in the workplace may be diverse along several dimensions of personal characteristics. For example, they may be diverse in terms of demographics and cultural background (gender, ethnicity, age, race, gender, color,

[1]Harriet Landau, J.D., served as coauthor for this chapter.

Work groups will continue to grow in diversity.

religion, national origin), psychological attributes (values, beliefs, knowledge, personality) or organizational attributes (tenure, occupation, hierarchical level, degree of power) (Jackson & Ruderman, 1995).

The existence of a diverse workforce and diverse work groups is increasingly becoming the norm in organizations. Furthermore, the reliance of organizations on work groups and their importance to the functioning of modern organizations has never been stronger (Guzzo & Shea, 1992). Thus, the impact of diversity on work groups is an important issue for organizations. Diversity in work groups, whether considering the entire organization or a small work unit, is often viewed as a two-edged sword. A culturally diverse work group provides many potential advantages for an organization as well as potential difficulties that must be addressed by the organization.

This chapter identifies the benefits and disadvantages for diversity within work groups. Subsequently we will turn to examining the theories that illuminate why diversity within groups can lead to dysfunction. We will pay special attention to those factors that lead to discrimination within groups as well as both minority and majority individuals' feelings of dissatisfaction, lessened commitment, and overall detachment.

Potential Advantages of Diverse Groups

Because most group activities require a variety of skills and knowledge, it is reasonable to assume that a work group composed of individuals with diverse skills and knowledge will be more effective and that dissimilar individuals are more likely to have such a variety of skills and knowledge (Robbins, 1998).

Work group diversity has been associated with a number of *potential* advantages (Brickson, 2000; Milliken & Martin 1996; Robbins, 1998; Schneider & Northcraft, 1999), including

- increased number of alternatives and perspectives considered
- increased opportunity to find errors or discover key information
- enhanced probability that an adequate solution will be proposed
- increased innovation
- increased connections to a more varied external network, which increases outside contacts and access to information
- increased likelihood that needed skills are present
- the possibility of specialized division of labor
- enhanced quality of reasoning due to consistent counterarguments from a minority
- increased likelihood of identifying creative, unique, or higher quality solutions
- increased time discussing issues, thus decreasing the chances that a weak alternative will be chosen

Work groups are most likely to reap the benefits of diversity when they are engaged in complex tasks or problem-solving and decision-making tasks.

Potential Disadvantages of Diverse Groups

It is also recognized that diversity in work groups *may* have negative consequences (Brickson, 2000; Milliken & Martin, 1996; Robbins, 1998), including

- increased individual dissatisfaction
- higher turnover
- more difficulty learning to work with each other and solving problems
- more difficulty unifying the group and reaching agreement
- decreased group integration and cohesiveness
- decreased commitment and attachment to the organization
- increased absenteeism
- increased ambiguity
- increased miscommunication

A recent study by Richeson and Shelton (2003) also suggests that majority group individuals with racially prejudiced attitudes may suffer a loss of cognitive functioning when required to interact with minority group members. Fifty-nine White college students were given a test to evaluate their degree of racial bias. They were then asked to converse with either a Black student or a White student, introducing themselves and discussing both a racially sensitive topic (racial profiling in light of the 9/11 attacks on the World Trade Center) and a neutral topic. After the conversation, the students were tested on a challenging mental task. The results indicated that the more biased the student, the worse he or she performed in the mental task if the intervening conversation was with a Black student. The researchers speculated that the interaction created a source of stress and anxiety for the more biased individuals, using up energy and depleting cognitive functioning. It is unclear whether this impaired functioning would continue over time or with repeated interactions.

Some researchers looking at the combined results of many studies believe the impact of diversity on work groups is still unclear and may be affected by many factors, such as type of diversity, type of task, size of group, difficulty of the task, organizational characteristics, group communication skills, conflict management skills, and type of measure (Bowers, Pharmer, & Salas, 2000; Jehn, Northcraft, & Neale, 1999; Williams & O'Reilly, 1998). Another reason for inconsistent results and small effect sizes is that demographic or cultural diversity does not always translate into the variety of skills and knowledge that are helpful for the task (Jehn et al., 1999). Furthermore, when diversity is present, members of diverse work groups must successfully deal with the difficulties arising from diversity before they can reap the benefits (Jehn et al., 1999).

Williams and O'Reilly (1998) provide a very comprehensive review of the demography and diversity in organizations literature. These authors examine how different forms of diversity such as age, background, race, and gender affect both group processes and performance. Overall their review demonstrates that common demographic variables studied such as race and gender are found to have inconsistent effects on work group performance. Laboratory research appears likely to conclude in positive effects on performance, whereas analyses of "real world" field data often result in small negative effects of diversity on group performance or no effects at all (Williams & O'Reilly, 1998).

Ely & Thomas (2001) suggest that diversity work group researchers should pay more attention to the conditions under which diversity appears to enhance or detract from work group functioning. These authors conducted a qualitative study of three different organizations in order to understand the diversity-work group performance relationship. They concluded that there were three types of diversity perspectives/conditions that organizations adopted, and that these perspectives and the organizational cultures that resulted, drove whether or not diversity was an asset or cost to work group processes and performance.

Some work groups adopted a traditional equal employment opportunity (EEO) perspective on diversity, which the authors referred to as the **discrimination and fairness perspective**. Other work groups seemed to embrace diversity only as an opportunity for enhanced marketing and profit. This perspective was titled the **access and legitimacy perspective**. Other work groups saw diversity as an opportunity to learn new ideas and ways of working. These groups adopted what the authors called the **integration and learning perspective** (Ely & Thomas, 2001). Each perspective affected the quality of intergroup relations experienced within the work group, the extent to which workers felt valued and respected, and the significance of workers' racial identities at work. As Diversity Figure 6.1 demonstrates, groups that had an integration and learning perspective were most likely to experience positive outcomes of work group

Figure 6.1 | Diversity Perspectives and Group Functioning

Mediators	Integration-and-learning	Access-and-legitimacy	Discrimination-and-fairness
Quality of intergroup relations	Conflict resulting from cultural differences in point of view; different groups accorded equal power and status; open discussion of differences and conflict	Conflict resulting from differential power and status accorded different races/functions; little open discussion of conflict	Intractable race-related conflict stemming from entrenched, undiscussible status and power imbalances; no open discussion of conflict or differences
Feeling valued and respected	All employees feel fully respected and valued for their competence and contributions to the organization	Employees of color question whether they are valued and respected equally; perceive devaluation of functions staffed predominantly by people of color	Employees of color feel disrespected and devalued as members of minority racial/ethnic groups

(continued)

diversity, both in regard to work group dynamics as well as performance. This study seems to support Williams & O'Reilly's (1998) assessment that more work on the moderators of the diversity–performance relationship must be undertaken in order to provide more conclusive evidence about this potential linkage.

Given our interest in how individuals, especially those who belong to minority groups, experience diversity in the workplace, it is worthwhile to revisit Williams & O'Reilly's (1998) analysis of this literature. Especially in regard to their conclusions regarding how race and gender diversity within work groups affect individuals. For example, their review illustrated that the gender composition of a work group is important in understanding individual reactions to gender diversity.

Williams and O'Reilly concluded that, "In general, gender diversity has negative effects on groups, especially on males. It is associated with higher turnover rates, especially among those who are most different. The studies also reveal that women and men respond differently, and may have different experiences as a minority. Men display lower levels of satisfaction and commitment when they are in the minority, while women appear less likely to have a negative psychological reaction. This is despite the fact that men in female dominated

Figure 6.1 | Continued

Significance of own racial identity at work	Source of value for people of color, a resource for learning and teaching; a source of privilege for Whites to acknowledge	Source of ambivalence for employees of color; Whites not conscious	Source of powerlessness for people of color; source of apprehension for Whites

Group functioning

	Enhanced by cross-cultural exposure and learning and by work processes designed to facilitate constructive intergroup conflict and exploration of diverse views	Enhanced by increased access and legitimacy; inhibited by lack of learning and exchange between racially segregated functions	Inhibited by low morale of employees, lack of cross-cultural learning, and the inability of employees of color to bring all relevant skills and insights to bear on work

From R. J. Ely and D. A. Thomas, "Cultural Diversity at Work: The Effects of Diversity Perspectives on Work Group Processes and Outcomes," *Administrative Science Quarterly* 46 (2001): Table 3, p. 261. Reprinted by permission.

groups are more likely to be accepted, less likely to be treated with hostility, and less likely to be stereotyped" (Williams & O'Reilly, 1998, p. 108).

Interestingly, a similar asymmetrical pattern was revealed when these authors examined the literature on individual reactions to racial/ethnic diversity in work groups. Williams and O'Reilly concluded that those who are different from the racial majority within a work group often demonstrate less attachment to the group as compared to those in the majority ethnic group. These individuals tend to be more likely to leave the group, are less satisfied, and are less committed to the organization. As was the case in their examination of gender diversity within work groups, these effects are more pronounced for White workers than for ethnic minorities (Williams & O'Reilly, 1998). When examining the literature on individual reactions to either race or gender diversity, these authors found dominant group members (i.e, men or Whites) seemed to have a more difficult time in coping with their "work group minority status" than those individuals who are themselves minorities within the larger society.

Social psychology provides ample scholarship to help us understand why diverse work groups can lead to poor organizational and group attachment and can even trigger discrimination. The following section reviews theories that help explain diverse work group dynamics.

THEORIES THAT EXPLAIN DYSFUNCTIONS WITHIN DIVERSE GROUPS

Social Identity Theory

Humans tend to categorize. That is, they place objects and events into meaningful categories or groupings that allow them to deal with new information more quickly, efficiently, and automatically (Brewer & Miller, 1996, Chap. 1). These categories may be based on natural characteristics such as plants, animals and minerals, or based on social categories, such as religion, political party, or ethnicity. Social categories are unique in that people are part of social categories, so that the act of placing another individual into a category means that such another individual is either a part of the group to which the person belongs (member of an ingroup) or is part of a group to which the individual does not belong (member of an outgroup) (Brewer & Miller, 1996, Chap. 1). According to Tsui, Egan, and O'Reilly (1992) individuals may use social characteristics such as age or race to classify themselves into social groups.

Social identity theory proposes that one's self-identity and sense of self-worth may be derived in part from group memberships (Tajfel, 1981; Tajfel & Turner, 1979). Individuals' social identity is based on those characteristics of their self-image that are associated with the social categories with which they identify and to which they see themselves as belonging (Tajfel, 1981; Tajfel & Turner 1979; Turner, 1985). Our social group identities play a role in how we see ourselves and how others see us. For many individuals, certain social group memberships are a significant source of personal pride and self-esteem (Cox, 1994).

When individuals join an organization, they bring their many social group identities with them. Thus work groups often comprise individuals with diverse social group identities. In fact, Nkomo and Cox (1996) define **diversity** as a "mixture of people with different group identities within the same social system" (p. 339). The effects of categorization and identification with specific social groups are viewed by many as the primary building block of social stereotyping and intergroup prejudice (Brewer & Miller, 1996, Chap. 1).

Ingroup/Outgroup Biases   The terms **ingroup** and **outgroup** are often used to refer to social groups to which one belongs or doesn't belong (Brewer & Miller, 1996, Chap. 2). To maintain a positive social identity, the people in the ingroup must be positively viewed as compared to some relevant outgroup (Tajfel, 1981; Tajfel & Turner 1979; Turner, 1985). This can lead to the development of two sets of rules for assessing other individuals; one set for the ingroup and another set for the outgroup (Tajfel, 1981; Tajfel & Turner, 1979). Accordingly, ingroup members and their accomplishments are likely to be regarded positively whereas outgroup members and their accomplishments are more likely to be regarded negatively (Turner, 1985).

In addition, individuals are more likely to be cooperative with members of their ingroup and more competitive with respect to members of an outgroup—

even if they share a common problem (Brewer & Miller, 1996, Chap. 2). Moreover, we tend to like ingroup members more than outgroup members even when we know nothing about their personal characteristics; and favoritism for ingroup members can occur without actual personal attraction (Brewer & Miller, 1996, Chap. 2). Ingroup members are perceived to be easier to communicate with, more predictable, more trustworthy, and more likely to reciprocate favors than outgroup members (Schneider & Northcraft, 1999). Some researchers believe that attachment, preference, and loyalty to ingroups over outgroups may be a universal characteristic (Brewer & Miller, 1996, Chap. 2).

The preference for ingroup members over outgroup members is also associated with certain attributional errors. Attributions are inferences; they may or may not be correct (Weiten, 2001). The inferences or attributions of interest with respect to ingroups and outgroups deal with inferred causes of actions and accomplishments.

Fundamental Attribution Error   When we observe another person performing some behavior or achieving some outcome, we may explain the behavior or outcome in terms of the person's personal characteristics or in terms of the situation or environment in which it happens. The tendency to attribute a behavior or outcome to personal characteristics and underestimate the impact of the person's environment or situation on that behavior or outcome is known as the **fundamental attribution error** (sometimes referred to as the **correspondence bias**) (Ross, 1977, as cited by Brewer & Miller, 1996, Chap. 1). We tend to overstate the importance of internal (i.e., personal) characteristics of others in part because the external or situational factors may not be obvious to us. Also, it is simple and requires little effort. Attempting to understand the situational factors requires more effort and energy (Weiten, 2001).

Self-serving biases reflect our tendency to make personal attributions for good or successful behaviors but to make external attributions when we fail (Brewer & Miller, 1996). For example, I could think that I receive job offers due to my intelligence and work ethic. However, when I fail to get a promotion or job offer, I am more likely to make attributions related to a poor economy or a hostile boss.

Ultimate Attribution Error   There is another attributional error that is often made when explaining the behaviors and outcomes of ingroup and outgroup members. Positive behaviors and outcomes of an ingroup member tend to be explained by stable, internal characteristics whereas negative behaviors and outcomes of ingroup members tend to be explained by situational factors, or unstable internal factors (I was having a bad day) (Brewer & Miller, 1996, Chap. 1). On the other hand, positive behaviors and outcomes of outgroup members are explained by situational factors or unstable internal characteristics whereas negative behaviors and outcomes are explained by stable, internal factors. This pattern of differences in explaining the behaviors and outcomes of ingroup members and outgroup members is known as the **ultimate attribution error** (Pettigrew, 1979, as cited by Brewer & Miller, 1996, Chap. 1). This can lead to attributing the success of ingroup members to factors such as effort, ability, or talent, but attributing the successes of outgroup members to luck, favoritism, or other situational factors. The reverse explanations would therefore be offered for failure. When my group fails it is due to bad luck. When others fail it is due to the lack of ability.

Unsatisfactory Social Identity   If social categories and group memberships are so important to our self-esteem and self-concept, what happens when our social identity is unsatisfactory? Generally speaking, if the group to which an individual belongs does not provide a sense of positive self-worth, then the individual will want to leave the group or increase the status of the group. Several different change strategies may be employed, including social mobility, social creativity, and social change (Tajfel & Turner, 1986; Sampson, 1999). **Social mobility**—or self-focused change strategies—are aimed at improving the individual's identity without necessarily improving the status of the relevant ingroup. Social mobility typically involves individuals attempting to leave or distance themselves from their group physically or psychologically. **Social creativity** and **social change**—or collectively oriented change approaches—involve attempts to increase the status of the entire group, not just the status of oneself (Tajfel & Turner, 1986; Sampson, 1999). Social creativity involves attempting to change the image of your group, whereas social change typically involves working toward changing conditions or the environment so that your group can gain equality. The research regarding which approach might be used under different circumstances remains unclear (Tajfel & Turner, 1986; Sampson, 1999).

The most obvious solution wtih respect to belonging to a low status group is to physically leave the group (social mobility). Although this may be possible in some situations (changing jobs or professions) it may be impossible if the group is based on unchangeable demographic characteristics, such as skin color or gender, or if the higher status group denies admission (Tajfel & Turner, 1986; Sampson, 1999). If members of a group cannot physically leave the group, then the members may try to leave the group psychologically, using one or more of several strategies (Tajfel & Turner, 1986; Sampson, 1999):

- Decreasing their identification with the group, such as not using the group's label in describing themselves
- Reducing similarity to other group members, such as by dressing or talking or otherwise acting differently from the other group members
- Imitating the behaviors and actions of members of a higher status group

Social creativity tries to improve the desirability or status of the very characteristics that makes the ingroup distinct. This approach may include various strategies (Tajfel & Turner, 1986):

- Comparing the groups on a new dimension (although it is often difficult to obtain validation of the value of the new dimension from the higher status group).

- Changing the value of the salient characteristic by which the groups are compared. Under this strategy, terms of derision are often co-opted by the members of the group. According to Sampson (1999), examples include "Black is beautiful," "Older is wiser," and "More weight brings more pleasure." This approach is not always successful because the majority outgroup does not embrace the extremity of these efforts, or because the ingroup minority members cannot accept terms that were for so long a source of derision (Sampson, 1999).
- Changing the outgroup with which one makes comparisons. Women may be dissatisfied if they compare their salaries to men, but satisfied if they compare their salaries to other women's groups or other lower status groups.

Social change—or social competition—involves mobilizing support to actually change the status of the disfavored group. This approach has resulted in many social movements aimed at equal treatment and acceptance (Tajfel & Turner, 1986; Sampson, 1999).

Relational Demography

Relational demography focuses on the relationship between an individual's demographic characteristics and the demographic characteristics of a group of which the individual is a member (Tsui, Egan, & O'Reilly, 1992; Tsui & Gutek, 1999; Tsui & O'Reilly, 1989). Thus individuals may compare their demographic characteristics with the demographic characteristics of their work group, and the perceived level of similarity or dissimilarity may affect the individuals' work-related attitudes and behaviors (Tsui, Egan, & O'Reilly, 1989). For example, the experience of a Black individual in a work group consisting of mostly Black members may be different from the experience of that same individual in a work group of mostly White members (Tsui et al., 1992).

Demographic similarity or dissimilarity has been studied with respect to many job-related variables. Tsui and O'Reilly (1989) looked at six demographic variables (age, gender, race, education, company tenure, and job tenure) with respect to superior–subordinate dyads. They found that increasing overall dissimilarity was associated with decreased perceived effectiveness by superiors, less personal attraction on the part of superiors for subordinates, and increased role ambiguity experienced by subordinates. Differences in sex and race were specifically associated with increased role ambiguity and unfavorable performance evaluations on the part of subordinates, and decreased attraction by the supervisors toward their subordinates.

Tsui et al. (1992) found that increasing work group diversity (especially sex and race) was associated with lower levels of organizational commitment, intent to stay, and psychological attachment among group members, and that Whites and men showed larger negative effects for increased heterogeneity than non-whites and women. Riordan and Shore (1997) studied gender, race-ethnicity, and tenure in 98 work groups in a life insurance company. Similarity in race-ethnicity (but not gender or tenure) affected perceptions of advancement, group productivity, and commitment to the work group. The patterns for Whites, Blacks, and Hispanics, however, were not the same. Blacks had consistent attitudes toward advancement and perception of productivity across all three types of demographic composition (mostly white, 50/50, mostly minority). Work group commitment for Blacks, however, increased as group similarity increased. Whites perceived higher levels of work group productivity, advancement opportunities, and work group commitment in mostly White and 50/50 groups. That is, Whites reported lower levels of work group productivity, advancement opportunities, and work group commitment only when in mostly minority work groups. Hispanic subjects reported higher levels of all three work attitudes in the 50/50 group.

Personal and social identity group histories can also affect the abilities of diverse group members to relate well to one another as well as be an effective team. Cox's (1994) discussion of legacy effects describes how history affects the present.

Legacy Effects

Cox (1994) argues that contemporary attitudes and feelings held by members of one cultural group about members from other cultural groups are based in large part by the history of intergroup relations between the relevant groups. He describes two ways in which this sociocultural history effect is shown: A micro effect and a macro effect.

Micro Legacy Effects   "The micro effect refers to group identity-based experiences that many of us have in our own personal histories that partly shape our attitudes toward other groups" (Cox, 1994, p. 68). For example, a Black teenager bullied by a group of White students because he is Black, or exclusion from a country club because one is Jewish may contribute to negative attitudes in the future if these experiences persist. Cox points out that the experiences are directly related to group identities and are not due to individual characteristics, nor to generalization based on one negative experience with a group member. These experiences are often numerous and outstanding in the recollections of minority group members, leading them to easily see the impact of their group membership on their relationship with majority group members (Cox, 1994). Majority group members, on the other hand, are often unaware of the impact of their majority group membership on their life experiences (Cox, 1994). These micro effects of sociocultural history can influence subsequent cross-group relationships (Cox, 1994).

Macro Legacy Effects   On the other hand, macro effects do not require personal participation (Cox, 1994). Certain significant sociohistorical events can influence the view of one group toward another just by awareness of the event. Cox gives two examples: (1) the confiscation of land from American Indians by

White settlers and the forced move of American Indians to reservations and (2) internment of Japanese Americans during World War II. Other examples include the enslavement of Blacks by White Americans and the use of concentration camps for Jews by Germans. In each of these cases, simply knowing the treatment of the minority group members by the majority group members can create an attitude of wariness and mistrust on the part of one group toward the other (Cox, 1994).

Stereotyping

At times these legacy effects may lead to the promotion of stereotypes. "**Stereotypes** are widely held beliefs that people have certain characteristics because of their membership in a particular group" (Weiten, 2001, p. 658). Stereotyping is a pervasive human tendency that increases the efficiency of perceptual and cognitive processes by simplifying our world in terms of social categories (Cox, 1994; Weiten, 2001). When someone use stereotypes, they judge and evaluate other people based on perceptions of the group to which the others belong, not on their specific, individual characteristics (Robbins, 1998). Stereotypes are often based on sex, age, race, ethnicity, or cultural background.

Stereotypes are very problematic because they can be widespread and frequently used in spite of the fact they may be inaccurate or irrelevant to the situation (Cox, 1994; Robbins, 1998). Furthermore, stereotypes ignore diversity among the members of social groups by assuming that all members will have the same characteristics (Cox, 1994; Weiten, 2001). There are many negative consequences of stereotyping in an organizational setting, including job segregation, differences in expectations and feedback, differences in training and relocation opportunities, and biases in performance evaluation (Cox, 1994).

Because members of outgroups are often viewed as similar and essentially interchangeable, there is little motivation to notice or remember information that distinguishes individual outgroup members or that might contradict inaccurate stereotyped perceptions of that person or group. This phenomenon of undifferentiation is an important factor in understanding how stereotypes about social groups are perpetuated (Brewer & Miller, 1996, Chap. 3).

Robbins (1998) provides the following examples of stereotypes in organizations:

- Women won't relocate for a promotion.
- Men aren't interested in childcare.
- Older workers can't learn new skills.
- Asian immigrants are hardworking and conscientious.
- Overweight people lack discipline.

Note the important distinction between stereotypes and acknowledging group differences for purposes of valuing diversity. The latter (a) is based on beliefs about characteristics of culture groups that are derived from systematic studies of reliable sources of data and (b) acknowledges the existence of intragroup differences and variations (Cox, 1994).

Figure 6.2 | Stereotypes of Various Groups

Jews	Blacks	White men	White women	Japanese men	French men	East Indian women
Rich	Athletes	Responsible for all of society's ills	Bad at math and science	Meticulous	Good lovers	Analytical
Miserly	Underqualified	Competitive	Emphatic	Studious	Frank	Passive
All support Israel	Good dancers	Intelligent	Easy	Humble	Dry-humored	Submissive
Money-grubbing	Greedy (food)	Insecure	Passive	Workaholics	Romantic	Always wear saris
Penny-pinchers	Uneducated	Racist	Money-hungry	Dedicated	Harass women	Very feminine
Well-educated	Expressive in communication	Power-hungry	Ruining the traditional American family	Polite	Egotistical	Religious
Complainers	Poor	Manipulative	Competitive	Family-oriented	Drink wine all the time	Quiet
Stingy	Militant	Insensitive	Change their minds frequently	Highly intelligent	Suave	Overachieving
Cheap	Untrustworthy	Aggressive	Talkative	Racist	Sexy	Subservient to men
Unified	Volatile	Ignorant	Timid	Anti-American	Do not shower much	Class-oriented
Family-oriented	Low IQs	Clannish	Selfish	Single-minded	Superior attitude	Mothering type
Good at business	Clannish	Arrogant	Nasty	Business-oriented	Hate Americans	Tradition
Run New York City	Hate Whites	Not really perceptive	Ambitious	Nationalistic	Arrogant	Uneducated
Self-centered	Lazy	Domineering	Individual-oriented	Disciplined	Extremely eccentric	Not ambitious
Status-conscious	Laid back	Like to brag	Gullible	Unemotional	Individualistic	Too concerned with social status
Hard to get in social circle	Defensive	Like beer	Trusting	Demanding	Unfaithful	
Racist	No ambition	Wear Dockers	Flaky	Sexist	Proud of country	
Snobbish	Unmotivated	Not literate	Shallow	Drink a lot, especially scotch		
Hates other religions	Have lots of friends	Cold	Non-aggressive	Productive		
Take care of their own	Content with life	Handed everything on a silver platter	Do not care about careers	Power-hungry		
Manipulative	Love talking	Oppressive		Vindictive, hold grudges		
Nonrhythmic	Oversexed	Greedy		Good at math and science		
Girls are JAPs— Jewish American Princesses	Violent	Always trying to keep non-Whites down		Secretly envious of American life style		
Separatists	Very emotional	Out for themselves		Defer to authority		
Cliquish	Warm	Elitist		Cameras		
Too sensitive to group criticism	On welfare	Dishonest				
	Funny	Backstabbers				
	Spendthrifts, too much concern about clothes	Opportunistic				

Stereotype Threat

Stereotypes not only affect how individuals relate to one another within groups, they also can have consequences for the behavior of the stereotyped. According to Steele (1997), **stereotype threat** is the social–psychological threat that arises when a widely known, negative stereotype about a group to which one belongs could be used to interpret one's performance. "This predicament threatens one with being negatively stereotyped, with being judged or treated stereotypically, or with the prospect of conforming to the stereotype" (p. 614). Stereotype threat is not dependent on internalization of the stereotype or a worry that the stereotype is true of oneself. Stereotype threat can occur without feelings of inferiority or lowered self-worth. It is triggered by the realization that a negative stereotype could apply to oneself in a given situation (Steele, 1997; Steele & Aronson, 1995). A necessary condition to stereotype threat is that individuals must find the negative stereotype relevant to their self-definition; they must identity with and be concerned about their performance in the relevant domain (Roberson, Deitch, Brief, & Block, 2003; Steele). This means that stereotype threat may be most commonly experienced by those individuals who are motivated, qualified, and successful (Roberson et al., 2003; Steele; Steele & Aronson).

When activated, stereotype threat is hypothesized to interfere with performance and intellectual functioning because attention is redirected from the task at hand to a concern with the significance and implications of one's performance in light of a negative stereotype (Roberson et al., 2003; Steele & Aronson, 1995). For example, African Americans who experienced stereotype threat underperformed on a diagnostic academic test, relative to Caucasians and to African Americans who were told the test was not diagnostic of ability (Steele & Aronson, 1995). Over time, stereotype threat may also result in disidentifying with achievement in the previously important performance domain. This helps to protect the individual from stereotype threat, but also results in reduced interest, motivation, and achievement (Steele & Aronson, 1995). Stereotype threat has been found to generalize to other groups such as women with respect to mathematical tests, the elderly with respect to memory tasks, and Hispanics with respect to cognitive ability tests (Roberson, et al., 2003).

Additionally, stereotype threat has been found to operate in the workplace. One study found that with respect to a sample of African American managers, being the solo or token African American in the work group was positively associated with perceptions of stereotype threat (Roberson et al., 2003). The relationship was significant but not strong, and Roberson et al. suggest that several other organizational context factors may increase the experience of stereotype threat in the workplace: the number of African Americans and other people of color at senior levels of the organization, group differences in the distribution of organizational power, the extent to which stereotypes are reinforced, and the organization's approach to diversity. Of more interest is the fact that increased experience of stereotype threat was associated with

Diversity in Practice 6.1	**Stereotype Threat in the Eye of the Storm**

Former third grade teacher Jane Elliott is responsible for the classic blue eye–brown eye case that demonstrated how prejudice can be ignited by any arbitrary division of people; even something like eye color. The video *Eye of the Storm* demonstrates the striking ease by which young children will engage in prejudice. During the late 1960s, after Dr. Martin Luther King was murdered, Jane Elliott gave her third grade students a lesson on prejudice by dividing the students by eye color. On one day the children with brown eyes were designated as inferior and on another day the children with blue eyes were designated as inferior. The group designated as inferior was forced to wear a special collar so that they could be identified as inferior even from a distance. Despite this arbitrary division among the students, classmates easily began to mistreat and discriminate against one another. The division of students also led to unexpected performance differences.

Consistently the "top" group demonstrated prejudice toward the inferior group. In addition, Jane Elliott noticed that when students were in the designated inferior group, their performance on class assignments, such as those involving flash cards, suffered. When asking students to explain the dip in their performance on the inferior days and the rise in their performance on the days when they were on top, they mentioned that they were thinking about that collar and how much they hated having it around their neck. Having the collar caused them physical and psychological discomfort and interfered with their performance.

Jane Elliott has traveled the world delivering seminars in which she takes adults through this experience as well. *A Class Divided*, a follow-up video, demonstrates that the same scenario can take place with adults and yield the same unfortunate behaviors and outcomes. Watch *A Class Divided* at http://www.pbs.org/wgbh/pages/frontline/shows/divided/etc/view.html.

---

increased use of indirect feedback seeking (monitoring, as opposed to direct feedback seeking) and with increased discounting of performance feedback (viewing feedback as less informative and useful for improving performance). Both indirect feedback seeking and discounting are in turn associated with poorer performance because indirect feedback is open to misinterpretation and discounting can be associated with failure to comply with suggestions for improvement (see Roberson et al., 2003).

Self-Fulfilling Prophecies

Robbins (1998) describes a **self-fulfilling prophecy** as the phenomenon that occurs when one person with inaccurate expectations and perceptions about another person causes the other person to behave in ways consistent with those perceptions and expectations. It is a situation in which expectations become reality. For example, the beliefs of teachers about their students can unintentionally influence the performance of their students, and the expectations of

Diversity Learning Point 6.1	Self-Fulfilling Prophecies in Job Interviews

An important study by Word, Zanna, and Cooper (1974) demonstrated how self-fulfilling prophecies can invade a job employment context. In Study 1, the researchers videotaped mock employment interviews of Black and White job seekers. The videotapes revealed that Black job seekers performed less well than their White counterparts. Black job seekers appeared distant, disinterested, and often appeared unprepared for the interview as compared to White job seekers. The researchers also noticed, however, the White interviewers themselves seemed to behave differently with the White job seekers as compared to the Black job seekers. The White interviewers appeared more interested in the applicant when the applicant was White, established greater eye contact, leaned forward toward the White applicant, and overall indicated more immediacy. The opposite occurred with Black job seekers. When interviewing Blacks, White interviewers made several verbal slips, appeared nervous, lacked eye contact, and physically distanced themselves from the Black applicants. Clearly, no conclusion could be drawn from these initial data.

In the second study the researchers trained student confederates to act with low or high immediacy toward White job seekers. The data revealed that when White job seekers were treated with low immediacy by the White interviewers they behaved as did the Black job seekers in Study 1. Likewise, White job seekers given high immediacy by the trained interviewers excelled. This classic study is a great example of how self-fulfilling prophecies can impair performance in the workplace.

psychological researchers can unintentionally influence the responses of their research participants (Rosenthal, 2002). Expectations of individuals in authority are communicated in at least four ways (Rosenthal, 1974, as cited in Cox, 1994):

- The overall climate (favorable or unfavorable responses, positive or negative tone)
- Amount of input given relevant to the job at hand
- Amount of feedback given
- Amount of expected output

In an organization, managers and supervisors may inadvertently change their behaviors toward employees as a consequence of their preconceived perceptions and expectations regarding the abilities of such employees. A low level of expected outcomes can result in a lack of opportunity to show otherwise, such as the situation in which a minority employee is never given challenging goals, authority, visibility, or a position of responsibility. The performance of such employees is then indirectly and subtly influenced by the behaviors and expectations of the managers and supervisors. One source of the inaccurate expectations of managers and supervisors is bias in favor of ingroup members and against outgroup members (Cox, 1994). For example, lower expectations for members of minority groups can result in reduced performance by minority group members. Cox suggests the self-fulfilling prophecy is the mechanism by which prejudice does its greatest harm to organizational performance.

Cultural Differences

Finally, the cultural differences that individuals bring with them into their work groups can result in poor work group processes and subsequently poor performance. Cox (1994) identifies six areas of behavior where a lack of understanding of cultural differences may have a significant negative impact on the functioning of diverse organizational groups:

- *Time and space orientation.* Examples: Some individuals from Arab or Latino-based cultures are more comfortable sitting or standing close to each other and with physical touching than Anglo-Americans. Anglo-Americans often place more importance on adhering to strict time expectations and timelines than individuals from other cultural groups where the timing of an event may be less important than the people's participation in an event.
- *Leadership style orientation.* Examples: Mexican Americans may place more importance on relationship building in leadership, and consider Anglo-Americans too abrupt in their business interactions. Women tend to have a more democratic approach to leadership than men.
- *Individualism versus collectivism.* Example: Anglo-Americans tend to value autonomy and self-reliance (as opposed to the needs and goals of the group) more than individuals from Asian, Hispanic, or African backgrounds.
- *Competitive versus cooperative behavior.* Example: Anglo-Americans (especially men) tend to be more competitive than Mexican Americans, African Americans, and Chinese Americans, who are more likely to demonstrate cooperation and helping behaviors.
- *Locus of control.* Locus of control refers to the extent individuals believe they are in control of their own fate. Individuals with a high locus of control believe they have a significant impact on the events in their life. Individuals with an external locus of control tend to believe more in fate and the influence of factors outside of their control. Example: Anglo-Americans tend to believe they are individually responsible for their success and failures while many individuals from Arab, Asian, African, and Latino cultures are quicker to believe their successes and failures are due to influences other than their ability and effort.
- *Communication styles.* Examples: According to Tannen (1990, as cited by Cox, 1994), conversations are viewed by women as an opportunity to share support and reach consensus; conversations for men are viewed as an opportunity to seek the upper hand in a hierarchical social order. Eye contact in Asian cultures is considered rude, while Anglo-Americans expect eye contact during conversation.

In addition to differences in behaviors and style, Cox (1994) points out that cultural differences in perceptions and worldviews can also increase conflict among social groups in the workplace. For example, Blacks and Whites in the same organization may have very different perspectives on whether the organization discriminates against Black employees, whether promotions are based on qualifications, or whether support groups are racist. Because of in-group and outgroup biases, many believe that their perspective is "the right one." A lack of understanding of these cultural differences in behaviors and worldviews can lead to misunderstanding, miscommunication, and unsatisfactory workplace experiences (Cox, 1994).

The literature reviewed suggests that there are many opportunities for work group diversity to result in negative work group processes and outcomes. Therefore I would like to conclude our discussion of group diversity by focusing on strategies for improving diverse work groups.

IMPROVING DIVERSE GROUPS

Researchers and scholars recommend several strategies to decrease the potential problems of diverse work groups and increase the likelihood of potential benefits.

Diversity Training and Increased Awareness

Miscommunication and conflict between social groups arising from diversity in work groups can sometimes be reduced by formal diversity training. This type of training can help build mutual understanding and respect for cultural differences. The goal is not to eliminate such differences but to improve interpersonal relations between coworkers (Cox, 1994). Diversity training is more likely to reduce conflict when it includes the following:

- A focus on group behavior and organizational values and norms that create barriers and difficulties for minority groups, rather than a focus on changing or improving minority groups (Frost, 1999)
- Discussions of privilege, racial identity, race, racism, and worldviews to encourage self-exploration and the development of a mature racial identity (Kirkland & Regan, 1997; Thomas, Philips, & Brown, 1998)
- An opportunity to learn about other cultures (Cox, 1994; Triandis, 1995)
- Open discussions about group differences, the impact of group differences on group dynamics, and the sources and causes of stereotypes, biases, and intergroup conflict (Cox, 1994)
- Training on many different types of conflict management techniques (Cox, 1994)
- Trainers with a highly developed sense of their own racial identity (Kirkland & Regan, 1997)

- Commitment from senior management to the goals of diversity and diversity training (Kirkland & Regan, 1997; Ferdman & Brody, 1996; Rynes & Rosen, 1995)
- Techniques to build a sense of similarity (Thomas, Philips, & Brown, 1998)

Organization and Group Culture

Organizations and work groups that have a culture supportive of diversity are more likely to maximize the benefits of diversity and avoid the destructive conflicts that arise between social groups (Robbins, 1998; Schneider & Northcraft, 1999). Diversity training, discussed above, is one way to help build this type of culture (Schneider & Northcraft). But more than training is required to encourage a culture supportive of diversity. Leaders and top management must be committed to diversity and clearly show their support, such as by issuing a statement that clearly states management's commitment and support, allocating resources to achieve diversity goals, considering diversity training part of business strategy, and modeling appropriate behavior for employees (Kirkland & Regan, 1997).

Furthermore, a culture that supports diversity will also have an expectation of high performance from all employees (it will not expect less from minority employees, because of the danger of self-fulfilling prophecy), stimulate personal development, welcome openness, promote a high tolerance for debate and constructive conflict on work-related matters, make workers feel valued, and appreciate new perspectives and ways of performing work (Thomas & Ely, 1996). Moreover, cultural differences will be viewed as opportunities not problems (Cox, 1994).

Selection

Another way to reduce conflict between different social groups is to alter the organization's or work group's personnel. In addition to accomplishing such changes through diversity training, the organization can hire and promote persons who are tolerant, flexible, and open to new perspectives and who understand and appreciate different cultures and the advantages of diversity (Cox, 1994).

Superordinate Goals

Social group differences can be made less salient and important, thus reducing ingroup/outgroup effects, if the work group has a superordinate goal. This means focusing on the importance of the work group's objective and making it clear that it is in the best interest of diverse members to cooperate and work together because the objective can not otherwise be accomplished (Schneider & Northcraft, 1999). At the organizational level, superordinate goals can be created with employee ownership, meaningful profit sharing, and incentive programs (Triandis, 1995). Superordinate goals can foster a superordinate identity (the organization or the work group) that may reduce the importance of social identities while members are working toward the superordinate goal (Brickson, 2000).

Decrease Power Imbalance

Conflict between social categories is less likely when social category diversity is not highly correlated with functional diversity or the distribution of organizational power (Cox, 1994; Schneider & Northcraft, 1999). A work group consisting of majority group managers and minority group nonmanagers is more likely to have difficulty in working together than a group where both the managers and nonmanagers are represented by both minority and majority groups.

Encourage Nonwork Interactions

Social outings (picnics, baseball games) and socializing prior to tackling work tasks can provide an opportunity for group members to form friendships and to have a good time together. These events may then allow group members to get to know each other, increase familiarity with the norms and language of other cultures, increase respect for the culture of other members, and create an opportunity to dispel stereotypes (Cox, 1994; Schneider & Northcraft, 1999; Triandis, 1995).

CONCLUSION

Organizations expend great effort, time, and resources to evaluate individuals in organizations for the purposes of selection, development, and promotion. Despite organizational attempts to focus on job relevant attributes such as one's knowledge, skills, and abilities, prejudice and discriminatory behaviors based upon social group memberships persist in and outside of organizations. Attempts to rid organizations of bias due to group membership, and to improve the performance of diverse groups are dependent upon creating work cultures that are cooperative and which help organizational members work productively across different sources of diversity.

Discussion Items

1. Social categorization undermines many organizational attempts regarding diversity. Brainstorm as a class what organizations can do in order to help employees adopt a superordinate identity and thereby diminish the occurrence of prejudice based upon social group membership.
2. Review Figure 6.1. Stereotypes exist for every group. Choose five stereotypes listed and explain how each stereotype can impede individual as well as group performance.
3. This chapter has focused upon race and gender and dominant social categories by which Americans divide society. However, these attributes may

not be meaningful in other parts of the world. Research the cultures of Brazil and Taiwan. What group differences matter there? Why?

4. As you research the cultures of Brazil and Taiwan, also describe why prejudice occurs in those societies and in their organizations. What are the similarities to and differences from your own culture?

 ## InfoTrac College Edition

Be sure to log on to InfoTrac College Edition and search for additional readings on topics of interest to you.

Conflict, Perceptions of Justice, Privilege, and Diversity

Read Diversity Case 7.1 on page 112. How would you respond if you were Bob or Vanessa? How would you feel if you were a team member, and how would their disagreements affect your ability to work? Bob and Vanessa seem to be experiencing **conflict**. Cox (1994) defines *conflict* as an expression of the tensions between the goals and concerns of one group and those of another. In this case, the disagreements that Bob and Vanessa experience are conflicts. However, their perspectives about how their disagreements should be resolved are in conflict also.

Given that organizations are systems comprised of people, conflict is a natural (and often costly—see Diversity in Practice 7.1) part of organizational life (Proudford & Smith, 2003), especially since the work that organizations engage in is increasingly interdependent and often team or group based. Increasing diversity in the workplace (see Chapter 1) enhances the probability that work groups and teams will likewise be more diverse as well. Although work group diversity can facilitate group creativity and decision making, it can also increase the opportunity for **diversity conflict** (Friedman & Davidson, 2001, Proudford & Smith). That is, conflict is rooted in differences.

This chapter focuses on diversity conflict and the many ways in which it may manifest itself within the workplace. Diversity conflict not only occurs between different groups at work, it can also present itself within an individual. Diversity conflict is evidenced in silence as well as in loud arguments. It occurs as obvious forms of discrimination as well as in differences in perspectives and worldviews (Friedman & Davidson, 2001). After reviewing the many ways in which diversity conflict may occur we will consider the triggers for di-

All work groups experience conflict.

versity conflict. Special attention will be paid to the issue of privilege in the workplace and how privilege can be the source of different forms of diversity conflict. Finally we'll think more broadly about diversity conflict and its place within organizations. This discussion will center on the benefits of conflict that is rooted in diversity and how to capitalize upon diversity for organizational effectiveness.

Diversity Case 7.1	Bob and Vanessa

Bob, a fifty-something White male, is a senior manager of a small management consulting firm and leads a growing staff. Bob seems to have good relationships with everyone except for Vanessa. Vanessa, a thirty-something Black female, is a project leader and is second to Bob in authority and leadership. The two seem to have a different perspective on everything that the team and Bob discuss. Their constant disagreements create tension for the entire team. Bob doesn't understand why they view everything so differently; they both grew up in the New York City tri-state area, they both have worked for the organization for the same amount of time, and they even share similar educational backgrounds. Vanessa doesn't understand why Bob is so uncomfortable with their disagreements. He seems to want to put an end to every discussion before they really get started. Vanessa feels disrespected every time Bob puts an end to what she feels are important discussions and his lack of interest in engaging in these conversations threatens her credibility with her team. Bob feels as though Vanessa is just a drama queen looking for conflict and that she doesn't know when to walk away. He wouldn't be surprised if Vanessa was using all of these disagreements as a way to demean and demoralize him so that she could steal his job.

| Diversity in Practice 7.1 | Costs of Conflict |

Stewart Levine, founder of Resolution Works (www.resolutionworks.org), a firm that provides training, facilitation, and conflict resolution services, suggests that conflict is a major resource drain for organizations. He identified four costs associated with conflict in organizations:

- *Direct costs* are the financial costs associated with using lawyers and mediators to resolve conflict.
- *Productivity costs* refer to the time lost (that could have been used to pursue other issues) addressing workplace conflict. Too often loss of time also results in loss of income or profit.
- *Continuity costs,* according to Levine, refer to "Loss of ongoing relationships including the community they embody." Continuity costs refer to the loss of relationships that help to sustain a work group or a community.
- *Emotional costs* are the emotional pains suffered during conflict. The anger, fear, and blame that arise during conflict take away energy that could have been directed toward more job relevant tasks.

From S. Levine, "The Many Costs of Conflict," found at www.mediate.com. Reprinted with permission.

THE MANY FACES OF DIVERSITY CONFLICT

Diversity conflict presents itself in many (sometimes unexpected) ways. Diversity conflict can occur within and between individuals, within and between groups, and throughout an entire organization. For example, at times, individuals have a minority status social identity (the group to which they belong) that does not match their professional identity; the result is **intraindividual conflict** (Ibarra, 1999). That is, as individuals we experience conflict related to how we negotiate our social identity, such as our cultural self with our professional identity. Minority group members who are often highly underrepresented within various professions are prone to experience intraindividual conflict as they break into new fields.

Ibarra (1999) suggests that individuals who experience intraindividual conflict are often forced to engage in **social identity impression management** by attempting to project an image of themselves that is more in line with their professional identity. For example, female leaders who may elect to use more democratic and participative methods of influence may find that these inclinations do not fit with their professional identity and expectations. The pressure to present an alternative identity that is more authoritative may then create inner turmoil for these women that decreases their sense of well-being and may also promote stress and depression.

The social identity conflict experienced by minority group members like Blacks, women, and gay and lesbian workers makes it difficult for these groups to succeed in organizations that reflect traditional, Eurocentric, and patriarchal values given that each day they must experience the dissonance of social identity conflict (Elmes & Connelley, 1997). For example, Elmes and Connelley suggest, "Many members of lower status groups face a classic double bind rooted in identity conflict: If they fail to act with decisiveness and power, they are seen as not being aggressive enough to manage the challenges of executive roles; however, if they do act with decisiveness and power, they are seen as threatening and aggressive" (p. 159).

Diversity conflict may also occur at the interpersonal level. Jex (2002) discusses **interpersonal conflict** as being reflected in those negative interactions with anyone you may have contact with as part of your job. This may include coworkers, supervisors, clients, as well as suppliers. Interpersonal conflict may be rooted in prejudice or it may simply reflect personality differences. Diversity Case 7.1 is a typical example of interpersonal conflict.

Cox (1994) focuses upon **intergroup conflict** as the conflict that can arise between whole groups of individuals, such as the majority group and a minority group, or among various minority groups (e.g., African Americans vs. Latinos) within a work setting. Ohlott, Chrobot-Mason, Dalton, Deal, & Hoppe (2003) suggest that when conflict reflects the level of value placed upon the social groups to which individuals identify, **identity-based conflict** results. These conflicts are rooted within society, but they impair relationships between members of different groups within the workplace. Identity-based conflicts can present challenges to both minority and majority groups. When minority group identity is devalued or a source of stigma, minority group members feel pushed to embrace their minority group identity given the threat posed by majority members to dismiss it. Majority group members in turn feel themselves threatened when it appears the minority group is rejecting *their* social identity (Thomas & Chrobot-Mason, in press).

Two other forms of intergroup conflict more frequently studied in the organizational sciences are **emotional/relationship** or **task** oriented (see Figure 7.1). Task conflict results when individuals with different functional backgrounds (e.g. engineering, sales) work together on a task. When this conflict promotes the sharing of knowledge and information about the task, task conflict results in improved performance (e.g., Pelled, Eisenhardt, & Xin, 1999).

Emotional/relationship conflict often develops out of differences in value systems or when members rely upon superficial attributions or stereotypes to define others with whom they work (Jackson & Joshi, 2001). Emotional/relational conflict can frequently result in worker absenteeism, turnover, and low job satisfaction; however, neither Pelled et al. (1999) nor Jehn (1995) found that it affected group performance. Pelled et al. suggest that perhaps when diverse group members do experience emotional conflict they simply find ways to cope with the conflict, or maybe they simply avoid working with one another. Therefore it appears that the emotional/relationship conflict that is produced by demographic differences in the workplace, such as racial differences,

Figure 7.1 | Task and Emotional/Relationship Conflict

A taxonomy for describing the content of diversity

	Attributes that are more likely to be task-related	Attributes that are more likely to be relationship-oriented
Readily detected attributes	Department/unit membership Organizational tenure Formal credentials and titles Education level Memberships in professional associations	Sex Socioeconomic status Age Race Ethnicity Religion Political memberships Nationality Sexual orientation
Underlying attributes	Knowledge and expertise Cognitive skills and abilities Physical skills and abilities	Gender Class identity Attitudes Values Personality Sexual identity Racial identity Ethnic identity Other social identities

From S. E. Jackson, K. E. May, and K. Whitney, "Under the Dynamics of Diversity in Decision-Making Teams" in *Team Effectiveness and Decision-Making in Organizations*, R. A. Guzzo and E. Salas (eds.) (San Francisco: Jossey-Bass, 1995). Reprinted by permission.

has its impact upon individuals and their ability to effectively adjust to a diverse work context rather than group performance.

Both interpersonal and intergroup conflict reflect what Friedman and Davidson (2001) call **first-order conflict.** First-order conflict involves discrimination and is experienced mainly by minority group members. Majority group members are typically not involved in first-order conflict unless they are being accused of discrimination. Discrimination related to access to jobs and resources and the subsequent conflict that can result are examples of first-order conflict. These forms of conflict are typically unambiguous and the organization may already have procedures in place to deal with them. However, at times the procedures or practices chosen to address or prevent first-order conflict may reveal more pervasive and deeper forms of diversity conflict. Friedman and Davidson refer to conflicts related to remedies for first-order conflict as **second-order conflict.**

**Diversity
in Practice 7.2**

Diversity Conflict
and Sexual Diversity

Differences in social attitudes, religion, and political orientation at times make organizations' support of gay and lesbians in the workplace an opportunity for diversity conflict. Cox and Beale (1997) suggest some methods for lowering tensions among employees who differ in their level of support for organizational initiatives that support gay and lesbian workers.

- These authors suggest that organizations pay close attention to how they convey their messages regarding sexual diversity practices and initiatives. All efforts that support the gay and lesbian workforce should do so out of a commitment to equal opportunity. The organization must make clear that their commitment to equal opportunity is pervasive, and that this organizational commitment is distinct from individual-level opinions regarding the personal acceptance of homosexuality.
- At times conflict related to sexual diversity initiatives brings up questions regarding whether a gay or lesbian identity is a choice or not (however, this same question never comes up for heterosexuals). Organizational representatives must defuse these issues by asking employees to consider if the origins of one's sexual identity are relevant to equal opportunity (they are not!).
- Organizations should also provide all workers with the opportunity to select themselves out of positions in which they feel that they will have to compromise their religious or moral sentiments.

Second-order conflicts are typically rooted in differences in individuals' and groups' understanding of issues such as identity, justice, and **privilege**. Second-order conflict is manifested in backlash and resistance to programs and practices to prevent or resolve first-order conflict. Affirmative action programs are one very visible source of second-order conflict (see Diversity Learning Point 7.1). Friedman and Davidson (2001) suggest it often plays out in organizations in subtle or hidden ways such as through gossip or veiled hostility. Given that second-order conflict is often invisible, there are no procedures in place to deal with it. When differences in opinion about first-order conflict end open communication in organizations, Friedman and Davidson indicate that **autistic hostility** is the result. This lack of communication silences issues related to diversity and conflict, thus making the opportunity for change extremely difficult.

Whereas first-order conflict typically is only felt by minority group members, second-order conflict is widespread and felt by both minority and dominant group members (Friedman & Davidson, 2001). For example, second-order conflict often makes dominant groups feel disadvantaged and perhaps even discriminated against. Dominant groups then blame minority group members as the source of the sense of unfairness or injustice they experience. Minority group members experience second-order conflict too; however, they see the dis-

Diversity Learning Point 7.1	Affirmative Action and Second-Order Conflict

Affirmative action is probably the leading source of second-order conflict within institutions today. It creates conflict and resistance throughout society, including institutions of higher education (Crosby, Iyer, Clayton, & Downing, 2003; Thomas, Mack, & Montagliani, 2004). Most of the conflict related to affirmative action is a result of the public's ignorance regarding what affirmative action entails (Thomas et al., 2004; Hays-Thomas, 2004). Often the public believes that affirmative action involves quotas and the hiring of unqualified members of minority groups (Hays-Thomas, 2004; Jacques, 1997) when this is rarely the case (Jones, 2002).

When I think of affirmative action, I see it as a verb rather than as a noun. The American Psychological Association (1996) defined affirmative action as "voluntary and mandatory efforts undertaken by federal, state, and local governments; private employers; and schools to combat discrimination and to promote equal opportunity in education and employment for all" (p. 2). Crosby et al. (2003) describe affirmative action as an active attempt to redress discrimination of the past and confront the discrimination of the present. Affirmative action therefore can involve a variety of different efforts including improving one's recruitment strategy in order to recruit a more diverse applicant pool and engaging in an aggressive public relations campaign in order to create the image that your organization is diversity friendly.

comfort experienced by majority group members as a necessary step for organizational change (Friedman & Davidson, 2001).

TRIGGERS OF DIVERSITY CONFLICT

There are numerous triggers of diversity conflict. Broadly, these antecedents of diversity conflict are often related to competition, cultural differences, and differences in expectations. Although I have structured these triggers into three broad groupings, the reader will quickly realize that these triggers are often related to one another. For example, feelings of competition in the workplace may stem from cultural differences, and differences in expectations that trigger conflict may themselves be rooted in differences in culture. The triggers are often related to one another given that in some way they all highlight the issue of **privilege** in the workplace. Our discussion of conflict triggers will therefore conclude with a discussion of privilege, what it is, how it manifests itself at work, and how it can promote conflict. However, before we get into the sometimes contentious issue of privilege, let's review three common sources of conflict, beginning with competition.

Competition

Conflict is often related to the real or imagined competition that individuals or groups may feel toward one another. Within organizations diverse groups may have to compete for access to jobs or promotions, or access to the information, mentoring, or networks that can lead to jobs and promotions.

In a classic study of **realistic group conflict**, Sherif, Harvey, White, Hood, and Sherif (1988), examined the role of competition in producing conflict among boys attending a summer camp. These authors found that simply dividing the boys into groups and having them compete against each other in sporting events produced prejudice and discrimination. Furthermore, once identified, the conflict was difficult to extinguish. Attempts to eliminate the conflict by getting the boys to relate on a personal level simply backfired and often resulted in fights. The conflict was finally resolved when the researchers gave the boys a **superordinate goal** on which to work. By having the boys work together cooperatively, the conflict eventually subsided (Thomas & Chrobot-Mason, in press). Similarly, other social identity theorists (e.g., Tajfel and colleagues) have demonstrated the **minimal group paradigm effect.** That is, even the arbitrary assignment of individuals into groups can lead to ingroup and outgroup categorization that subsequently result in bias and discrimination. These tendencies simply become heightened when competition is introduced (see Chapter 6 for more on social identity and group dynamics).

If the mere arbitrary division of individuals into groups can lead to hostility and conflict, it would seem that the context for conflict simply becomes intensified once the identity groups with which individuals identify have some kind of historical tension or competition between them. In Chapter 6, we discussed Cox's (1994) concept of legacy effects and how they affect group processes. **Macro legacy effects** refer to when the collective history of two groups are manifested in contemporary relationships between members of those groups (Cox). For example, Black and White employees may experience conflict due to their shared history of the enslavement of Africans in the United States. Perhaps a White employee doubts the competence of a Black coworker, given that the legacy of slavery does not place Blacks in roles of competence and authority. Black employees may likewise use the legacy of slavery as justification for their distrust or dislike of White colleagues. History can also produce a **micro legacy effect** when personal experience with members of other groups affects future relationships with members of those groups.

Cultural Differences

Bowman (1991) and Cox (1994) each list a number of ways in which cultural differences can lead to conflict. Among these are leadership style orientations, individualism and collectivism values, and communication styles. If you refer back to Diversity Case 7.1, you could interpret differences in Bob and Vanessa's communication and styles of handling conflict as reflecting differences in culture. For example, communication styles of African Americans are usually identified as being highly assertive and emotionally expressive (Cox). Furthermore, in analyzing cultural differences in responses to conflict, Davidson (2002) found that Whites preferred to initiate a cooling off period before a

Diversity Learning Point 7.2	**Understanding Perceptions of Justice in First-Order Conflict**

Differences in perceptions of justice can be a source of conflict among individuals as well as groups. There are three different types of justice perceptions, **distributive,** **procedural,** and **interactional** (Colquitt, Conlon, Wesson, Porter, & Ng, 2001). *Distributive justice* refers to the perception that the rewards or outcomes distributed by an organization to its members are fair. The worker must consider, "Is the reward or outcome received (such as pay) fair compared to what I expected to receive?"

Procedural justice refers to the perception that the procedures by which a reward or outcome is distributed are fair. That is, "Are the rules, regulations, and procedures that are in place fair to me?" Finally, *interactional justice* refers to the fairness and sensitivity with which employees are treated by their employer. Employees' perceptions of interactional justice often result from how communication occurs between the organization and its employees. Colquitt et al. (2001) suggest that interactional justice can be further divided into two dimensions, **informational** and **interpersonal justice.** *Informational justice* refers to the extent to which an organization conveys information to employees regarding the policies and procedures related to rewards and other outcomes. *Interpersonal justice* addresses the extent to which the organization treats employees with respect.

heated discussion could escalate and that walking away from conflict is a likely indicator of respect for the other party. Blacks in the study on the other hand expressed a desire to continue and work through the conflict. Clearly the cultural differences represented in this case demonstrate how conflict can escalate due to a lack of knowledge about cultural differences.

Training is one way to help make workers aware of how cultural differences can result in conflict. However, increasing awareness of cultural differences is not enough (Chrobot-Mason & Ruderman, 2004). Training should also help trainees to develop behavioral skills for communicating across groups and engaging in conflict resolution. Seeking feedback about how one is perceived across groups and the level of fairness and justice perceived in one's policies and practices is also critical (Chrobot-Mason & Ruderman, 2004).

Expectations

Differences between the expectations of diverse newcomers and those of workplace insiders can be a frequent source of conflict. Bowman (1991) suggested that minority workers, specifically African Americans, often find themselves in a **triple quandary** as a result of differences in expectations that derive from differences between their minority culture and that of the larger mainstream culture. The **mainstream quandary** faced by African Americans reflects their aspirations for upward mobility in a mainstream culture that may have lower expectations for them. The **cultural quandary** reflects the differences in expectations that are a reflection of differences in culture. We have already discussed one example of this, Davidson's (2002) work on Black–White differences in responses to conflict. Likewise differences in cultural dimensions such as individualism–collectivism mean that Blacks must often subdue their collectivistic values in exchange for the larger mainstream individualistic values. Likewise, Bowman (1991) identifies a **minority quandary** that reflects differences in African Americans' cultural tendency to pursue organizational activities related to social change and activism as compared to mainstream culture's less active style for coping, especially in regard to coping with inequality. Experiencing this triple quandary likely results in the internal, intraindividual conflict of which Ibarra (1999) speaks.

Another example of differences in expectations across groups that may result in conflict deals with how groups become socialized into a work group or organization. Minority group members often expect integration, whereas majority group members may expect assimilation (Cox, 1994). Furthermore, the level of difference that individuals bring into their work group or team may be reflected in the level of conflict experienced during this important process of socialization. For example, Bell and Nkomo (2001) found that newcomers often present challenges to organizational insiders about how things are done and the overall culture of the organization. They found that demographic differences between newcomers and insiders created conflict that lengthened the amount of time it took for newcomers to feel fully socialized and integrated within their new work environment. In comparing the experiences of Black and White women, these authors found that Black women experienced more conflict than their White female counterparts as they attempted to integrate into a predominantly White male work environment and culture.

Within diverse settings, conflict can also result from differences in perspectives. At times, differences in realities set the context for conflict. A lack of understanding and appreciation for each other's unique reality can promote conflict that stems from differences in privilege.

PRIVILEGE: AN OVERARCHING THEME

Privilege is an invisible source of conflict in the workplace. Organizations' inability to see and understand privilege creates hidden inequities in the workplace. It is these hidden inequities that promote conflict.

When most people hear the word *privilege,* they think of financial wealth and power. However, the privilege that I believe most often results in conflict within diverse workplaces is of a more psychological nature. Privilege is the luxury to ignore aspects of one's identity that confer unearned advantages and power. It is easy to talk about *others'* disadvantages. However, rarely do we discuss how one group's disadvantage is an advantage for another group. To discuss how we as members of a group may benefit from another group's suffering likely causes too much discomfort and anxiety.

What Is It?

Peggy McIntosh (1993) defines privilege as "an invisible package of unearned assets that I can count on cashing in each day, but about which I was 'meant' to remain oblivious. White privilege is like an invisible weightless knapsack of special provisions, assurances, tools, maps, guides, codebooks, passports, visas, clothes, compass, emergency gear, and blank checks" (p. 31). We all have some form of privilege, although we take it for granted. Yet those without a particular type of privilege (e.g., privilege based upon sexuality) can easily see it in others.

> The invisibility of privilege strengthens the power it creates and maintains. The invisible cannot be combated, and as a result privilege is allowed to perpetuate, regenerate, and re-create itself. Privilege is systemic, not an occasional occurrence. Privilege is invisible only until looked for, but silence in the face of privilege sustains its invisibility. (Wildman & Davis, 1996, p. 8)

How Do You Know Who Has Privilege?

Often we can tell who is privileged and who is not by asking about the extent to which certain groups must think about or negotiate their identity at work. Wildman and Davis (1996) suggest that privilege has two elements; invisibility/normalization and the choice to fight against oppression. Those who have privilege represent the norm and the status quo. They are never defined as different, they just are. The characteristics of the privileged define what is normal, often in ways that benefit and reinforce their privilege. "Privilege is not visible to its holder; it is merely there, a part of the world, a way of life simply the way things are. Others have *a lack,* an absence, a deficiency" (Wildman & Davis, 1996, p. 17).

Furthermore, many of the issues that we have discussed in this book are topics that the privileged can choose to address or to ignore. However, if you are a target of racism, sexism, or heterosexism in your workplace, you have little choice but to deal with it in some way.

> Members of privileged groups can opt out of struggles against oppression if they choose. Often this privilege may be exercised by silence. . . . Depending on the number of privileges someone has, she or he may experience the power of choosing the types of struggles in which to engage. Even this choice may be masked as identification with oppression, thereby making the privilege that enables the choice invisible. (Wildman & Davis, 1996; p. 16)

Manifestations of Privilege in the Workplace

There are many ways in which privilege manifests itself in the workplace, creating a climate ripe for conflict. For example, when people of color are also the numeric minority in their organizations (as well as the cultural minority), they are often defined by their color or culture rather than their credentials. For example, a chief executive officer (CEO) who happens to be African American

Diversity Learning Point 7.3	**Understanding Privilege**

Privilege is a difficult concept to grasp without examples. Both McIntosh (1993) and Maier (1997) provide numerous examples that can apply to the workplace. Thomas and Landau (2002) offered the following:

Examples of Race Privilege
- If I receive a poor performance evaluation, I can be confident that it was not due to my race.
- I can speak to the top management team of my workplace, and not put my race on trial.

Examples of Gender Privilege
- I can choose to have a family and no one will consider my ability to remain a contributor to my workplace.
- I can seek mentoring from a senior colleague, and not raise suspicions that I am interested in a romantic relationship.

Examples of Heterosexual Privilege
- I feel confident that my relationship with my significant other will not damage my career.
- I can bring my significant other to work-related social functions and not feel harassment or discrimination because of my partner's identity.

will be referred to as a Black CEO. Rarely have I heard someone refer to a CEO of European descent as a White CEO. Whites (especially men) who are CEOs are the norm and thus defined as normal. People of color aspiring to the chief executive's office must constantly consider how their race, color, or culture impacts their upward mobility in the organization. Whites need only consider their effort and credentials; that is their privilege.

We can identify gender-based privilege based upon the extent to which workers must consider their gender as they go about the business of their work. For example, take the example of family pictures in the workplace. I would think for men who want to have pictures of loved ones in their office or cubicles, this would be a no-brainer. Men would likely not think about the extent to which pictures of loved ones around one's office could stymie one's career. Yet for women, the issue is often more complex. Many women (myself included) might consider the message that family pictures may convey to one's coworkers or superiors. For women, family pictures in the workplace may convey a lack of commitment to or focus on one's work. Men with pictures of loved ones at their desk are likely just considered caring husbands or fathers.

The same example is useful when considering heterosexual privilege in the workplace. Within your workplace or institution, in what way is heterosexuality privileged? That is, in what ways is it reinforced as normal? Certainly gay and lesbian workers must consider the extent to which their sexuality is revealed, and to whom. Again, this is a privilege that heterosexual workers rarely consider. Likewise, many gay and lesbian workers may be hesitant to display pictures of their partners (gay and lesbian workers do not have the heterosexual privilege of marriage in most U.S. cities and states). Because of heterosexist privilege in the workplace, gay and lesbian workers often carry the burden of intraindividual conflict. Their conflict is between negotiating their personal identity and their presumed "heterosexual" professional identity and when and if to reveal their gay identity and to whom (Day & Schoenrade, 2000).

Now the issue of whether or not one is comfortable having photographs of loved ones in the office may seem insignificant, but in fact it is a reminder to those lacking privilege of the extent to which they have to manage their identity at work and continually try to fit in. Mark Maier (1997), a White male, writes about his privilege:

> As a person who is both "white" and "male," I not only fit the normative profile of the competent, to-be-taken-seriously "manager,"—but precisely because I do— I am not likely to be aware that I do, nor how I am privileged by it. I do not have to deal with a whole range of additional pressures beyond those associated narrowly with my job performance. I do not have to expend the type of substantial emotional energy trying to "fit in" and justifying my presence that my female and "non-white" colleagues do. (p. 30)

Privilege is often a trigger of diversity conflict, especially when majority groups and minority groups just can't seem to see things from the same perspective. Yes, cultural differences and differences in expectations that come out of culture or socialization result in differences in perceptions, interpretations, and worldviews. But the inability of majority group members to accept the existence, experiences, and perspectives of minority group members as legitimate, reflects privilege.

It is easy to see how White privilege, for example, impairs some White peoples' ability to accept a racial minority experience that is different from their own as equally important and valuable. Many racial minorities have had the experience of not being heard by their nonminority colleagues and friends, especially when claims of discrimination or harassment are made. Often the response to those claims are, "You're being too sensitive," or "You're taking the statement out of context, Joe really didn't mean it that way." The conflict comes about due to differences in cultural norms or expectations, but also because privilege allows the nonminority friend or colleague to ignore the racist offense.

Privilege can also impair relations and create conflict between minority group members too. Privilege comes in many different forms. Within American society we see privilege resulting from being male, White, heterosexual, middle-class, Christian, and so forth. Therefore a member of a minority group can be privileged in one way, but denied privilege in other ways.

Proudford and Smith (2003) provide an example of this in their analysis of a conflict between Black and White women. The executive women's group (comprised of White women) within the organization was pushing leadership to embrace and enact more diversity initiatives that would support women's leadership. However, their conversations and their proposal to the management never addressed issues of race or racial privilege within the organization, and this created a conflict between the executive women's group and more junior Black women in the organization (who subsequently organized their own group). Although the executive women's group pushed for greater opportunities for women in their organization, their white privilege permitted them to ignore the ways in which racial minorities (many of whom were women) faced additional barriers related to race. The conflict was finally resolved when new leadership in these women's groups was able to communicate and find a more inclusive agenda to support.

Privilege can undermine any relationship, within or outside of organizations. The challenge for organizations is to understand what privilege is, and in what ways organizational norms, policies, and practices can privilege some groups and not others. Organizational norms that support business dealings in strip bars (male and heterosexual privilege), or some private country clubs (male or White privilege) will deny opportunities for some organizational members while providing opportunities to others.

DIVERSITY CONFLICT: GOOD OR BAD?

Although conflict may be inevitable in any situation in which people come together, conflict need not be solely negative. In fact, effectively managed conflict can have quite positive consequences, even within a diverse workplace. Earlier, the chapter highlighted research which found that functional diversity within teams can lead to better task understanding and subsequently enhanced performance. Emotional conflict, however, which can be promoted by demographic differences, can lead to dissatisfaction, lowered commitment, and other forms of withdrawal. However, no performance detriments were found in relation to emotional conflict (Pelled et al., 1999). The challenge for diverse organizations then is how to decrease the opportunities for emotional conflict.

REDUCING INTERGROUP CONFLICT

Social psychology offers many lessons for reducing the occurrence of intergroup conflict. Allport (1954) early on discussed the need for intergroup contact. His reasoning was that prejudice and conflict often grew out of ignorance and that with greater contact between groups prejudice would decrease. Of course, nothing is that simple (especially when it comes to human behavior). Subsequent researchers have examined the boundaries of Allport's recommendation. They too agree that contact is important to decreasing prejudice and conflict; however, they also suggest a number of conditions that are necessary to make the contact meaningful within the context of prejudice reduction.

Cooperation

Competitive contact fosters prejudice and conflict rather than eliminating conflict. The Sherif et al. (1988) study of campers was a superb example of this. In order for contact to reduce prejudice and conflict, the contact itself should be pleasant, rewarding, and cooperative.

Equality

Contact should also occur between diverse individuals who are equal in status. Certainly contact between diverse individuals in which the majority group member is always in a position of control and authority, and the minority individual is the subordinate simply reinforce societal stereotypes and dominant group privilege. Exposure to people who are different from you on one dimension like sexuality, but the same as you in regard to family background and education, help to break down the perceived barriers between us.

Intimacy

In order for contact to reduce prejudice, it must also allow for opportunities for the individuals involved to develop personalized relationships (McDaniel & Walls, 1997). That is, having diverse individuals share space within a seminar room or classroom is not enough. The contact should facilitate the opportunity for individuals to communicate with one another at a level where the potential for friendship is possible.

Support

The contact should also be supported by the institution. That is, for contact to reduce prejudice it should be supported and facilitated by the organization. Diverse decision making teams or diverse mentoring relationships that are sanctioned and supported by the organization can be one mechanism for reducing conflict.

Aronson's jigsaw method uses these very principles within diverse classrooms. Students work in small and diverse groups. Like a piece of a puzzle, each student is given the opportunity to develop niche expertise in an area that is needed by other group members in order for the group to complete their task. Students therefore become equals despite their differences and they are motivated to communicate and cooperate with one another to be successful on their assignment.

In addition to reinforcing intergroup behavior that is cooperative, between equals, intimate, and supported, organizations should also make sure that the diversity in their work teams and groups do not create strong **group faultlines**.

According to Lau and Murninghan (1998) group faultlines reflect the extent to which member attributes align themselves in ways that subdivide a group. The strength of these faultlines then is dependent upon the number of attributes that align themselves. Therefore, when in a work group all of the engineers are White, male, and fifty-something and all of the support staff are women and in their twenties, we see a faultline produced by function, age, and gender that could subdivide the group into conflicting factions when faced with a task that is faultline related. One such example could be a review of the organization's new maternity leave policy. Faultlines are only dangerous and promoting of conflict when the larger group is faced with a task that is related to some dimension of the faultline. Faultlines are created early in a work group's history given that newcomers typically look for similar members with whom to establish relationships. With time, however, group members can move beyond their surface similarities and differences and grow to appreciate their deeper-level diversity that occurs in regard to perspectives and talent (Harrison, Price, & Bell, 1998).

Faultlines, like conflict, are not always bad. Faultlines can help us recognize ways in which types of individuals are directed into certain career paths and not others. Likewise conflict can help organizations facilitate learning and communication when it is effectively managed (Church, 1995; Thompson & Gooler, 1996). Conflict in and of itself should not be defined as destructive because these interactions may provide an opportunity for more constructive relationships in the future (Proudford & Smith, 2003).

CONCLUSION

McDaniel and Walls (1997) offer an interesting perspective related to diversity and conflict. Rather than focus on conflicting relationships as bad, these authors offer the benefits of weak relationships (produced by diversity) in organizations. They refer to the "strength in weak ties" among diverse individuals.

> Specifically, weak ties can lead to more effective bridges between subgroups, richer sets of interactions within and outside of the organization, better diffusion of information throughout the system, and a higher probability that the organization will discover critical information. . . . People with weak ties may be more willing to share innovative ideas, to be early adopters of new ideas and to be less subject to social pressure to conform than those with strong ties. (p. 368)

It would appear then that the weak ties produced by diversity may help organizational members be more authentic and more willing to step outside of organizational norms and boxes in ways that benefit creativity and risk taking.

Likewise Powell (1998) suggests that perhaps too much value is placed upon cohesion within organizations. Cohesion in regard to core values may indeed help to create strong cultures needed to move organizations forward. But over time, organizations need to have more flexibility to keep up with rapidly changing environments. This flexibility can in fact come from diverse workforces whose unique backgrounds and perspectives are valued rather than si-

Diversity in Practice 7.3	**Resolving Diversity Conflict**

A number of diversity consulting groups specialize in diversity conflict. Wealth in Diversity Consulting Group (www.wealthindiversity.com) is one such firm. According to their Web site this firm sees "conflict as an opportunity for personal and professional growth, inspiration, learning and transformation through facing both the positive and negative aspects of conflict . . . conflict ignored and unresolved will lead to stress, pain, personal and professional loss and in some instances irretrievable damage to individuals and teams." This firm provides consultation, education, and training to organizations who want to develop their conflict resolutions skills. They offer several workshops including the following:

- Whose Problem Is It Anyway? Valuing and Managing Differences
- What to Do When Customers and Employees Collide
- Discovering Sources of Team Conflict: An Ounce of Prevention, and
- Managing Workplace Negativity: Creating a Positive Environment

lenced. A core value of the organization must ultimately include an appreciation of diversity as an opportunity for greater learning and effectiveness.

Elmes and Connelley (1997) suggest that understanding those issues that are at the foundation of diversity conflict has a variety of implications for change agents and managers who want to create a supportive climate for diversity. Change agents need to understand the influence that intergroup relations have on organizational processes. Subordinate and majority group members may not share the same perspectives or interpretations of the majority in the organization. In fact, faced with differences in opinions and perspectives, majority group members may behave in ways to reinforce and sustain their own group privilege (Proudford & Smith, 2003). Managers must be willing to encourage (rather than discourage) minority group members to be true to their own backgrounds and heritages. It is their uniqueness that provides organizational assets (McDaniel & Walls, 1997).

Organizations must be willing to complicate (rather than simplify) themselves in order to match the level of complication that exists in their environments (McDaniel & Walls, 1997). Diversity can be a source of complication when organizations are willing to hear and listen to the different perspectives and interpretations that a diverse workforce can offer (McDaniel & Walls, 1997). Leaders have to foster an environment in which differences are appreciated and rewarded, and find a balance of promoting productive conflict that reflects differences in perspectives regarding work and not debates over individual differences (Chrobot-Mason & Ruderman, 2004). Minority group members therefore need to be involved in decision making at every level of the organization. Again, effective training can provide a diverse workforce with the tools needed to interact in rich and meaningful ways (despite their weak ties), in order to reap the decision-making benefits that can be offered through diversity (McDaniel & Walls, 1997).

Leaders must also understand their own social identities and group memberships in order to understand how their identities influence what they see and how they respond to diversity issues (Elmes & Connelley, 1997). While leaders need to construct structural opportunities (e.g., take affirmative action) for diversity and dismantle barriers such as the glass ceiling, leaders must also be willing to engage in the difficult work of uncovering and resolving the emotional issues (e.g., second-order conflict) tied to differences in group membership and those legacies related to identity and work (Church, 1995; Elmes & Connelley, 1997).

Discussion Items

1. Review Case 7.1 What types of conflict are presented? How would you work to resolve the conflicts presented?
2. As mentioned, privilege can be a difficult concept to grasp. In what ways are you afforded or denied privilege due to your identity? What organizational practices afford one unearned privileges in your organization?
3. Affirmative action is often a source of second-order conflict in organizations. What other triggers exist for this type of conflict? How is this conflict manifested?

 InfoTrac College Edition

Be sure to log on to InfoTrac College Edition and search for additional readings on topics of interest to you.

Stressors in a Diverse Workplace[1]

CHAPTER 8

Stress is inevitable. It is all around us and comes in many different forms. The sources of stress we encounter are extensive and range widely for different individuals. The workplace can present many opportunities to encounter and experience stress. Today's organizations and employees encounter new sources of stress from toxins in the environment, the rate of technological change, threat of downsizing and the economy, as well as the growing escalation of violence at work (DeFrank & Ivancevich, 1998). DeFrank and Ivancevich also suggest that diversity itself may be a source of stress for all workers: "The stress in a setting with a diverse workforce may result from differences in beliefs and values; a lack of clarity in regard to decision-mking, especially surrounding issues such as performance appraisal and promotion; differences in opportunities for advancement, reward and recognition; and conflict among the various role expectations that exist within an employee population that varies in ethnicity, gender, age, and many other factors. In addition, perceptions by minority employees of either discrimination or a lack of fit between themselves and the organizations have been found to be related to both stress and job satisfaction" (p. 56). It seems likely that there may be different sources of stress for different individuals and groups of people in the workplace, particularly within a diverse organization (Marsella, 1994).

The stress and diversity literatures are slowly becoming integrated and providing a better understanding of stress for a diverse workforce.

---

[1]Kimberly L. Williams served as coauthor on this chapter.

Many workers experience stress on the job.

Given the growing diversity of the population and of the workforce, it will be necessary for organizations to understand groups traditionally underrepresented and ignored in academic research. Also, understanding the sources of stress as well as the impact that stress has on minority workers and women is important if we want to prevent job stress for all workers (Keita & Hurrell, 1994).

This chapter focuses on stressors for women and minorities. Based upon the literature available on the stress-related experiences of these groups we will also inquire about stressors for sexual minorities in organizations. In addition, we will define and characterize general stress, job stress, and stress-related concepts and review the traditional or "common" sources of stress at work. Next, we'll review the potential unique sources of job stress for a diverse workforce.

WHAT IS STRESS?

Stress is defined differently by all types of experts. Ivancevich and Matteson (1980) define **stress** as an adaptive response, mediated by individual characteristics and/or psychological processes, which is a consequence of any external action, situation, or event that places special physical and/or psychological demands upon a person. Sagrestano (2004) encourages us to think about stress as the outcome when the demands of a particular situation (such as work) exceed the resources that we may have available to cope with the situation. Stress also results when there is a substantial difference between the rewards from meeting the demands of a situation and the costs of succumbing to them (Nelson & Quick, 1985).

Stress is a fact of life and can affect all aspects of our daily existence. Stress can have a negative impact on one's mental, as well as physiological, function-

Diversity Case 8.1	**Trina's Tension**

Trina was proud to be working for one of the most prestigious consulting firms in the world. She had visions that this "dream job" was going to help her make a name for herself. Trina appeared to have it all including a great high-paying career that afforded her the ability to rent a loft in Manhattan. Trina graduated Magna Cum Laude, went on to receive her Ph.D., and was consistently recognized for her research. However, this was Trina's second year at the firm and she still didn't feel the connection that she desired. Others who had been hired at the same time she was were being coached by their mentors. Trina desperately wanted a mentor, but no one seemed to take interest in developing her career. She thought if she had a mentor she would have a better chance of getting a promotion in the coming year (the colleagues in her cohort had already received their promotions this year). Although Trina tried to cultivate relationships with the senior leaders in the firm, she was never appointed to "high-profile" projects, which are almost always guaranteed to advance one's career. Instead, she was always pitched for projects with a minority project sponsor, which made Trina feel like she had been included on the projects so that she could "relate" to the client, never because of her skill set.

Trina spent many sleepless nights thinking about how she could change her situation. She continuously tried to dispel the idea that this was all due to her race. Being one of two African American women in the firm, it was hard to think differently, especially since she repeatedly received satisfactory performance reviews. She increasingly became unproductive at work due to her insomnia coupled with her frequent tension headaches and the inability to concentrate. After weeks of experiencing headaches, Trina decided to go to the doctor. Five visits later and a dozen or more tests, Trina's doctor diagnosed her with high blood pressure and depression. Her doctor informed her that it was necessary for her to change her lifestyle because her elevated blood pressure could in fact lead to a stroke, even at the age of 29. Trina was puzzled because blood pressure problems did not run in her family; she was extremely health conscious and avoided many salty foods. She realized that the job was taking its toll on her heath. She had become very stressed about her lack of career development/progression, not having a mentor, not being positioned to use her skills. In addition to her physical health, she was suffering emotionally. She felt pressure to attend after-work functions with her coworkers even though they did not seem to have a real interest in her likes and dislikes. One of her colleagues made a comment that all of the lawsuits against colleges regarding reverse discrimination of affirmative action were absolutely justified and that most African Americans have been lucky to get this far with affirmative action.

ing. An important issue here is the way that employees handle stress. For some individuals, stress motivates and challenges them to excel; this is **eustress.** For others, however, excessive stress diminishes the capacity to function and can have severe medical ramifications; this is **distress.** Even though stress is inevitable, the negative and dangerous consequences associated with it are not.

Diversity in Practice 8.1	The Stress Epidemic

A study conducted by Northwestern National Life Insurance Company (1991) (cited by the National Institute of Safety and Health, 1999; www.cdc.gov/niosh/stresswk .html), demonstrated that job stress is increasing to epidemic proportions. The findings of the survey include the following:

- Seven of every ten workers said that job stress caused frequent health problems.
- Fifty-three percent of workers reported that they were required to work more than 40 hours a week either "very often" or "somewhat often."
- More workers reported high levels of job stress. Forty-six percent of workers said that their jobs are highly stressful. An earlier study in 1985 reported that only 20% of workers experienced a high level of job stress.
- One-third of workers seriously considered quitting their jobs during the previous year and 14% changed jobs in the previous 2 years due to job stress.
- Almost half of the workers reported that their jobs were "very" or "extremely stressful," and over one-fourth perceived their jobs as the single greatest cause of stress in their lives.

Therefore, it is necessary to examine potential sources of stress, especially in the workforce, in order to prevent unnecessary and unhealthy outcomes for the individual, as well as the organization.

THE IMPORTANCE OF UNDERSTANDING JOB STRESS

It is imperative that our workforce be physically and mentally healthy. Yet, according to the National Institute of Occupational Safety and Health (NIOSH), job stress frequently results in significant psychological, physical, and financial costs to both organizations and the workers they employ (NIOSH, 1999). **Job stress** originates in the organization and is related to aspects of the job, the work environment, the relationships at work, or any number of variables that are associated with one's occupation. Job stress can have very negative implications for both work and nonwork environments.

Stress in the workplace can be a serious threat to the overall well-being of an individual and to an organization. The individual consequences of job stress may be categorized as physical, psychological, or behavioral and can include coronary heart disease, neuroses, ulcers, cancer, asthma, hypertension, depression, backaches, anxiety, and drug and alcohol abuse (Beehr & Newman, 1978; House, 1974; Schuler, 1980). Sagrestano (2004) identifies other physiological effects of stress as including elevated lipid levels, elevated blood pressure, and increased hormonal activity. Stress produces the physiological, psychological, and behavioral changes that predispose workers to illness and lower immunity and it can promote risky behaviors such as excessive drinking of alcohol, smoking, and use of illegal drugs that further threaten safety, health, and well-being (Sagrestano, 2004).

Typical psychological consequences of stress include anxiety and depression. Common behavioral effects of stress are violence in the workplace, eating disorders, family problems, and accidents (Quick & Quick, 1984). Negative cognitive effects of stress impair performance within and outside of the workplace. These detriments include deteriorating or decreasing concentration and attention span, short- and long-term memory deficits, and impaired organizational and long-term planning. Distractibility and error rates greatly increase as well (Fontana, 1989).

Job stress results in many other productivity barriers within the organization. Problems such as dissatisfaction, withdrawal, high turnover, absenteeism, and low productivity at an estimated annual cost of $10 to $20 billion often result from job stress (Schuler, 1980). Many companies have reported drastically increased medical claims due primarily to stress-related medical and psychological conditions (Bassman & London, 1993).

Stress and Individual Differences

Although stress affects people individually, there are a variety of demands that serve as stressors for groups of individuals. What one may perceive as a stressor, another may perceive as a stimulating factor of the job. For example, the job stress literature (Keita & Hurrell, 1994; Jick & Mitz, 1985), supports the argument that identified stressors for women on the job may vary from the reported stressors for men. Other evidence suggests that the identified job stressors for African Americans and White Americans may be different (Guiterres, Saenz, & Green, 1994; K. James, 1994). Various cultural groups may not only perceive and define stressors differently but may also handle stress differently than the mainstream or dominant culture. An actual or perceived cultural difference, for example, may affect the health of minority workers in majority-dominated organizations because of the stress of having to assimilate into the majority culture (DeFrank & Ivancevich, 1998; K. James, 1994; Keita & Hurrell, 1994).

IMPLICATIONS OF JOB STRESS

The relationship between workplace stress and detrimental consequences has recently been recognized as highly complex. Not all stressors have the same impact on all individuals. Characteristics of the job, the degree of perceived control, the presence or absence of other roles, and the amount of social support available all appear to be important in determining how well individuals cope with job-related stressors (Sagrestano, 2004).

Research supports the argument that certain sources of work stress adversely affect both women's and men's health (Nelson & Hitt, 1992). Developing programs and effective policies to decrease stress levels requires an understanding of the sources of stress that working women and minorities experience. A review of research on the consequences of stress has found that women tend to report higher levels of psychological distress and minor illnesses than men, whereas men are more prone to severe physical illnesses (Jick & Mitz, 1985). Yet, as women move into more male-dominated occupations, they have begun to suffer the same stress-induced maladies as men, including ulcers and gastrointestinal illnesses (Winter, 1984). Research has shown that different racial groups are affected by stress differently (Keita & Hurrell, 1994). Keita and Hurrell suggested that African American women have a greater chance of sustaining work-related illnesses, and African American women and men have a higher percentage of dying from their work-related illnesses.

TRADITIONAL SOURCES OF JOB STRESS

Research supports the claim that stress in the workplace is a serious problem (Keita & Hurrell, 1994; Schuler, 1980). Much of the organizational research in this area has focused upon identifying and understanding the sources of stress at work. Generally, five types of demands have been identified as sources of stress in the workplace that are likely to affect any one employee in the workforce (Quick & Quick, 1984): **Task demands, physical demands, role demands, interpersonal demands,** and **career development.**

Task Demands

A person's job is typically defined by the specific tasks and activities that they are assigned. Economic, technological, and business factors such as downsizing, the skills shortage, and low employment have forced American workers to work 150% or more just to keep up with the work (Laabs, 1999). Jobs that demand too much of the employee in terms of the demonstration of skills or the utilization of knowledge and experience can lead to stress for an employee (Quick & Quick, 1984). Situations that underutilize employees' skills and abilities, such as repetitive work, can be very stressful and lead to boredom, shifts in attention, and associated physiological problems (Quick & Quick, 1984).

Employees may experience stress when they are given too few tasks (**quantitative work underload**) or too many (**quantitative work overload**) to complete in a given period of time. Stress also results when one feels unable to complete a given task (**qualitative overload**); this is different from **qualitative underload,** which results when individuals engage in tasks that do not utilize their skills or potential (Ivancevich & Matteson, 1980; Hurrell, Murphy, Sauter, & Cooper, 1988). Another work overload factor, overtime, has been connected with stress and ill health (Smith, 1985).

| Diversity in Practice 8.2 | **Language, Diversity, and Well-Being** |

In June 2003 the U.S. Labor Department initiated a nationwide effort to protect Latino workers and their safety. The program, "Justice and Equality in the Workplace," provides Latino workers with training to avoid on-the-job injuries. The at-work fatality rate has dropped for all ethnic groups except Latinos; their workplace death rate rose from 1992 to 2001 by 53% (Zeilberger, 2002).

There are many reasons why Latino workers suffer more workplace injuries and deaths. Immigrant Latinos are likely to take more high-risk jobs according to Daniel Morales, spokesperson for the Department of Labor (Brown, 2003). Immigrant workers and other Latinos may not be offered safety training due to language barriers between supervisors and workers. For example, a 25-year-old day laborer in Florida died from suffocation when a 9-foot-deep trench collapsed on top of him. The hiring contractor who hired him had simply picked him up from a street corner and provided no instructions on safety procedures for the job site (Zeilberger, 2002).

Some organizations are being proactive in finding ways to enhance worker safety regardless of language. The Dallas–Forth Worth International Airport provided a 40-hour safety training program to its 4,200 employees (at a cost of $900.00 per person) working on the airport's expansion (Zeilberger, 2002). Half of those workers received training in Spanish. Although the training is costly, accident rates have decreased. Furthermore, the airport saves money related to potential future costs due to hospitalization, potential lawsuits, and the recruitment and selection of replacement workers.

In addition to safety training, bilingual supervisors help to produce safe workplaces. The Occupational Safety and Health Administration (OSHA) has begun specialized outreach services to multilingual community coalitions in order to understand the hazards in the workplace. These efforts extend beyond the Spanish-speaking population. For example, the Chicago OSHA office is engaged in an effort that includes Polish-speaking workers. The OSHA offices in the western United States provides assistance in Spanish and Korean (Zeilberger, 2002).

Physical Demands

Stressors associated with the physical conditions of work elicit fairly consistent stress responses. Physical demands include noise, vibration, temperature variation, humidity levels and ventilation, lighting and illumination levels, hygiene factors, and climate. Ivancevich and Matteson (1980) suggest that excessive noise (approximately 80 decibels and above) on a recurring, prolonged basis can induce stress. Related research identified unpleasant working conditions due to noise as a significant predictor of job dissatisfaction (Hurrell et al., 1988).

A clean and orderly work environment influences worker satisfaction as well. Office designs should facilitate effective social interaction.

Role Demands

Within an organization certain behaviors and demands are associated with the role that the individual fulfills. **Roles** are typically defined in terms of the expectations of an individual or groups of individuals (Quick & Quick, 1984). Two types of roles identified as major stressors for workers include role conflict and role ambiguity (Sagrestano, 2004). **Role conflict** occurs when following one set of procedures makes it difficult, unacceptable, or impossible to comply with another set of procedures (Ivancevich & Matteson, 1980; Sagrestano). **Role ambiguity** results when employees are not given adequate information or clarification concerning their role, job objectives, and the scope of the responsibilities of the job (Ivancevich & Matteson; Sagrestano).

The primary source of job stress under role demands emerges from a lack of person–job environment fit resulting in role conflict, role ambiguity, role overload, underutilization of valued skills, and resource inadequacy (Gupta & Beehr, 1979; Abdel-Halim, 1981). Some research suggests that role conflict and role overload present particular difficulties for working women because of their traditional roles as mother, homemaker, wife, and professional (Bhaget, 1983; Quick & Quick, 1984). Others researchers (e.g., Barnett & Hyde, 2001; Sagrestano, 2004) suggest that women with more roles may have higher self-esteem and take better care of themselves. Apparently, the characteristics of these roles are more important than the actual number of roles that a woman occupies. The relationship between the number of roles occupied by women and its effect on their health may be mediated by the degree to which they receive support from their supervisors and families (Barnett & Hyde, 2001; Sagrestano, 2004).

In fact Hewlett's (2002) research on executive women appears to suggest that when these women are supported (both at home and by their employers), there are significant payoffs for these women as well as for their organizations. When women have partners who do their share of housework and childrearing, and also have organizations embracing diversity by implementing work-life policies, there are clear benefits.

> Companies offering a rich array of work-life policies are much more likely to hang on to their professional women than companies that don't. High achieving mothers who have been able to stay in their careers tend to work for companies that allow them access to generous benefits: flextime, telecommuting, paid parenting leave, and compressed workweeks. In contrast, high-achieving mothers who have been forced out of their careers tended to work for companies with inadequate work-life benefits. (Hewlett, 2002, p. 27)

Barnett and Hyde (2001) took an expansionist perspective of women's competing roles and concluded that multiple roles may actually benefit both men and women by leading to enhanced mental, physical, and relationship health. This seems especially true for individuals who are equally committed to their multiple roles. Furthermore, these authors cite research that suggests that roles in one domain (such as work) may provide a buffer to the effects of stress that one experiences in another domain, such as one's home life (Barnett &

Diversity in Practice 8.3	**Reducing Executive Women's Stress**

Nelson and Burke (2000) outline a number of ways in which both organizations and individual women can take steps in preventing and coping with the stress experienced by female executives. The following table outlines strategies for prevention and coping.

	Individual	Organizational
Prevention	• Use exercise facilities • Network • Employ mind–body techniques such as yoga or meditation • Take advantage of employee assistance programs if available	• Support alternative work arrangements • Provide assistance with childcare and eldercare arrangements • Establish "zero-tolerance" for harassment • Develop and reward systems that promote equity • Develop social support and networking programs
Coping (enhancing health)	• Identify stressors and work toward eliminating them • Take advantage of developmental opportunities that provide a sense of challenge and growth • Adopt the perspective that work-life conflict is inevitable and then deal with it • Develop a network of qualified professionals that you can rely upon	• Provide exercise facilities • Encourage networking and opportunities for social support • Provide counseling support through employee assistance programs

Hyde). For many women, having the role of employee may help to buffer them from stressors that stem from economic hardships as well (Barnett & Hyde).

African Americans also tend to experience more chronic role stress than their White counterparts (Matteson & Ivancevich, 1987). This may result from working in environments in which they are a "solo," or one of a few members of their ethnic group. These workers must meet the exaggerated expectations (both high and low) of the majority (Pettigrew & Martin, 1987) and deal with the fact that expressions of their cultural identity may not be welcome in the work environment. As such, they must take on the roles imposed on them by the majority in the organization (Cox, 1994; Pettigrew & Martin), as well as fulfill their own work-related role, which may cause a considerable amount of stress.

Female managers also report stress from having stereotyped roles imposed on them (Davidson & Cooper, 1983; Nelson & Quick, 1985; McDonald & Korabik, 1991). They experience role conflict from occupying an executive role that some may perceive as being more appropriate for men than for women (Davidson & Cooper).

Interpersonal Demands

Interpersonal stressors at work arise from demands experienced during the course of normal social, personal, and working relationships in the organization. Within an increasingly diverse work context, the diversity itself may be a source of stress if workers lack the experience, competence, and skills to relate and communicate with one another across various dimensions of diversity such as race, gender, and sexuality. For example, DeFrank and Ivancevich (1998) suggest that when organizations fail to provide employees with opportunities to develop the ability to work in a multicultural environment, negative interpersonal consequences may occur. "If diversity is not managed effectively it may lead to interpersonal stress, competition among different groups for attention and resources, and decreased interaction because of the perceived need for political correctness in speech, interaction, and recognition" (DeFrank & Ivancevich, 1998, p. 56).

Career Development

Efforts to engage in developing one's career can be stressors. Even individuals' own personal assessment of their career progress can evoke stress (Ivancevich & Matteson, 1980). Career choices can serve as stressors when they constantly cause concern, anxiety, or frustration for the individual. The employee often feels a lack of job security and concern over real or imagined obsolescence. Fear that promotion is out of reach and general feelings of dissatisfaction with the match between career aspirations and the current level of attainment has been linked to job stress and illness (Sagrestano, 2004).

Career development may be stressful for women and minorities because they may feel threatened by their coworkers in the majority groups (Glowinski & Cooper, 1987) and they often lack the social support available to majority group peers (K. James, 1994). Women and minorities often feel as though they must work twice as hard to prove that they are equally capable of succeeding (Ivancevich & Matteson, 1980). Although mentoring is often a beneficial career development tool, it too can be a stressor.

Recall from chapter 5 that **mentoring** is defined as a relationship between a less experienced employee (protégé) and a more experienced employee (mentor) and is believed to provide numerous career benefits (Cox, 1994). The mentor's role is to provide direction, support, and advice to aid in the success of the protégé (Kram, 1985). *Mentoring* in this chapter refers to power-based career and psychosocial support (Cox; Kelly & Streeter, 1992). Mentors may help reduce career-related stress by providing protégés with advice and networking opportunities, as well as information and resources that may not be obtained otherwise. Kanter (1977) noted that protégés are affected by the power of their mentor, in that the same power is also assumed to be possessed by them.

However, we also reviewed evidence in chapter 5 that women and ethnic minorities sometimes lack access to mentors. Ragins and Cotton's (1991) research, for example, demonstrates that women report greater barriers to mentoring than do men. Furthermore, research by Lyness and Thompson (2000) into the barriers and facilitators of career advancement for managers working in a multinational financial services corporation revealed that mentoring facilitated men's careers but did not provide the same level of facilitation for women. In fact, more successful women were less likely to report that mentoring facilitated their advancement than were less successful women. In addition, their results indicate that other common career issues were likely stressors for these executive women. Women in their sample, as compared to the men, were more likely to report that they perceived a lack of culture fit, they felt excluded from important informal networks, and they experienced difficulty in getting developmental assignments (Lyness & Thompson, 2000). These authors suggest that in comparison to men, women must overcome social isolation, stereotyping, and performance pressures as well as the reluctance of organizational leaders to take risks on them (Lyness & Thompson).

Summary of Traditional Sources of Stress

The five types of sources of stress discussed in this chapter are important when assessing the different sources of stress for women and men of different racial groups. Early investigations of work stress failed to examine the possibility of gender differences. The job stress literature has also failed to address ways that different racial groups experience stress. However, this chapter takes a deeper look into the potential existence of additional and unique stressors for a diverse workforce. In addition to the five sources of stress examined, other sources of stress exist in a diverse workplace. These stressors reflect societal barriers such as discrimination and stereotyping, but these additional sources of stress for a diverse workforce also reflect coping strategies and issues that one must face as a minority group member at work.

SOURCES OF STRESS FOR DIVERSE POPULATIONS

Much of the literature suggests that women and minorities do not encounter any differences in sources of stress, such as time pressures and work overload, than do nonminorities or men. However, the diversity literature suggests that they may face several unique stressors such as discrimination as a result of sexism, racism, and tokenism in the workplace (Kanter, 1977; Pettigrew & Martin, 1987).

Prejudice, Discrimination, and Harassment

Racial group differences have a complex and constantly changing impact on relationships in the workplace. Minority groups represent subcultures, which often have norms and values that are not always understood by the majority group (Bowman, 1991; Quick & Quick, 1984). These cultural differences often cause minorities to be more distinctive within an organization and expose them to discrimination based on their noticeable differences from the majority (Gutierres et al., 1994).

With regard to organizational stress, a substantial majority of researchers and therapists believe that minorities are disproportionately affected by prejudice and discrimination (K. James; Clark, Anderson, Clark, & Williams, 1999). Blatant racial prejudice is the most obvious source of stress for ethnic individuals. The impact of racist attitudes and behavior at work can magnify some minority workers' feelings of inferiority, inadequacy, or low self-esteem (Quick & Quick, 1984). This may be especially true when a minority is hired into a supervisory or management-level job in a predominantly White organization with no previous examples of successful minorities in those positions (Quick & Quick).

Similarly women who are underrepresented within their work context are more likely to face sexual harassment. Sexual harassment and discrimination also is a significant stressor for women (Fitzgerald, Hulin, & Drasgow, 1994). Experience and the threat of harassment result in lowered levels of satisfaction, self-reported decrements in job performance, job interruption, and even job loss (Fitzgerald et al.).

Employees of minority status may also suffer from a lack of support from the formal organization and a lack of role models, which creates stressful situations that intensify responses to other stressors (K. James, 1994). This can lead to role conflict and role ambiguity (Hurrell et al., 1988). Constant exposure to stressors resulting from unfair employment practices, discrimination, and harassment erodes minority employees' coping skills and places them at greater risk for psychological and physical illness (Marsella, 1994).

Secondary victimization is another stressor for those that encounter discrimination or harassment in the workplace. Secondary victimization occurs when stigmatized groups such as gay or lesbian workers feel that they cannot seek justice for the discrimination or unfairness they face in the workplace due to the reactions of those in charge (Murphy, 2001). For example, if a gay or lesbian worker has come to supervisors in the past with claims of discrimination and those supervisors do not take the worker seriously, ignore the person's complaint, or attempt to minimize the complaint by claiming the worker is being "too sensitive," these supervisor reactions "silence" the worker and provide the person little or no opportunity to find justice. No wonder so many workers experience harassment and discrimination in silence in order to avoid a second layer of injustice they may encounter from their managers or supervisors.

Solo or Token Role

Organizations are often unwilling to create an equal balance in their work environment. This disproportionate environment leads to unfavorable consequences for the individuals of the underrepresented group (Cox, 1994). A **solo** is defined as an individual who is the only one or one of a few that is representative of a particular group. Solos are expected to be representative of their entire group. Research demonstrates that solo status causes uneven scrutiny, extreme evaluations, and highly stereotyped impressions of the minority by the majority members (Kanter, 1977; Pettigrew & Martin, 1987; Sagrestano, 2004). Solos are unlikely to feel as though they have social support in their workplace (K. James, 1994).

Minority members are frequently viewed as **tokens;** that is, majority group members may attribute the selection of minority group members solely to affirmative action (Gutierres et al., 1994; Pettigrew & Martin, 1987). Tokens experience three sources of stress: **performance pressure, boundary heightening,** and **role entrapment,** that may lead to adverse mental health outcomes (Sagrestano, 2004). Tokens experience performance pressure due to the amount of visibility they may face in their workgroup or department due to their solo status. This heightened visibility increases attention to their performance. Tokens then experience pressure to perform well, to know their job well with minimal or no help or guidance, and to avoid making mistakes. This is an impossible situation, especially given that employees that are categorized as tokens are also assumed to be incompetent (due to **affirmative action stigma**). Tokens are then placed in double jeopardy; they are subject to the same pressures, stereotypes, and prejudices as those with solo status but also have the additional stigma of being categorized as incompetent.

Boundary heightening is similar to the **outgroup homogeneity effect.** That is, majority group members may exaggerate the similarities among their in-group members as well as the differences between the token and themselves. Exaggerating these differences can lead to improper jokes and other inappropriate comments that reinforce a sense of social isolation for the token employee (Sagrestano, 2004). **Role entrapment** simply involves an inability to see the token employee beyond a stereotype. Majority group members who buy into a stereotype of the token have less of an opportunity to get to know the token employee as an individual.

Social Isolation

Women and ethnic minorities suffer from social isolation when they are underrepresented in their workplace; especially when these workers occupy positions of power (Kanter, 1977; Nelson & Quick, 1985). These stressors have been associated with a lack in organizational commitment, low job satisfaction, and high likelihood of job turnover among managerial women (Rosin & Korabik, 1991). Other stressful effects related to the social isolation of female managers include role ambiguity, the lack of same-gender role models and the unavailability of mentors, exclusion from "old boy" networks, and the unwillingness of men to share job-related information with women (Cahoon & Rowney, 1984; McDonald & Korabik, 1991; Nelson & Quick, 1985; Nelson et al., 1989).

Gay and lesbian workers are also highly vulnerable to social isolation. Several national polls of worker attitudes demonstrate that heterosexual workers remain uncomfortable with the possibility of working closely with a homosexual employee (Day & Schoenrade, 2000). For example, a study by the National Defense Research Institute demonstrated that 27% of respondents would prefer not to work with someone who is gay and another 25% indicated that they would strongly object to this work arrangement (Day & Schoenrade). Heterosexual employees are often silent when gay employees and their allies seek inclusion and justice within organizations, further strengthening the isolation that gay workers experience (Fletcher & Kaplan, 2000). Organizations also seem to be hesitant to share power with sexual minorities. A *Wall Street Journal* survey of chief executive officers (CEOs) indicated that 66% of respondents would be reluctant to include a homosexual on a management committee (Day & Schoenrade, 2000).

These studies have important implications for understanding the workplace pressures that gay and lesbian workers experience related to managing their identity at work. These studies seem to suggest that heterosexuals would prefer to assume that all of their coworkers are heterosexual (**heterosexist privilege**). Furthermore, employers who reinforce this privilege by locking openly gay workers out of positions of power reinforce their privilege and strengthen the solo status and social isolation that other gay employees likely experience.

Stereotypes

Stereotyping is a perceptual and cognitive process in which people assign certain traits to an individual because of that individual's membership to a particular group (Cox, 1994). Widespread stereotyping behaviors in organizations adversely affect the career development of both women and minorities. Not only do stereotypes hinder members of certain groups from being hired, they also result in extensive problems and assumptions once they are on the job. Stereotypes may result in role status incongruence, role conflict, obstructed career mobility, biased evaluation, poor feedback opportunities, distribution of power and choices of jobs against women and minorities (Cox, 1994).

McDonald and Korabik (1991) noted that women tend to report problems in the area of managing subordinates. This may be the result of very real difficulties that women encounter with the authority aspects of leadership (Butler & Geis, 1990). Researchers have suggested, for example, that women find it more difficult to be assertive in employment situations because such behavior is inconsistent with societal stereotypes about appropriate behavior for women (Davidson & Cooper, 1983; Nieva & Gutek, 1981).

Affirmative Action Stigma

Despite the good intentions of its advocates, affirmative action may compound work stress for minorities because many workers who are members of more dominant groups feel that as a result of legislation, Black Americans get preferential treatment in securing employment (DeCarlo & Gruenfield, 1989). This stigma attached to affirmative action has severe ramifications for racial minorities and women and greatly hinders performance on the job.

Heilman and Block (1992) found that minorities and women who are in nontraditional roles are perceived by their organization as being in that particular role as a result of affirmative action. Subsequently, they are also perceived as being incompetent by their coworkers. Evidence supports the fact that minorities and women who experience this form of affirmative action stigma internalize those negative perceptions of incompetence. Also, women or minorities in this position who are not given specific information as to the reasons they were hired, perceived themselves as being beneficiaries of this policy. Minorities and women in the stigmatized position then may begin to act in ways that reinforce others' misconceptions and low expectations of them (Cox, 1994). These **self-fulfilling prophecies** lead to the avoidance of challenging tasks and other assignments in which women and minorities have increased interactions or visibility among their coworkers (Heilman & Block). Unfortunately, these same tasks are crucial to career advancement. Some critics of affirmative action argue that, although organizations invest a great deal in recruiting and locating minorities, they fail to recognize the ongoing professional development and training needs of these workers (Quick & Quick, 1984). The stigma attached to affirmative action and the lack of continuous support by the organization tend to limit the career development and advancement of minorities and women.

John Henryism

S. James (1994) coined the term *John Henryism* to refer to many African Americans' propensity to actively cope with the discrimination, prejudice, and stereotypes they often face. This active form of coping drives many Blacks to outperform their counterparts with the hope that they will subsequently be perceived as "just as good as" and "equal" to their nonminority peers and counterparts. In the African American folktale John Henry is a "steel-drivin' man" who competes against a steel drill to see who can lay railroad tracks faster. John Henry wins the race but dies seconds later of exhaustion. James's research has also demonstrated that Black Americans who score highest in measures of high-effort coping, like John Henry, have physiological profiles that suggest that they are at risk for stress-related diseases such as hypertension.

Bicultural Stress

As mentioned in chapter 6, many African American women are bicultural boundary spanners. That is, their life is composed of a series of transitions between their predominantly White professional life and the Black social system that they depend upon to succeed in their professional life. In Bell and Nkomo's (2001) *Our Separate Worlds: Black and White Women and the Struggle for Professional Identity,* one respondent talks about the separate lives she leads:

> . . . two separate drawers, two separate faces, and two separate uniforms. I get up Monday through Friday and I think about acting, behaving, and interacting with one group of people where I am more formal and maintain an emotional distance. Then on Friday evenings, I close the door to my office. The weekend is back to me, back to family, back to being in safe territory. It's not that I don't do things with white folks from time to time, but my worlds are not very integrated, they are separate and distinct. . . . It's just two closets: they both work and I know what to expect in both of them. (p. 231)

Another of Bell and Nkomo's (2001) respondents talk about the transition between Black and White worlds as similar to being a guest:

> The white world, as best I can describe it, is me being a guest in someone else's home. . . . When I am around white people . . . I am much more aware and alert about everything that is going on around me. . . . It takes a lot of energy to be around white folks all day. (pp. 232–233)

Although these women discuss their biculturalism as a career-enhancing strategy, they also discuss stress-inducing issues related to isolation, being on constant alert, and depleting one's energy. Bell (1990) refers to the tension of leading a bicultural life as **bicultural stress.** Bicultural stress is most pronounced when the cultures one is trying to negotiate are very different from one another. Thomas and Gabarro (1999) suggest that bicultural stress mandates that minority professionals strive to develop an integrated sense of self to avoid lacking *any* kind of sense of self. Having an integrated self may also provide one with an opportunity to use experiences gathered across cultures to one's professional benefit.

Intergroup Anxiety

At times anxiety represents a fear of the unknown. Here diversity is often a stressor for dominant group members who lack experience and history with individuals from groups other than their own (Thomas & Chrobot-Mason, in press). Preconceptions of outgroup members also heighten anxiety about interactions with these individuals. Stephan and Stephan (1985) present a model of intergroup anxiety in which they argue that group-based stereotypes, a lack of personal history with outgroups, or a negative history with outgroup members can create anxiety that impairs intergroup interaction.

Refer back to Diversity Learning Point 6.1. You'll recall that Word, Zanna, and Cooper (1974) demonstrated that White interviewers acted with less immediacy (little eye contact, shorter interviews, more verbal slips) when interviewing Black applicants as compared to White applicants. Furthermore, a second study by these authors demonstrated that White applicants who were treated with low immediacy performed less well in an interview scenario as

Diversity Learning Point 8.1	Reducing Workplace Stress	

Individual and Organizational Strategies for Reducing Stress

	Strategy	Description
Individual	Behavioral intervention	Teaches individuals to behave in a different way
	Physiological intervention	Treats the physiological effects of stress through the use of biofeedback and relaxation techniques and exercise
	Cognitive intervention	Helps individuals change their perception about the work environment or stressor
Organizational	Job design and redesign	Changes aspects of the job or work environment that are contributing to the stress of employees
	Organizational structure	Changes the structure of the organization itself in order to reduce burdens on employees
	Team building	Provides employees with the opportunity to improve work group functioning and it can include activities such as role analysis
	Mentoring programs	Provides a vehicle for individuals to discuss their experiences and gain advice from more senior-level professionals

For more information on the reduction of job stress, see NIOSH's (1999) report, *Stresss . . . at Work* or Quick & Quick (1984).

compared to other White applicants who were in a high immediacy condition. These results certainly exemplify the power of self-fulfilling prophecies but they also demonstrate that intergroup anxiety may be a power force in initiating the self-fulfilling cycle.

STRATEGIES FOR INDIVIDUALS AND ORGANIZATIONS FOR STRESS MANAGEMENT

Understanding the various sources of stress will allow organizations to engage in program development to target the specific sources of job stress through managing diversity initiatives or through teaching individuals how to cope with these sources of stress that could minimize their negative effects. This research helps to validate the necessity of proper implementation of diversity programs as well as stress management interventions. There are several ways that both the individual and the organization can help to prevent or alleviate the negative effects of stress. Diversity Learning Point 8.1 identifies several methods for stress management.

Companies have spent millions of dollars annually on stress management. Many have questioned the success of the interventions. The evidence is mixed, although it is still promising. Organizational and job redesign has not typically been measured as it relates to decreases in stress levels, yet it is probably the most effective in terms of sustaining the positive benefits of a stress management intervention. However, stress management interventions must be coupled with a diversity management program. This requires organizations to be committed to creating a climate in which members of all groups can excel. This begins with the hiring process. New hires must possess the values that facilitate this type of environment. The organization must be committed to reinforcing the values of the culture through the reward system and the appraisal system. Other ways organizations can help reduce the stress that minorities experience is by implementing support groups.

CONCLUSION

The potential differences in the vast number of sources of job stress demonstrate that we cannot simply generalize findings from one population to another because various groups of people experience different sources of job stress (K. James, 1994). It is important that the individual differences are considered when examining the sources of stress that are experienced by individuals and groups. It is not simply a person's demographic identity that is a source of stress for individuals, but instead it is the situations in which they find themselves outnumbered and unsupported that create a context for stress.

Other ways to expand this research include examining the differences in the sources of stress with respect to the demographic makeup of the organization. Will women and minorities still experience the same sources of job stress when they are no longer in a minority position in an organization but actually make up the majority? Examining the racial and gender composition of the organization may affect the sources of stress that the different groups experience. For African American women it would appear likely that the more diverse an organization is with respect to race and gender the less they may be affected by the unique sources of stress outlined. The local environment or the profession also needs to be examined more carefully. In addition, professions must take responsibility for adding to the pipeline of minority talent that will someday become practitioners of their profession, and must also provide training and professional development opportunities for all members of the profession so that they learn the skills needed to be effective within a diverse world.

When researching job stress, we must not only consider the experience of workers as it relates to their lack of job opportunities, relationships, and treatment at work, but we must also consider an even larger concern, which is the health implications of stress. It has been found that minorities experience a greater degree of heart disease and high blood pressure as a result of stress (Gutierres et al., 1994; K. James, 1994). An article in the *Atlanta Journal* (July 1996) reported that African Americans experience a higher health risk as a result of racism. Researchers found that heart rates and blood pressure increased after racial confrontations with their White counterparts. This may have serious ramifications for those employees who experience a great deal of prejudice and discrimination in their work environment as well as strained interpersonal relationships in the workplace.

Factors such as prejudice and discrimination, stereotyping, interpersonal relations with coworkers and supervisors, social isolation, pressure to assimilate, lack of mentoring, as well as affirmative action stigma have severe ramifications for the overall diversity climate of an organization. Minorities and women experiencing these additional sources of stress do not have a positive environment conducive to working. According to Cox's (1994) Interactional Model of Diversity, the work environment has direct effects on several organizational outcomes such as innovation, problem solving, work group cohesiveness, and communication. The type of work environment that minorities encounter and whether or not it is stressful may therefore have negative health and career-related consequences for individual workers, but subsequently may also result in negative outcomes for the organizations that employ them (Cox, 1994).

Discussion Items

1. Refer to Diversity Case 8.1. What sources of stress did Trina encounter?
2. What strategies could Trina and her organization pursue to prevent and reduce workplace stress?
3. How does the stress experienced by visible minorities such as women and ethnic minorities differ from the stress experienced by invisible minorities such as sexual minorities? Discuss.
4. Employee assistance programs (EAPs) often provide services to prevent or reduce worker stress. Use the Internet to identify three firms that outsource EAP services. How do these firms help organizations resolve worker stress?

 InfoTrac College Edition

Be sure to log on to InfoTrac College Edition and search for additional readings on topics of interest to you.

9

CHAPTER | # The Leadership–
Diversity
Dynamic

*Breaking Barriers
and Developing
Multicultural Leaders*

Effective leadership is critical to organizational effectiveness (French & Bell, 1999). Unlike **management,** which focuses upon the more mundane organizational work of planning, budgeting, and problem solving, leadership appeals to the more universal needs of people working in organizations. Effective **leaders** motivate, inspire, act as a role model, communicate, and provide vision (French & Bell). Cox (1994) argues that diversity is at the core of every organization and thus should be on the mind of every leader—diversity facilitates achieving the organizational goals of moral, ethical, and social responsibility, fulfilling legal obligations, and maintaining solid economic performance. The challenge for leaders today is to accomplish all of these goals with a workforce that is increasingly more diverse in terms of complexion and gender and more open in regard to sexuality. However, to use diversity as a competitive advantage, organizations and their leaders must work at eliminating the glass ceiling for nontraditional workers so that they themselves can become leaders. It is also necessary for present and future leaders to develop the psychological readiness and competencies for effective leadership of multicultural workplaces.

This chapter focuses on the diversity–leadership dynamic from two different perspectives. The first perspective will look at the barriers to inclusive leadership in organizations. The focus here will be on the glass ceiling. This discussion will focus on defining and understanding what is meant by the term and identifying the causes for the glass ceiling from the perspective of both minorities within organizations and those that lead them. Likewise a discussion of organizational and individual strategies for breaking the glass ceiling will be covered.

148

Effective leadership is critical for diverse workplaces.

The second perspective of the diversity–leadership connection will center on the importance of "multicultural leadership" for the success of diversity initiatives. This discussion will focus on the importance of committed leadership for diversity success and models that are informative in the development of multicultural leadership. Specifically we will cover Thomas's (1998) model of readiness for multicultural leadership and its components, Sue's (1995) and Chrobot-Mason's (in press) multicultural competencies for leadership, and Corson's (2000) engaging model of emancipatory leadership for diverse institutions.

LEADERSHIP AND ITS ROLE IN DIVERSITY EFFORTS

Leadership is key to the success of any diversity initiative (Sue, 1995). Without leadership support many diversity efforts falter. Elsie Cross, the president of the very well regarded diversity management consulting firm Elsie Cross Associates Inc., addressed corporate chief executive officers (CEOs) and senior executives on this very issue. She said, "Unless the corporate CEO and his [sic] senior executives take the diversity initiative seriously by devoting the necessary time, attention, and leadership to the issue, then this issue will go nowhere" (Hinton, 2002).

In order to take diversity initiatives to the next level, "leaders must understand the implications of diversity, ask tough questions in performance reviews, and provide ongoing communication about the priority of the work. They must also explain how managing diversity is connected to other aspects of the business model. They must give guidance on process—how those whom they influence should approach work on diversity" (Cox, 2002, p. 19).

In addition to strong leadership commitment, diversity efforts rely upon the understanding and commitment of workers as well. Without their comprehension of the importance of diversity to organizational survival (and thus the survival of their jobs), diversity efforts become stale rather than empowering and these efforts often face resistance (Winters, 2002). Ben Jenkins, then president and CEO of the now defunct First Union National Bank of Florida concurs, "even though I recognize responsibility, as the leader of my organization for taking charge of the initiative, it's important for me to work with people who are supportive. None of us can take this on alone—we have to have people around us who believe in the subject and are strong proponents" (Cross & Jenkins, 1999, p. 15).

Although there is overwhelming agreement about the value of leadership to organizational functioning and health, there is not much agreement in regard to how leadership is defined. In fact, leadership continues to be a popular area of study given the ambiguity involved in identifying what makes a successful leader. The evolution of the study of leadership is complex and has not followed a clear and predictable path. Krumm (2001) provides a useful history of the leadership research and presents its different phases, which have included identifying key leadership "great man" traits and effective behaviors (e.g., consideration, initiation of structure, democratic, authoritarian) and analyzing the extent to which there is a contingency nature to effective leadership (e.g., Fiedler's contigency theory and leader–member exchange theory) (see Den Hartog & Koopman, 2001, for another recent review of the leadership literature). The goal of this chapter is not to dissect popular leadership models in regard to how they address diversity (in fact, most do not explicitly address how diversity impacts leadership effectiveness). Instead this chapter seeks to identify barriers to leadership for minority group members and contemporary approaches for developing multicultural leaders—leaders who successfully lead diverse workplaces.

Mendez-Russell (2001) suggests that **multicultural leaders** work "to create and maintain a safe, accepting, and respectful workplace with creative, innovative, and productive employees—unencumbered by barriers that impede growth" (p. 16). A primary responsibility of the multicultural leader is to dismantle barriers that impede the career development of any aspiring leader regardless of race, gender, and sexuality. Diversity requires leaders who are sensitive to the influence of culture and history and the needs, expectations, and even the stereotypes of others (Chemers & Murphy, 1995). Effective multicultural leaders understand that glass ceilings are not fictitious and that organizations must be proactive in order to rid themselves of these barriers to leadership diversity.

BARRIERS TO LEADERSHIP FOR A DIVERSE WORKFORCE: THE GLASS CEILING

Despite the growing numbers of diverse individuals in the workplace and increasing numbers of people who are seeking advanced training and education, there remain many barriers to their advancement to highly visible and powerful leadership roles. The **glass ceiling** refers to the invisible barrier within organizations that prevents members of minority groups such as women and people of color from ascending to top levels of management and leadership.

Evidence of the Glass Ceiling

Evidence of the glass ceiling is visible everywhere. The worlds of business and even higher education provide ample evidence that women and people of color face invisible organizational barriers to their upward mobility. The glass ceiling is most readily apparent when examining the numbers of women and African Americans who are CEOs in major organizations. Allow me to provide you with an exhaustive list of the names of women who are CEOs within the *Fortune* 500:

- Carleton S. Fiorina, Hewlett-Packard
- Marce Fuller, Mirant
- Patricia Russon, Lucent
- Anne Mulcahy, Xerox
- Andrea Jung, Avon Products, Inc.
- Marion O. Sandler, Golden West Financial Corporation

If we expand the list to include women who lead companies in the *Fortune* 1000, other female CEOs include:

- Pamela Forbes Lieverman, Truserv
- Cinda Hallman, Spherion
- Dorrit J. Bern, Charming Shoppes
- Pamela Kirby, Quintiles Transnational
- Jody Odom, Software Spectrum.

Are you exhausted yet? That's it. Catalyst, an important think tank that researches issues related to gender and leadership, identifies only 11 female CEOs in the *Fortune* 1000; and only one of those women leads a company within the *Fortune* 50! If we examine the same career path, the road to the CEO office, the picture is even worse for African Americans.

There are currently three Black Americans who lead organizations in the *Fortune* 500. All three are men. A January 2002 issue of *Newsweek* magazine featured these three men on its cover with the title *The New Black Power*. A more accurate title would have been *The New Black Male Power*. In the many discussions of glass ceilings and other workplace injustices that impact women and ethnic minorities, women of color are often forgotten and thus career and leadership barriers for them persist (Bell & Nkomo, 2001).

We have examined evidence for the glass ceiling in the corporate sector. At this point you may be thinking that the cutthroat world of big business likely reinforces biases and injustices that help sustain the glass ceiling, and that this barrier is just characteristic of the business environment overall. Clearly, there could be no glass ceiling for women and minorities in the ethical and moral world of higher education. Or could there be?

The level of representation of female and ethnic minority faculty members continues to grow within the field of higher education, yet female and minority faculty remain disproportionately represented at the lowest levels of academe. Previous upward mobility trends experienced by women are actually reversing; their numbers holding tenured or tenure-track positions are actually *decreasing*. According to a recent report from the American Association for University Professors (2002), when compared to their male counterparts new female faculty are most likely to be found outside of the tenure track in part-time positions or as instructors or lecturers. The pipeline for White and Black women in higher education administration seems to be closing. Women who are able to progress to the highest levels of administration as CEOs in educational institutions are grossly underrepresented in comparison to their share of all faculty and senior-level administrative positions (American Council on Education (ACE), 2000). The overwhelming profile of the American college president remains that of a fifty-something, married, White male who has held the position for an average of 7 years (ACE, 2000).

Reasons for the Glass Ceiling

So why does the glass ceiling exist? Opinions regarding the glass ceiling differ widely. For example, when interviewed about why the glass ceiling exists in corporate America, executive women and their male employers differ significantly in what they report. Male CEOs fault women's supposed lack of interest, family responsibilities, and lack of numeric representation (women's absence within the leadership pipeline) as keeping women outside of the core of corporate leadership. Executive women in contrast discuss lack of access to male-dominated networks, lack of mentoring, as well as the lack of access to line positions that afford women budget authority (Ragins, Townsend, & Mattis, 1998).

Persistent notions regarding appropriate gender roles for men and women also likely support the existence of a glass ceiling. Alice Eagley's research on **the social-role theory of sex difference** contributes important insight to this issue. This theory asserts that as a population we assume that the stereotypes we hold about group members are intrinsic and involve issues that are basic and essential to their very being, such as our notions regarding women and nurturance. Furthermore, we expect group members to occupy positions or roles that fit with our stereotypes of them (Sampson, 1999). For example, consider our image that all women desire to be mothers. Given our need to sustain gender role stereotypes and our expectations that some people are best for particular roles, it is not difficult to see how women are constantly steered (or steer themselves) toward roles that include providing support for others (often men). Most striking about the influence of gender roles and stereotypes is that even within industries in which women make up the vast majority of the workforce, those women are led by men! How does this happen?

One explanation is that men who work in female industries such as the helping professions of teaching or nursing are moved into management because parents and patients are uncomfortable with men who teach or nurse. These men are put into leadership positions that are perceived as more *appropriate* for men. Pharr (1988) would also argue that men gain an advantage in female industries due to **heterosexism** (privilege based upon heterosexuality) and that men (and women) who challenge their socially assigned gender roles risk public scrutiny and being devalued and labeled abnormal. This pressure to reinforce the norm may keep both men and women in roles that are perceived as being more socially appropriate.

Eagly and Carli (2003) also suggest that, although women may be gaining an advantage in access to leadership and an appreciation of a more feminine leadership style (i.e., promoting democracy, involvement, and inclusion), prejudice against women persists. Even today evaluations of women's competence as leaders is vulnerable to sexist bias, especially in masculine organizational contexts (Eagly & Carli).

Even within the field of banking where women make up the majority of the industry's workers, men lead banks because they may be seen as having the *innate characteristics* that benefit leadership roles. Women on the other hand are valued for having interpersonal skills that are only seen as beneficial to their roles as tellers and clerks rather than also enhancing their potential for leadership.

Morrison, White, and Van Velsor and the Center for Creative Leadership (1992) have found in their leadership development work with corporate leaders that leaders' expectations of female employees place women in very limited and difficult positions. Organizations send all women the message that they are to take risks but consistently be outstanding at their jobs, and that women are to be tough but not macho. In addition, women should be ambitious but not expect to be treated equally to men, and women should take responsibility while following others' (likely men's) advice (Morrison et al.). In other words it appears that organizations tell (and perhaps need) women to reinforce traditional gender roles and female stereotypes while also demanding that these women excel at their job even though the stereotypes women are asked to reinforce ultimately work against their ability to lead.

Thomas and Gabarro's (1999) six-year study of minority and nonminority career advancement in three organizations indicates that race impacts "fast-trackers'" movement into the executive suite. Even when identified by organizations as being on the fast track, minority employees hit plateaus early in their careers that create the perception that they are "off track" for executive leadership positions. Managers of color received as many promotions as their White colleagues; however, these promotions were oftentimes lateral or to positions that did not increase the minority manager's development, visibility, or perceived value to the organization. Those managers of color that did make it to the executive suite faced fewer career hurdles than their White colleagues and many times reached higher levels within the corporation. However, their numbers were relatively few compared to the number of minority managers who were initially identified as being on the fast track.

Thomas and Gabarro (1999) suggest three barriers that block the development and advancement of people of color to the executive suite. These include the prevalence of prejudice, leaders' levels of comfort with people of color, the perceived risk involved in sponsoring ethnic minorities, and leaders' difficulty in identifying high-potential people of color. All leaders, like all people, have some prejudice that can potentially impact how they perceive and relate to dissimilar others around them. At times this prejudice can be very overt; however, the traditional old-fashioned forms of prejudice in our politically correct world are rare. Most likely the prejudice that we all confront is subtle and not easily identified nor resolved.

One example of a more contemporary and subtle prejudice that likely manifests itself in organizational settings is **aversive racism** (Dovidio & Gaertner, 2000). Aversive racism is characteristic of individuals who hold very egalitarian values and beliefs and who view themselves as nonprejudiced but who have also learned racist stereotypes of ethnic minorities and hold negative feelings and beliefs toward them. Aversive racists discriminate in very subtle ways that are often rationalized in order to protect these individuals' self-image as nonprejudiced and fair while also preventing them from engaging in behaviors that would be evaluated by others and themselves as prejudiced. Aversive racist beliefs and tendencies do however manifest themselves in situations in which a prejudiced act or judgment would be perceived as ambiguous and could thus be rationalized as fair. Many promotion decisions in organizations are themselves subjective and at the discretion of higher-level managers and executives. Subjectivity in organizational decision making by primarily majority group members leaves ethnic minority employees vulnerable to aversive racism. In fact, Dovidio and Gaertner's (2000) review of racial bias in selection decisions over a 10-year period revealed no prejudice against Blacks whose credentials were clearly superior or inferior. However, this study did reveal a preference for White candidates when the differences between Black and White candidates' credentials were perceived as ambiguous.

Likewise, women are made vulnerable by many decision makers' benevolent sexism. Like aversive racism, **benevolent sexism** is a subtle form of sexism that disadvantages women in the workplace. Glick and Fiske (2001) define benevolent sexism as having a dual nature. Benevolent sexism involves the tendency to view women in a seemingly positive light such as portraying women as people to be cherished and put on a pedestal. However, these beliefs have detrimental consequences for women's subsequent career development. For example, beliefs that women should be cherished and protected deny women the opportunities to confront challenges in order to develop their strengths and identify their weaknesses. Benevolent sexist beliefs subsequently lock women out of much needed developmental opportunities that are required for their upward mobility.

No glass ceilings allowed.

High-level leaders may have deeply ingrained beliefs and stereotypes about women and people of color that make them uncomfortable around members of these groups. Discomfort with dissimilar others and avoidance of these individuals likely limits the roles in which leaders are willing to place women and people of color. Similarly, aversive prejudice and stereotypes will limit leaders' ability to identify women and people of color as appropriate for high-level roles in organizations. Furthermore, decision-making bodies such as top management teams, which are often homogeneous, may subsequently limit advancement opportunities for women and people of color, given that decision makers (like all people) evaluate people like themselves in a more favorable light. This **"similar to me bias,"** our natural bias to respond favorably to those we feel are like us, negatively impacts women and people of color in regard to selection decisions, promotion, and needed developmental opportunities in majority-dominated organizations.

As women and people of color increase in their representation in the workplace, won't the glass ceiling go away? Not necessarily. Maume's (1999) research supports the continued existence of a glass ceiling for women and people of color as well as a **glass escalator** for White men to the leadership suite in those careers in which diversity is increasing. Like glass ceilings, glass escalators are invisible. Unlike glass ceilings, glass escalators provide opportunities and advantages that assist members of the dominant or majority group in their career-related goal attainment. In his analysis of Black and White adults' career mobility over a six-year time period, Maume confirmed the increasing representation of White women and Black men and women in the workplace. However, he also found that for careers in which women or people of color were

Diversity in Practice 9.1	Breaking the Glass Ceiling

Eyring and Stead (1998) investigated the "best practices" of companies that were distinguished in their attempts to dismantle the glass ceiling. These companies

1. established and maintained a task force to address issues of concern to women
2. communicated goals for women's upward mobility
3. made sure women were represented on task forces that addressed issues salient to women
4. explicitly included women of color in programming geared toward women's issues
5. regularly surveyed employees on a variety of issues, including issues of concern to women
6. established and maintained minority networks and support groups to provide support for women of color
7. held management accountable for women's development
8. established systems for identifying high-potential women
9. encouraged the movement of women into line management positions
10. provided awareness-oriented diversity training to managers

From A. Eyring and B. A. Stead, "Shattering the Glass Ceiling: Some Successful Corporate Practices," *Journal of Business Ethics*, 17(3): 245–251. Reprinted with the kind permission of Kluwer Academic Publishers.

increasing in numbers, White men gained an advantage relative to those groups in regard to their career progression. For example, compared to their female counterparts, men working in female-dominated occupations or industries were often more likely to become managers (likewise for Whites within those career paths in which Blacks were most visible). The increasing representation of women and people of color may actually give White men's career advancement a boost!

Gender and racial stereotypes, inflexible gender role ideology, and aversive and benevolent prejudice are likely explanations for why glass ceilings persist for women and people of color. Given the subtle nature of these biases, proving their existence and avoiding these biases are difficult tasks for those that must confront them. Yet some people of color and women have been able to break through the glass ceiling. The following section identifies both individual and organizational strategies that have been identified as helping to shatter the glass ceiling.

Strategies for Breaking the Glass Ceiling

Despite differences in how executive women and CEOs see the glass ceiling in organizations, these parties do come to common conclusions regarding how the glass ceiling can be dismantled. Their suggestions point to individual strategies and choices by women and other underrepresented groups as well as commitments on the part of organizations to ensure equity.

Individual Strategies

Although women and minorities confronting the glass ceiling have indicated that inhospitable climates and work cultures that favor Whites and men create the glass ceiling, those facing this barrier still must challenge its existence. A number of studies have identified the strategies used by female and minority executives in their own career advancement. Consistently the strategies identified have included exceeding expectations, making others comfortable, seeking developmental opportunities, and having a mentor.

Ragins et al. (1998) found that 99% of their executive female respondents indicated that consistently exceeding performance expectations was a "critical" or "fairly important" career advancement strategy. These women reported that they needed to exceed performance expectations in order to overcome negative and sexist beliefs by male peers and superiors. Women of color too report the need to perform "over and above" the expectations of those around them (Giscombe & Mattis, 2002). Additionally, White women and women of color also report adopting a style to help them fit into their surroundings. For example, Black women report needing to adjust their managerial style to fit into the corporate environment (Giscombe & Mattis). Other executive women discuss this strategy more specifically. These women report developing a "style that men are comfortable with" to further their career advancement (Ragins et al.).

These initial career development strategies, to me, seem somewhat oppressive. They appear to require women to take on extra roles and work in order to compensate for others' problems, biases, and insecurities. Although performing over and above others' expectations and adopting work and interpersonal styles to make others comfortable are reported as strategies adopted by successful female leaders, the very success of these strategies suggests that workplaces are resistant to women's presence. These strategies also work to reinforce an organization's existing negative climate for diversity when women work to adjust to it rather than challenge it. Other strategies identified by executive women speak to the importance of organizations providing equal access to women in regard to developmental opportunities and mentoring. Women's access to important developmental opportunities and to mentors are less oppressive and more empowering strategies that enhance both women's career advancement and the climate for diversity in organizations.

Organizational Strategies

Developmental experiences that afford women enhanced visibility and the opportunities to demonstrate budget accountability are rare but extremely important for women's career mobility. These "stretch" opportunities expand women's skill sets, allow them to establish new professional relationships, and enable them to experience success in new domains (Giscombe & Mattis, 2002; Ohlott, Ruderman, & McCauley, 1994; Ragins et al., 1998). Powell and Butterfield's (1994) study of a potential glass ceiling in the federal workforce for women revealed the importance of experience for women. In this study women were actually *advantaged* compared to men in regard to promotion decisions, in part due to their increased levels of experience as well as education. Interestingly, a replication of this study that examined a race-based glass ceiling in the federal workforce revealed that race indirectly *disadvantaged* ethnic minority candidates for promotion due to their lower levels of experience relative to White candidates (Powell & Butterfield, 1997).

Mentors are also important. Forty-four percent of the respondents in Giscombe and Mattis's (2002) study of Black women in corporate management reported that having an influential mentor was important to their career advancement. Thirty-seven percent of executive women in the Ragins et al. study said it was critical and another 44% indicated that influential mentors were fairly important. Mentors likely serve important functions in keeping protégés informed of stretch assignments and they often act as advocates for their protégés when important decisions are being made that may be vulnerable to modern and dangerous biases.

Parker and Ogilvie (1996) suggest that despite their daily confrontation with sexism *and* racism, Black female leaders use unique career development strategies to break the glass ceiling that include boundary spanning, creativity, and behavioral complexity to promote their distinct model of leadership. Additionally, Proudford and Thomas (1999) and Thomas, Proudford, and Cader (1999) further argue that minority women's marginal positions as "organizational outsiders within" provides them with the potential to engage in innovation that can potentially benefit both their employers and their careers. The message from the limited research on Black female leaders is that one can include aspects of one's unique experience as a double minority both inside and outside of the workplace to become an effective leader. For example, Bell's (1990) study of Black professional women identified that their lives were bicultural and that these women spend a significant amount of time and energy negotiating two worlds. These women must manage their relationships with the Black community, which provides them with support, encouragement, psychosocial mentoring, and belonging, and their relationships with their mostly white professional community, which provides them with work-related information, instrumental mentoring, and status. This **bicultural boundary spanning,** that is, the ability to negotiate two different cultures, allows Black professional women the opportunity to build effective networking skills that benefit subsequent leadership opportunities and roles (Bell).

Morrison's (1992) research on female and ethnic minority executives indicates that organizations' attempts at developing future leaders from nontraditional leadership groups must include a balance of challenge, recognition, and support. All job seekers need the opportunity to learn new skills and demonstrate their value. Challenging stretch assignments allow for this to happen. Challenge may come in participating in task forces, troubleshooting stints, overseas assignments, or short-term assignments to corporate offices that allow budget accountability. Recognition and rewards for one's achievement are important as are access to resources in order to continue achieving in the form of promotions, salary increases, and awards (Morrison).

The challenge aspect of Morrison's leadership development model is not unique. Many fast-trackers are given these types of assignments. However, for female and minority employees there may be a lack of support for taking on challenging assignments. Also these challenges present a layer of job stress that underrepresented workers must overcome, such as stress due to discrimination and affirmative action stigma, in addition to the typical job stressors of role overload or ambiguity. Support can come from employee groups such as a Black managers network, or through the advocacy expressed by one's superior. Bosses' willingness to allow employees to learn from mistakes is also supportive. Access to information and feedback also provide minority fast-trackers with the insight needed to continue along the leadership path. Flexibility in one's job allows one to better balance work and nonwork demands. Opportunities for stress relief are also supportive and can allow employees enhanced opportunities for work/nonwork life balance.

Organizations that are able to dismantle these barriers to women and people of color's upward mobility view diversity as presenting opportunities for organizational learning, innovation, and competitiveness (Thomas & Ely, 1996; McDaniel & Walls, 1997). Leaders of organizations *without* glass ceilings are led by unique leaders who have unique models of leadership.

LEADERSHIP FOR A DIVERSE WORKFORCE

Once glass ceilings are broken, organizations must be sure that workers who rise to leadership are adequately developed for leading multicultural workplaces. Building diversity into management and executive leadership development programs is critical to the development of leaders as well as to dismantling glass ceilings (Kram & Hall, 1996). Therefore, we now turn to the question of how to develop multicultural leadership. Having leaders who look like and who represent different demographic groups is not any guarantee that those individuals will be successful in leading others different from themselves. The remainder of this chapter highlights three different approaches to identifying and developing multicultural leadership. The alternatives reviewed include a discussion of psychological readiness for multicultural leadership, an identification of multicultural competence for leadership of diversity, and the behaviors indicative of emancipatory leadership—a promising model of multicultural leadership.

Readiness for Multicultural Leadership

Thomas (1998) proposed that leaders who are most effective in multicultural workplaces are those who are psychologically ready. Leaders who are psychologically ready for multicultural environments are those who are aware of their

| **Diversity in Practice 9.2** | **Demonstrating Diversity Readiness** |

Martin Davidson, an associate professor and diversity management expert, was recently interviewed regarding strategies for exhibiting diversity readiness or consciousness for aspiring leaders (Cole, 2002). According to Davidson, many employers wrongly assume that people of color, women, and openly gay and lesbian employees are predisposed toward diversity and have an advanced understanding of the complexities involved regarding diversity given their own minority experience. Minority employees may indeed have a unique experience, but like *all* employees, minority employees differ in the extent to which their identity is perceived as meaningful, important, or instructive to their ability to initiate and maintain productive work relationships with diverse others.

This presumption also places White males in a precarious position. This assumption suggests that White males lack diversity readiness and that they are not predisposed to knowing about diversity nor are they interested or able to learn about it. Davidson offers suggestions for *all* aspiring leaders in regard to demonstrating their diversity readiness and consciousness, regardless of their minority or majority status. Among these suggestions are that we learn to appreciate our own uniqueness and be willing to share that with others, see experiences that will broaden one's diversity perspective, and learn to use diversity related mistakes as a source of personal and organizational learning (Cole, 2002).

Cole, Y. (2002, Feb. 19). How to market yourself as a diversity-consciousness professional. DiversityInc.com.

own identity, privilege, and ethnocentrism and the potential for how each of these issues can create barriers for minority individuals within diverse workplaces.

Leaders who are self-aware in regard to their own identity work to explore how different forms of identity (due to race, gender, or sexuality) shape experience (in and outside of organizations) (Phinney, 1996). Leaders who lack identity development mistakenly believe that everyone's experience is the same (like theirs) and they fail to take into account the significance of race, gender, and sexuality as well as culture and economic status on one's education and other important opportunities. Instead, multicultural leaders have explored the significance of their own demographic membership—especially in regard to access to power—and they strive to create opportunities that are not bound to race, gender, or sexuality.

These leaders are also aware of **privilege** and how the lack of privilege can deny one access to opportunities that subsequently create barriers to individual performance and career development for members of minority groups. McIntosh (1993) refers to privilege as an invisible knapsack of provisions upon which one relies each day. An example of a race-based (and gender-based) privilege in many organizations is, "I can aspire to become the CEO of my company and feel assured that my race (or gender) will not work against this goal." For many White Americans this statement would be true. However, for people of color this statement highlights the extent to which their racial dissimilarity denies them an equal opportunity to become CEO. Leaders who reinforce privilege in the workplace due to gender, race, or sexuality never question the extent to which belonging to the dominant group in the workplace affords one advantages and that dissimilarity is punished.

Multicultural leaders also work to resist **ethnocentrism.** That is, these leaders resist the tendency to view the world and dissimilar others through their own cultural frame of reference. Ethnocentric leaders judge and evaluate their workers based upon their (the leader's) own cultural reality. These biased evaluations place minority workers in precarious positions since they must reinforce the cultural norms, values, and behaviors of their leaders in order to be perceived as competent and valuable to their workplace. Nonethnocentric leaders instead want all workers to use their uniqueness as a means of contributing to the organization.

In short, leaders who are psychologically ready for multiculturalism are not threatened by diversity but instead see it as an opportunity for their own personal learning. Diversity is perceived as an organizational learning opportunity as well. Davidson provides insight regarding how to demonstrate one's readiness for multicultural leadership.

Developing Multicultural Competence

According to Day (2000), "The primary emphasis in leadership development is on building and using interpersonal competence" (p. 585). **Building multicultural competence** in future and current leaders is therefore a must (Cox & Beale, 1997); of the *current* entrants to the labor force, almost 75% are racial and ethnic minorities (Sue, Arredondo, & McDavis, 1992). Hansen, Pepitone-Arreola-Rockwell, and Greene (2000) provide a two-part definition of multicultural competence for practicing psychologists that is useful in thinking about the competencies needed for multicultural leadership, "(a) awareness and knowledge of how age, gender, race, ethnicity, national origin, religion, sexual orientation, disability, language, and socioeconomic status are crucial dimensions to an informed professional understanding of human behavior, and (b) clinical skills necessary to work effectively and ethically with culturally diverse individuals, groups, and communities" (p. 653). If we apply this definition to leaders of diverse organizations (or those aspiring to positions of leadership), we can retain part (a) of the definition given that leaders too must have an understanding of human behavior (albeit informal) in order to build a motivated, loyal, and productive workforce. Part (b) of the definition is applicable as well. However, rather than focusing upon possessing clinical skills, organizations' leaders must have interpersonal skills to work effectively across groups both within as well as outside of organizations. Sue (1995) suggests that multicultural competence should address three areas: (1) the individual's beliefs and attitudes regarding minority groups; (2) the individual's level of knowledge of cultural differences, history, and values; and (3) the individual's development of skills to communicate and work effectively across difference.

Chrobot-Mason (in press) suggests that building multicultural competence is a developmental process that occurs over three stages. The first stage involves building awareness. Like Thomas (1998), Chrobot-Mason suggests that multicultural leaders must develop a greater understanding of the plights of other cultures and groups as well as come to a greater understanding of self in relation to other groups' experiences. The second developmental stage involves developing behavioral and coping skills (Chrobot-Mason). This stage is accomplished by actually practicing communicating and working with those who are different from oneself in safe environments. These opportunities may present themselves as part of diversity training (Ferdman & Brody, 1996); however, they may also come about through Davidson's suggestion of placing oneself around new individuals and cultures. Stage 3 of developing multicultural competence involves action planning. Chrobot-Mason suggests that this is a necessary step for organizations and individuals alike. These action plans focus on continuous learning so that multicultural leaders do not become complacent in their organization's diversity-related practices nor their own level of understanding and behavior regarding diversity. Just as workers must engage in continuous learning and improvement in order to be effective at their jobs, all workers (especially leaders) must continuously engage in developing multicultural competence in order to be continuously effective in their increasingly diverse work relationships (Chrobot-Mason).

Emancipatory Leadership

Corson (2000) introduced **emancipatory leadership** as a model of leading diverse educational institutions; however, the concept has promise for all diversity organizations. Whereas Thomas (1998) describes readiness for multicultural leadership in regard to the leader's diversity-salient attitudes, beliefs, and predisposition, and Sue (1995) and Chrobot-Mason (in press) focus on developing multicultural competence, Corson (2000) provides much needed insight regarding how "emancipatory leaders" *act and behave:*

- Emancipatory leaders know when they are out of their depth in complex sociocultural areas: they acknowledge the greater expertise of community members or their colleagues in certain situations, especially those linked to concerns for diversity; and they act accordingly.
- Emancipatory leaders can tell when they need to extend the circle of decision makers to include others whose interest might be at stake; they know when the in-group of the moment has severe limits placed on its understanding, or when it could be prejudiced in its views.
- Emancipatory leaders try to make their own presence a matter of small importance to the context of debate and decision-making: they step down from the chair, and they withdraw from centre stage by deliberately limit-

ing themselves to making consultative contributions to debate, perhaps by offering their opinions last, rather than first.

- Emancipatory leaders remove the effects of their own power from the process of decision-making: they make it clear that they will accept any decision that is the outcome of a democratic consensus, and that they will try as much as possible to do so without voicing their reservations after the fact, or acting on any negative feelings they might have.
- Emancipatory leaders agree to leave the implementation of a decision in the hands of those chosen for that task by the group. (p. 117)

Emancipatory leaders appear to understand their own boundaries and biases. Furthermore, they resist stereotypes and limits that impede the progress and power of members of minority groups. Emancipatory leaders appear to share power and empower their employees rather than rule them. These leaders also respect the unique contributions that members of minority groups offer organizations and dismantle the barriers to these contributions. Although this emancipatory leadership model is not appropriate for the more mundane managerial tasks for which leaders are responsible, it does provide leaders with much needed flexibility in regard to how they work with diverse management teams and issues related to diversity. Good leaders surround themselves with knowledgeable individuals who are trustworthy and competent in regard to the business at hand. Likewise, multicultural leaders must pursue knowledge regarding diversity and understand that this knowledge is likely incomplete. By adopting an emancipatory leadership approach, multicultural leaders appreciate the diversity expertise among their employees and use it to their individual and organizational advantage.

CONCLUSION

Thomas and Gabarro's (1999) study of the opportunities for development and advancement of high-potential managers suggests that successful leaders create a diversity strategy that reflects and is compatible with corporate culture while also improving upon it. These leaders monitor and ensure that opportunity exists for all workers regardless of their demographic makeup, and that promising leaders are developed in order to avoid glass ceilings (Chemers & Murphy, 1995; Thomas & Gabarro, 1999).

Multicultural leaders must also be visibly involved in diversity initiatives and take charge in forming partnerships with diverse employees who can facilitate accomplishing diversity and nondiversity-related goals (Thomas & Gabarro, 1999). Leaders like Ted Childs (of IBM) and Judith H. Katz (of the Kaleel Jamison Consulting Group) are two examples of multicultural leaders. Dr. Katz, author of *White Awareness: Handbook for Anti-Racism Training*, is a renowned scholar and practitioner who has created outstanding partnerships with many *Fortune* 100 companies to bring about corporate change related to diversity (www.kjcg.com). Ted Childs champions diversity efforts internally at IBM and is responsible for tremendous growth in the number of female and

ethnic minority executives there. Much of his work revolves around supporting minority employee networks and career development. Largely due to his efforts, the Catalyst organization (a research and advocacy group for women)
has awarded IBM with its corporate achievement award three times within the
last 15 years (Hammonds, 2000).

Bell, McLaughlin, and Sequeira (2002) view members of minority groups,
such as executive women, as important change agents for organizations and
leaders confronting barriers to diversity such as sexual harassment. Multicultural leaders are aware of the contributions that all workers are able to make
to their workplace, and these leaders work to ensure that barriers to these contributions do not exist.

Discussion Items

1. Review the section on the glass ceiling; how prevalent is it at your institu-
    tion? Consider its existence among faculty, administration, and even stu-
    dent leadership.
2. Brainstorm some strategies for dismantling the glass ceiling at your institu-
    tion. What would need to change in order for women and people of color
    to be better represented in positions of authority at your institution?
3. Is there a multicultural leader in your life? If so, describe that individual
    and indicate what makes that person's leadership effective for diverse envi-
    ronments.
4. Davidson advises aspiring leaders to "Be contrite as opposed to wrong and
    strong" when it comes to learning lessons from diversity missteps. What
    diversity mistakes have you experienced or witnessed? What was the les-
    son learned?

 ## InfoTrac College Edition

Be sure to log on to InfoTrac College Edition and search for additional readings on topics of interest to you.

Diversity Orientations

CHAPTER 10

Organizations

Organizations respond to diversity differently. The approach by which organizations choose to address the diversity around them affects the experiences of minority workers and subsequently the ability of these organizations to use diversity as an organizational advantage. Many organizations have implemented successful diversity initiatives and have found their diversity to be an organizational asset. Examples of these initiatives and these organizations will be highlighted throughout this chapter.

To help us understand how organizations differ in their diversity readiness we will review three different models of organizational diversity. These models can help organizational practitioners and employees understand where their companies are in their diversity readiness and competence. Specifically, Sue's model of multicultural development, Cox's acculturation model, and Thomas and Ely's diversity paradigms will be reviewed. After covering the highlights of each, we will think about the common message they send to organizations on their path to both embracing diversity and reaping its benefits.

SUE'S MULTICULTURAL DEVELOPMENT

Sue (1995), a counseling psychologist, is concerned about how to make organizations healthier for all types of individuals, not just those who fit the **mythical norm** (Tatum, 1999). By *mythical norm* I am referring to those individuals who are presumed to have the most potential to contribute to organizations. In our society the mythical norm is typically White, male, Christian, heterosexual, and middle class. Rather, Sue is concerned about the pressures and prac-

Kevin R. Morris/Corbis

Different organizations pursue diversity differently.

tices of organizations that suppress diversity. There are several broad societal beliefs and myths like the mythical norm that suppress diversity. Diversity Learning Point 10.1 describes three diversity myths that resist diversity.

Sue approaches the topic of organizational diversity from an **organizational development** perspective. Organizational development is a broad discipline concerned with improving organizations and their employees through applied research (e.g., organizational surveys, interviews, focus groups, or the analysis of archival data) and interventions that may be directed at the individual, group, or organizational level. Sue (1995) refers to his unique model of addressing diversity issues in organizations as **multicultural organizational development (MOD)**.

The basic premise of MOD is that organizations differ in the extent to which they are aware and concerned with basic social justice issues like oppression and discrimination. When inequities in an organization arise, organizational development (OD) practitioners traditionally focus on communication patterns or leadership as common areas to study. However, from Sue's MOD perspective, we must also examine the extent to which organizations contain and reinforce "monopolies of power" and privilege in order to understand the root of inequity and discrimination (Sue, 1995). Like other organizational perspectives, MOD views conflict as inevitable but not necessarily desirable.

According to MOD, organizations can escape conflict and cultural misunderstandings and discrimination by recognizing and valuing diversity. However, organizations have to progress to this awareness by moving through a

Diversity Learning Point 10.1	Myths That Resist Diversity

Thomas, Mack, and Montagliani (2004) review and confront arguments against diversity. These authors also point out broader cultural myths that support diversity resistance. Each of these myths support privilege and reject the notion that diversity matters, that it should be attended to, and that it can be a critical opportunity for success. The myth of meritocracy, the myth of the colorblind ideal, and the melting pot myth all support dominance and resist diversity.

The Myth of Meritocracy
This myth posits that anyone who works hard enough can be successful, in or out of work. According to this myth, our station in life is simply a function of our investment in the effort we direct to our work. Failure to achieve goals, or society's notions of success, is therefore simply due to a lack of ability and effort. Thomas et al. confront this myth by illustrating how histories of exploitation and exclusion support the privilege and achievement of dominant groups and blame subordinate groups for their inability to live up to the American dream. The myth of meritocracy is supported by the American value of individualism, which suggests that we can all pull ourselves up by our bootstraps. Those who hold on to this myth reject the notion of privilege and systems of oppression that stifle opportunities for minority group members.

Myth of the Colorblind Ideal
Many organizations adopt this myth as part of their diversity perspective. The sentiment is that everyone is equal and everyone should therefore be treated the same. Like the myth of meritocracy it ignores the influence of historical oppression. It also devalues and ignores diversity. This myth presents a positive front but has negative consequences:

> While the colorblind premise is a positive one, the reality of ignoring individual identity, culture, and minority status often has very negative consequences for minority groups. The underlying hypocrisy of the colorblind perspective is that its perpetuation tends to encourage subtle and even overt forms of discrimination against minority groups. . . . When individuals are not allowed to recognize and appreciate differences between themselves and others, there is instead a reliance upon ethnocentric standards and on stereotypes for explanations of differences that inevitably perpetuates rather than ends discriminatory behavior. The result is increased tension and segregation and the positioning of race as taboo. (Schofield, 1986) (Thomas et al., 2004, p. 49)

Melting Pot Myth
This myth is rooted in our immigrant history. The belief is that those who come to the United States do so to be a part of a new American identity and culture. Yet the reality for many people of color is one of expected assimilation. The true melting pot would be a nation in which *everyone* embraces a new identity. For many people

continued

**Diversity
Learning Point 10.1** | Continued

of color, especially linguistic minorities and immigrants, the experience has been one in which they are expected to reject their culture, values, language, holidays—in short, those things that may make them unique. Furthermore, opportunities to develop and succeed may only be available if people in these groups are willing to reject their uniqueness and instead embrace those values and assumptions that dominant groups define as important.

developmental-stage process. Sue's developmental model describes organizations at three different stages of development: **monocultural, nondiscriminatory,** and **multicultural.**

Sue (1995) describes monocultural organizations as primarily Eurocentric and ethnocentric. By this he means that organizations are grounded in a White European culture and value system and that these organizations have difficulty valuing any person, behavior, values, or practices that do not resemble or reinforce that cultural perspective. Because of the organization's inability to step out of its own cultural frame of reference and its inflexibility, it is not surprising that people of color and other "nonright types" (Deal & Kennedy, 2000) are excluded. The human resource practices of these organizations often leave minority groups out and reinforce White privilege. In these organizations there is a prevailing belief that there is "one best way" to everything, which further suppresses diversity and the benefits it may offer. These organizations are very much rooted in the belief that the country and its organizations are melting pots. However the actual practices of these organizations do not promote equal assimilation in order to become a new identity, but instead reinforce the expectation that people of color, women, immigrants, and other "different" others must assimilate in order to be accepted.

At the next stage of MOD, Sue (1995) describes nondiscriminatory organizations. These organizations are somewhat more aware and enlightened than monocultural organizations, yet they encounter difficulties in translating this awareness into organizational practices. Leadership in fact may recognize the need for the reconsideration and redesign of human resource systems and organizational practices but may also be hesitant to implement any systemic policy or program regarding workplace prejudice and discrimination. Therefore nondiscriminatory organizations may have inconsistent policies and practices throughout the organization so that some divisions or functions of the organization are better at embracing diversity than others based upon who is in charge. Even equal opportunity and affirmative action efforts may be pursued with hesitation. Those diversity efforts that are promoted and visible are often done for public relations purposes (Sue).

Unlike nondiscriminatory organizations, multicultural organizations do have a consistent culture that embraces diversity. At this developmental stage, organizations value diversity and see it as a strategic advantage and so they work to diversify the organizational environment. Within these organizations the contributions of a diverse workforce are visible. One mechanism by which this is accomplished is through the frequent collection of data within the organization in order to ensure that equal opportunity really exists. Unlike monocultural organizations, there is no best way. In fact the value here is that equal access and opportunities do not necessarily mean equal treatment (Offerman & Phan, 2002; Sue, 1995).

From this MOD perspective there are many barriers to valuing diversity in organizations. One barrier concerns the lack of multicultural knowledge. In organizations where leaders and employees lack this knowledge, distinct communication styles and other cultural differences may be misunderstood by dominant group members. Prevailing organizational ethnocentrism prevents these organizations from attempting to understand and value differences. Even when minority group members do attempt to assimilate to the dominant culture, their attempts are viewed with suspicion (Sue, 1995).

Another barrier to organizational movement in MOD is simply ongoing interpersonal and organizational discrimination. Organizations cannot move forward in their diversity attempts when they continue to use recruitment strategies that interfere with achieving a diverse workforce or when they tolerate individual discrimination and workplace cultures that make retention of a diverse workforce problematic. The glass ceiling interferes with diversity retention and keeps organizations from becoming multicultural workplaces. Sue (1995) also encourages organizational leaders to examine the broad assumptions and practices that disadvantage minority workers and create dominant group privilege by asking themselves, How do organizational expectations impede diversity and its benefits?

Sue's MOD model offers many lessons for diversity practitioners. His model itself is a different way of analyzing where organizations are in their diversity maturity. Because he takes an OD perspective in this work, he reminds practitioners that organizations are complex systems that have formal and informal rules that work toward **homeostasis;** that is, that all organizations work to maintain balance and stability. In fact, according to Sue (1995) it isn't only minority workers who are under pressure to conform in organizations, it's everyone (White males included). These norms prevent everyone from thinking and working in ways that may be different but creative and productive. Therefore, diversity efforts must be pervasive in order to be effective. You cannot intervene in only one area, one system, or with one target and expect that the entire organization will improve. Furthermore, the targets of our interventions, often employees, will understand diversity missions and philosophies, but they will *respond* to actions. Again, it is therefore important that emerging diversity philosophies and value statements be manifested in organizational practices and become part of the organization's culture (Sue, 1995).

Diversity Learning Point 10.2	Diversity Traps

Holvino, Ferdman, and Merrill-Sands (2004) identify several diversity traps that frequently put corporate leaders on the wrong road to moving their organizations forward in their efforts to manage diversity. Many of these traps reflect a dependence on diversity messages or images rather than actions.

Trap	Solution
Assuming short-term diversity training is sufficient	Diversity training and education are frequent and lifelong.
Assuming diversity is not connected to the company's mission, products, services	Diversity is infused and connected to all major goals and functions of the organization.
Waiting to collect data on employee perceptions or attitudes in order to avoid airing dirty laundry and voicing employee's dissatisfaction	Data should be viewed and welcomed as a valuable tool that provides needed information and direction to diversity efforts.
Waiting for everyone to support diversity efforts	Start movement regardless of who is or is not on board. With education and success, employees will eventually see the value of diversity efforts.
Ignoring resistant people, especially in top positions	Identify resistance and understand how it influences other organizational members. Provide education and resources to those individuals.
Relying upon good intentions and rhetoric	Tie goals to actions.
Ignoring dominant group members	Include all employees in your efforts as partners and allies.
Assuming that managing diversity is simply common sense and good management practice	Understand that the effective management of diversity requires education, self-awareness, exploration, and skill development.
Viewing effective diversity management as evidenced by the number or magnitude of diversity activities or events	View diversity management as evidenced by the effect diversity strategies have on workers.

Another major contribution of this work is the issue of what equal treatment really means in diverse organizations. If we compare organizations at monocultural versus multicultural levels of development, they take on the issue of equality very differently. Organizations lower in their MOD take a more tra-

Diversity in Practice 10.1	**Mentor Up**

Organizations such as Proctor and Gamble that rely upon employees with backgrounds and knowledge of male-dominated disciplines like engineering, the sciences, and technology face many barriers related to recruiting (and subsequently retaining) a diverse workforce. Yet industries that rely upon these competencies must be able to connect with a diverse market in order to remain viable. For example, auto manufacturers, pharmaceutical companies, and financial services organizations all rely upon employee backgrounds that represent disciplines which have encountered difficulties in recruiting and supporting women and people of color.

Proctor and Gamble became a diversity leader in the 1990s by taking efforts to be more proactive in supporting diversity (Thomas et al., 2004). One example is their Mentor Up program (introduced in Chapter 1). This program helps to support gender diversity in the organization by pairing women who work in technology- and science-related functions within the organization, with some of the highest-level male managers. This mentoring relationship is an effective learning opportunity for both parties. The female employees receive all of the benefits that we expect of mentoring relationships. Namely, they receive career advice, support, increased knowledge of the organization, and increased access to networks throughout the company. In addition mentors gain firsthand knowledge of what it is like to be a woman in their organization and in their industry. These data provide these mentors and leaders with important information for diversity efforts that enhance the climate for gender diversity at Proctor and Gamble.

ditional approach to equality that assumes everyone is the same and thus should be treated the same. There is no responsiveness to individual differences. Yet multicultural organizations embrace the value of equality even while being responsive to individual backgrounds and needs.

COX'S ACCULTURATION MODEL

Cox (1991) offered a similar model that describes how organizations differ in their stage of diversity development. Cox's work is an adaptation of earlier work on cultural integration. Through examining organizations by each of the seven cultural integration dimensions, diversity practitioners can identify areas in which integration does not occur and where more attention should be paid.

The first dimension, **acculturation,** examines how diverse groups adapt to each other and resolve their differences. Is there the assumption of minority group assimilation? Or is there **pluralism?** That is, do *both* minority and majority groups adopt some values and norms of the other? Or is there **cultural separatism?** That is, is there little adaptation by either group?

Structural integration, another dimension of Cox's model, is concerned with the cultural profiles of employees. Where are people of color and dominant group members on the organizational chart? Are there centers of power in the organization that are largely occupied by White males? or is diversity represented throughout all levels, functions, and divisions of the organization? A similar dimension, **informal integration,** is concerned with how well minority group members are included in informal networks and activities such as lunch and dinner meetings, golf, and other athletic events and social clubs. Cox's model also examines the extent to which **cultural bias** is allowed to flourish in the organization through prejudice and discrimination.

Another dimension by which organizations are examined is concerned with **organizational identification;** that is, do all employees have a sense of belonging, loyalty, and commitment to their workplace or are some groups more identified than others? Finally, organizations are examined by focusing on the extent to which **intergroup conflict** persists. Do tension and power struggles exist between groups? And how does workplace heterogeneity decrease cohesion and promote dominant group backlash?

By analyzing organizations based upon these seven dimensions of integration, Cox (1991) argues that companies will likely fit into one of three acculturation models, **monolithic, plural,** or **multicultural.** Monolithic organizations have the least amount of integration. These organizations are very homogeneous and any minority group members that may be present in the workforce will be expected to assimilate. Minority group members in these organizations also face **occupational segregation;** that is, they face very real barriers to moving to different jobs or areas of the company if another minority group member has not previously held that job or position. Because of the lack of diversity and the emphasis on assimilation, diversity related conflict is low; however, this is an unrealistic model for modern organizations today (Cox).

Plural organizations have more heterogeneous membership and are more integrated both in the formal structure of the organization as well as in the informal structure of the company. Yet there may remain skewed integration across function, level, and work group. For example, it would not be uncommon to still see women and people of color facing a glass ceiling in plural organizations. These organizations may rely upon hiring initiatives, affinity groups, and training in order to promote diversity. However, even though these organizations may have less discrimination than monolithic organizations, their levels of increased diversity do promote greater occurrence of diversity-related conflict and backlash. Within these organizations dominant group members may feel that increased attention to diversity is creating disadvantages for them and that they should not be held accountable for prior organizational actions that were discriminatory (Cox, 1991).

Multicultural organizations meet all of Cox's (1991) seven dimensions of integration in organizations. Typically, diversity efforts in these organizations encompass diversity training, affinity groups, and task forces, and diversity is present in all key committees and is involved in all levels of decision making (Cox). What is probably the most instructive about this final stage of Cox's model is the emphasis put upon the structural integration of minority group

<table>
</table>

Diversity in Practice 10.2 | **Tracking Inclusiveness**

Organizations such as the Human Rights Campaign, Out and Equal Workplace Advocates, and the Visibility Project help companies create inclusive environments for gay and lesbian employees. According to Lubensky, Holland, Wiethoff, and Crosby (2004) these firms track three indicators of inclusiveness:

1. *Policies.* Are there nondiscrimination and harassment policies that protect gay and lesbian employees? Are these policies known and followed by everyone? Are there consequences for not adhering to these policies?
2. *Benefits.* Do gay and lesbian employees have the same employee benefits that are afforded to heterosexual workers? That is, do they have health and other crucial employee benefits that are extended to them as well as to their partners?
3. *Support.* Are there networks and support systems that are available to gay and lesbian workers? As discussed previously, affinity groups are important to providing underrepresented workers with the support and voice they need to be effective in their organization.

members, especially for the purposes of decision making. This emphasis provides the opportunity for diverse voices to be heard throughout the organization.

Cox (1991) provides many suggestions for helping organizations move to a multicultural identity (see Figure 10.1). These include training, specifically on managing and valuing diversity, new member orientation programs, explicit mention of diversity in mission statements, and the creation of diversity advisory groups to senior management. Like Sue (1995), Cox emphasizes data collection and feedback in order to assess the climate for diversity in the organization (see Diversity in Practice 10.2 for suggestions about assessing the climate for inclusiveness for gay and lesbian workers). Diversity Figure 10.1 exhibits Cox's full recommendations.

THOMAS AND ELY'S DIVERSITY PARADIGMS

Like Cox's model, Thomas and Ely's (1996) model comes out of a management background. Their model of organizational diversity focuses upon organizational paradigms related to diversity and how organizations differ in their perspectives about diversity that subsequently drives their ability to use diversity to their advantage. They argue that many organizations encounter difficulty linking diversity to valuable organizational outcomes because these companies have only focused on diversity as representing identity group membership. Instead Thomas and Ely suggest that diversity should be "understood as the varied perspectives and approaches to work that members of different identity groups bring" (p. 80).

Figure 10.1 | Tools for Multicultural Organizations

Model Dimension	Tools
I. Pluralism *Objective/s* —create a two-way socialization process —ensure influence of minority-culture perspectives on core organization norms and values	1. Managing/valuing diversity (MVD) training 2. New member orientation programs 3. Language training 4. Diversity in key committees 5. Explicit treatment of diversity in mission statements 6. Advisory groups to senior management 7. Create flexibility in norm systems
II. Full Structural Integration *Objective/s* —no correlation between culture-group identity and job status	1. Education programs 2. Affirmative action programs 3. Targeted career development programs 4. Changes in manager performance appraisal and reward systems 5. HR policy and benefit changes
III. Integration in Informal Networks *Objective/s* —eliminate barriers to entry and participation	1. Mentoring programs 2. Company-sponsored social events
IV. Cultural Bias *Objective/s* —eliminate discrimination —eliminate prejudice	1. Equal opportunity seminars 2. Focus groups 3. Bias reduction training 4. Research 5. Task forces
V. Organizational Identification *Objective/s* —no correlation between identity group and levels of organization identification	1. All items from the other five dimensions apply here
VI. Intergroup Conflict *Objective/s* —minimize interpersonal conflict based on group identity —minimize backlash by dominant-group members	1. Survey feedback 2. Conflict management training 3. MVD training 4. Focus groups

From T. Cox, "The Multicultural Organization," *The Academy of Management Executive 5* (1991), Exhibit 3, p. 41. Reprinted by permission.

According to Thomas and Ely (1996) members of identity groups bring value to the organization because of their diversity. Diverse employees bring "different important, and competitively relevant knowledge and perspectives about how to actually *do* work—how to design processes, reach goals, frame tasks, create effective teams, communicate ideas, and lead. When allowed to, members of these groups can help companies grow and improve by challenging basic assumptions about an organization's functions, strategies, operations, practices, and procedures. And in doing so, they are able to bring more of their whole selves to the workplace and identify more fully with the work they do, setting in motion a virtuous circle" (p. 80).

Thomas and Ely (1996) have found that organizations rarely adopt this holistic **learning and effectiveness paradigm** to diversity. Instead, organizations seem to embrace one of two more common paths in managing diversity efforts. They refer to these paradigms as **discrimination and fairness** and **access and legitimacy.** Each of these paths will be described followed by a description of learning and effectiveness in organizations.

Discrimination and Fairness

Diversity goals in discrimination and fairness organizations typically revolve around numbers. These organizations are preoccupied with recruitment and retention goals rather than with what diverse employees offer to the organization. According to Thomas and Ely (1996) the staff may become diverse in these organizations but the work does not, given that a "colorblind" perspective is reinforced. The underlying code of assimilation in discrimination and fairness organizations undermines these organizations' abilities to learn and improve their practices and strategies. Furthermore, the emphasis on conformity and assimilation keeps people from identifying with their work within these organizations (Thomas & Ely). Thomas and Ely suggest that the U.S. Army is one example of a discrimination and fairness organization. The army is an incredibly diverse organization; however, the emphasis in this group revolves around due process and equal treatment.

Access and Legitimacy

Whereas discrimination and fairness organizations focus upon assimilation, access and legitimacy organizations focus on differentiation (Thomas & Ely, 1996). That is, differences are highlighted and celebrated rather than suppressed. Organizations who adopt this paradigm embrace diversity because it is seen as an avenue to more revenue. Companies who operate from an access and legitimacy mindset see enhanced marketing and sales opportunities to a growing diversity of consumers. To take advantage of a diverse marketplace, diverse employees are brought in for their niche knowledge of their ethnic and cultural group. Although diversity seems to be appreciated from this paradigm, it is minimal to the potential value and subsequent advantage that could be offered from the learning and effectiveness approach. Although organizations

| Diversity in Practice 10.2 | **Can We Talk?** |

Eastman Kodak is an example of one organization that is frequently heralded for its diversity efforts. It has been especially successful in its efforts to support gay, lesbian, and bisexual (GLB) workers. One initiative, the Lambda Network, serves as an affinity group for GLB workers and this group helps to promote the concerns of these workers throughout the organization.

The Lambda Network has developed several tools for outreach to the Kodak community including, "Can We Talk?" workshops that occur annually to promote communication between GLB and non-GLB Kodak employees (Lubensky, Holland, Wiethoff, & Crosby, 2004). The Can We Talk sessions occur using a **fishbowl** format. Using this format, gay and nongay workers are divided and each group is allowed the opportunity to discuss its issues without interruption from other group members. For example, GLB employees sit in a circle and discuss issues raised by a moderator. A larger circle, outside of the GLB circle, of nongay employees listens to the fishbowl's conversation. After a dinner break in which all participants are allowed to mingle and follow up on the initial group conversation, the roles of the two groups reverse. The workshop concludes with a conversation among all workgroup participants regarding what occurred and what was learned. These workshops have also become a powerful force in enhancing the climate for GLB workers at Eastman Kodak.

---

may experience success in forming targeted marketing and sales groups for various ethnic or even international communities, the competencies that those employees bring to their work are never fully shared throughout the organization. This lack of learning may become especially painful for the organization when diverse talent leaves the organization. The organization suffers by not infusing these competencies throughout the organization, and minority workers suffer as well.

Organizations that work from the access and legitimacy perspective frequently pigeonhole workers (Thomas & Ely, 1996). The perceived benefits that minority employees bring with them are limited to cultural knowledge from this paradigm. Eventually many minority workers feel used and exploited rather than truly valued. Basing these employees' careers solely upon their ability to help the organization better relate to specific communities leaves minority workers vulnerable and on an unstable and unpredictable career path (Thomas & Ely).

Learning and Effectiveness

Like Cox's (1991) multicultural organization, the emphasis in the learning and effectiveness organization is integration. This paradigm encourages diverse perspectives and the critique of existing practices and policies by *all* employees. Thomas and Ely (1996) argue "this model for managing diversity lets the organization internalize differences among employees so that it learns and grows because of them. Indeed with the model fully in place, members of the organization can say, 'We are all on the same team, with differences—not despite them.'" (p. 86)

Leaders in learning and effectiveness organizations realize that increasing diversity in an organization does not automatically lead to enhanced effectiveness. Rather how a company defines diversity and what it does with the diverse experiences and competencies offered by diverse newcomers is how effectiveness is enhanced. How do leaders move their organizations to a learning and effectiveness paradigm?

Clearly trust is a major value in these organizations. Leaders must trust their employees, regardless of how they look, that they will give their best work to the organization. Employees must trust organizational leaders that there will be no negative repercussions for working in ways that may be innovative and which may not fit the existing organizational mold. Open discussion of how work is done is valued. Managers take responsibility in these organizations for identifying and eliminating any barrier that may be oppressive and that may prohibit employees from contributing to the full extent of their capabilities (Thomas & Ely, 1996).

BROAD LESSONS

Individually each of these models offers lessons to organizations about gaps in their diversity thinking and practices as well as about how to move forward. Sue's model takes a social activist approach to encourage organizations to think about dominance rather than simply business. Cox's model focuses on dimensions of integration that can be identified and supported in organizations. Finally Thomas and Ely center their work on positioning diversity as an opportunity for organizational learning. Leaders must therefore understand how that learning can get suppressed or enhanced.

Despite the differences in the foundation of their recommendations, there are some overarching themes present in these models. Each will be identified and discussed.

Stages of Development

Each of the models presented identified three organizational types. Yes, this is a simplistic and obvious observation, but it is something to consider, nonetheless. My educated guess is that these types/stages/paradigms are not as clear cut as either the other authors or I have presented. Rather they simply offer a framework within which to consider particular organizations and where they currently are in terms of diversity management. More likely, organizations may show signs of being in multiple stages or types, which itself provides organizational leaders with feedback regarding opportunities for growth and areas of diversity achievement.

Eliminate Assimilation and Conformity as Core Values

In each of the three models discussed, those organizations that were the least mature in their diversity thinking and management were those with a culture that reinforced assimilation and conformity. Clearly these are not values that reinforce diversity. Assimilation and conformity may rather reinforce dominance and exclusion. This is a difficult barrier to overcome, but this is a necessary step in order for organizations to become inclusive and to enable diversity to be an opportunity for learning and effectiveness.

New Thinking About Fairness

Related to the issue of assimilation and conformity is the issue of fairness. An organization may embrace conformity of its employees as well as in the implementation of its policies and practices in order to promote a value of fairness. Certainly organizations that embrace diversity embrace fairness as an antidote to discrimination and prejudice. But what does *fairness* mean?

According to Offerman and Phan (2002) some leaders may take fairness to mean that all employees are treated equally without regard for their individual differences. Yet that type of equality or fairness limits managers and leaders from providing the tools or environment that each individual employee may need to be successful. Organizations must begin to challenge traditional notions of fairness that promote blanket treatment of all employees as the same. Leaders must understand appreciating diversity as a core mechanism of promoting fairness that is also responsive to employee needs.

Full Integration

Organizations that seem to be most successful in their diversity efforts, regardless of the model, all seem to support the full integration of minority group members in their organizations. Both the formal and informal structures of these organizations are open to all employees. Furthermore, the organization often takes proactive steps to ensure that minority group members have the resources and support systems they need to be engaged in their work. Mentoring and networking programs, like affinity groups, are often the bedrock of diversity efforts in these organizations in their attempts to ensure that all workers feel supported and heard.

Identification and Engagement

One of the more subtle messages offered by these models is that, in order for any employees to be full contributors to their work, they must be able to identify with their workplace so that they may be fully engaged in their job. For workers who have a minority status, this is difficult to accomplish if the organization is pressuring them to assimilate and to conform to another group's reality. In fact, the opposite effect is likely to occur; these workers will feel disidentified and disengaged. Rather than seeing the organization as a partner to their having a meaningful work life, the company becomes the enemy and a barrier to meaningful work.

CONCLUSION

The three models summarized offer organizational practitioners, consultants, and even employees valuable information that can aid in understanding where a specific organization is in its multicultural development. There are successful models of diversity management that can be used as benchmarks and which can motivate other organizations to more aggressively pursue their diversity goals. Yet the ability of any organization to put these recommendations into action falls upon the shoulders of organizational leaders and their own diversity readiness and identity development (Thomas, 1998). Therefore, Chapter 11 will explore the issue of identity development as it relates to diversity and its management in organizations.

Discussion Items

1. Analyze an organization with which you are familiar using Cox's seven dimensions of integration. Identify those dimensions that impede your organization from being fully multicultural and make recommendations for how this organization can improve.
2. Examine this year's "Best Places to Work" list for any group (many popular business-related magazines such as *Fortune*, *Working Mother*, and *Black Enterprise* publish these lists yearly). What do the top three organizations have in common and how do they differ? How does each of these organizations fit with the three models described in this chapter?
3. Thomas and Ely (1996) position organizational diversity as an opportunity for organizational learning. Reflect upon their model and compile a list of how diversity can promote learning in an organization with which you are familiar. In addition, what are the barriers in your organization that prevent the diversity–learning link?

 InfoTrac College Edition

Be sure to log on to InfoTrac College Edition and search for additional readings on topics of interest to you.

11 CHAPTER | **Diversity Orientations**

Individuals

In the last chapter we discussed the different ways in which organizations may think and act when it comes to diversity. According to these models the success of an organization's diversity efforts not only has consequences for a company's ability to attract *and* retain diverse workers, it also has consequences for the ability of *all* workers to feel identified with the organization and engaged in their work. When workers are engaged at work they feel free to help the organization move forward through questioning implicit assumptions about how work is done and the decisions that are made, which subsequently allows organizational diversity to create a competitive advantage.

Other issues that also arose in this discussion are **diversity resistance** and **backlash.** Diversity resistance and backlash occur when organizational members feel threatened by discussions about diversity and the actions that are taken by the organization. Resistance and backlash manifest in both subtle and overt ways. Subtle indicators of diversity may be silence, aloofness toward minority workers or workers championing diversity efforts, or just the avoidance of the organizational conversation about diversity and ignoring leaders' mandates to engage in ongoing diversity efforts. More overt forms of resistance include verbal and physical conflict related to diversity, vandalism, graffiti, and the filing of lawsuits to prevent the organization from acting in ways that benefit diversity rather than the interests of the status quo.

Organizational members can therefore facilitate an organization's diversity mission or resist it. This chapter examines how worker identity development can facilitate or hinder diversity efforts. We will focus on the issue of

| Diversity Learning Point 11.1 | What's in a Name? |

What is in a name? African American workers have had a variety of names. Upon arrival they were mostly called slaves, but later they were called Negroes, Colored, Blacks, and now African Americans. Today Americans of African origin often refer to themselves as either African American or Black. African American is chosen frequently because it provides these Americans with a place of origin. Others like Tatum (1999) choose Black because of its universality and connection to other people of African origin who may live in Africa, Central or South America, the United States, and Canada, as well as the Caribbean. Workers whose first language is Spanish are also referred to by a variety of labels. *Latino/a, Hispanic,* and *Chicano/a* are at times used interchangeably, although these terms refer to specific groups. Arana (2001) provides direction in defining membership for those who have Spanish roots.

> *Chicano/Chicana.* Term popularized during the fight for civil rights in the 1970s that refers to Mexican Americans' dual culture and heritage.
>
> *Hispanic.* Broad-based term used to describe people of Spanish-speaking ancestry. The term is somewhat controversial and rejected given that it is often viewed as a government-imposed term since it was used in the 1980 census.
>
> *Latino/Latina.* Another umbrella term used to describe individuals of Spanish-speaking ancestry. Used by the U.S. Census Bureau in 2000.

Although these definitions are provided, they are in no way definitive. Individuals may reject one or all of these terms. Many individuals may prefer to define themselves according to their specific place of origin such as Mexico, Puerto Rico, Cuba, or Spain. Also, it is important to consider the region of the country or world in which you live or work. A broad term like *Latino/a* will in actuality refer to different groups depending upon where you are. Where I grew up in Northern New Jersey, the Latinos were primarily Puerto Rican (and American!), Cuban, and Dominican. Now that I live in Georgia, the Latinos where I live are primarily Mexican. Therefore we may talk about Latinos all over the country or the world, but we must still respect that Latinos are a diverse and multifaceted group.

---

racial diversity by examining two models of identity development—one for Blacks and another for Whites—as examples of how identity-related attitudes shape responses to diversity. Obviously, employees are not at similar levels of identity development. Therefore we will also discuss the implications of managers and leaders being at different levels of identity development when compared to their subordinates. We'll also tap into the emerging conversation about the implications of different organizational levels of diversity identity for minority workers. Finally we will consider the consequence of these different models of organizational diversity *and* identity development for enhancing the climate for diversity in organizations.

WHAT IS IDENTITY?

Earlier we reviewed the importance of group membership for both our **identity** and our esteem. By *identity,* I am referring to how we see and define ourselves. Often our identity is tied (to some extent) to the groups to which we belong. These groups may be rooted in ethnicity, culture, gender, religion, sexuality, socioeconomic status, or even profession. **Identity development** refers to the extent to which one has a sense of belonging and affiliation to a specific group and has explored what being a member of this group means (Phinney, 1996). For example, for Black Americans, Black identity development refers to the extent to which one feels a sense of belonging and affiliation to other Blacks and the extent to which an individual has considered, What does it mean to be Black in this country (or organization)? Cross in *Shades of Black* (1991) coined the term **Nigrescence** to refer to the process of becoming Black; the process of exploring and defining for oneself what it means to be Black.

There are a wide number of identity development models that correspond to different aspects of identity such as race, gender, and sexuality. Most of these models have been built in some way upon Cross's early work. We will review several popular models that are used to assess racial identity in Blacks and Whites. Comparable models for women and gay and lesbian workers are presented in Diversity Learning Points 11.2 and 11.3.

IDENTITY DEVELOPMENT MODELS

There have been a number of models developed to describe the racial identity development process for many ethnic groups found in the United States. Janet Helms, a counseling psychologist, has contributed greatly to the understanding of both Black and White identity development and the interaction of individuals at different identity statuses. Thompson and Carter (1997) review the lengthy history of work in the areas of racial identity for people of color (especially Blacks) and for Whites. A summary of their review follows.

Racial Identity Development: Blacks and Other People of Color

Blacks and other people of color face a unique challenge in their racial identity development. Their unique challenge is developing a healthy and positive identity within an environment that often portrays their racial groups quite negatively and uniformly. However, African American workers and citizens are diverse and likely to be at different levels in identity development (Cokley, Dreher, & Stockdale, 2004). Diversity in identity development among minority workers contributes to the diversity of their responses to their workplaces and to the diversity initiatives that these organizations may promote.

Preencounter/Conformity   Blacks and other people of color who are at the preencounter stage of their racial identity adopt society's messages about what it means to be Black. These individuals unquestionably accept negative stereo-

Diversity Learning Point 11.2	Womanist Identity Development

Janet Helms is not only responsible for developing and modifying models of racial identity development, she has also developed a model of **womanist identity**[1] (Carter & Parks, 1996). Womanist identity, according to Helms, refers to women's attitudes toward their own womanhood. Like models of racial identity, womanist identity occurs over a variety of stages (also referred to as statuses). Each stage has consequences for a woman's attitudes about herself, other women, diversity strategies that may promote women's interests, and diversity overall.

Preencounter. Women in this stage deny sexism and societal bias against women that privilege men. Traditional sex roles are accepted.

Encounter. Women experience something (most likely sexism) that challenges their worldview, especially in regard to gender relations and the pervasiveness of sexism. A stage of questioning and examination of men and women and their assigned roles in society ensues.

Immersion–Emersion. The initial part of this stage involves a rejection of men and patriarchy and an idealization of women. The latter part of this stage involves a search for a positive and realistic model of womanhood.

Internalization. The development of a personal definition of what it means to be a woman that is not dependent upon men or other women. Women who reach this stage do not rely upon others or their movements or political agendas for self-definition. Women who reach internalization may be heterosexual or homosexual and may not necessarily define themselves as feminist.

[1] *Womanism* is also used by African American studies and women's studies scholars to refer to a model of feminist identity espoused by Black women and other women of color. Authors bell hooks and Alice Walker use the term to refer to Black women's fight for equality. In many ways the term *womanism* came about to protest the women's movement's exclusion of Black women and its denial of racism.

---

types of having a Black identity and passively accept White dominance and privilege. For these individuals, racism may be looked upon as a thing of the past or simply be perceived as a fabrication that other Blacks fall back upon in order to explain their failures. Preencounter Black workers are likely to distance themselves from other Black workers and be suspicious of their competence and ability. They may attempt to align themselves instead with White workers and attempt to prove their "worth" to White colleagues. Black preencounter workers will also be suspicious of any other Black individual who has a leadership position within the organization, especially in regard to the leader's competence and ability.

Encounter/Dissonance   Preencounter/conformity individuals move to the encounter/dissonance stage once they encounter an experience with racism

Diversity Learning Point 11.3

Gay and Lesbian Identity Development

Walters and Simoni (1993) used the work of racial identity theorists to propose a model of gay and lesbian identity development. This model identifies the attitudes that are characteristic of gay men and lesbians at three different identity stages. Each stage also has consequences for one's willingness to disclose one's gay identity at work and responses to workplace initiatives targeted at the gay, lesbian, and bisexual (GLB) community.

> *Preencounter.* Individuals in this stage see heterosexuality as normal and themselves as deviant. Their attitudes demonstrate a desire to be "straight" and to assimilate into "mainstream" culture.
>
> *Immersion–emersion.* Individuals develop a fascination with gay identity and culture. Heterosexuals may be perceived as oppressive. There may be growing anger toward societal heterosexism.
>
> *Internalization.* Individuals have a sense of inner security with their identity. Heterosexuals are no longer perceived as an ideal nor as the enemy. Heterosexuals are not perceived as a standard by which one is judged.

---

that is so blatant and offensive that there is no dismissing it. Typically the experience is personal and shocking. The experience initiates self-questioning about issues around race, equality, and the like. Although encounter individuals may feel a sense of internal conflict about being saddled with a negative identity and accepting it, there is also a sense of emerging freedom that may be experienced. Thompson and Carter (1997) suggest, "Initially, the shocking event or events leave the person feeling confused and bitter. Gradually, the person experiences euphoria which is born out of his or her decision to see a Black or Asian or Hispanic identity" (p. 21).

Immersion–Emersion   Individuals in the immersion–emersion stage of their identity development are seeking a positive sense of a racialized self. At the first part of this stage, a Black worker may immerse herself in everything she identifies as Black—literature, music, art, fashion, and so forth. In fact this immersion is so intense that often these individuals may distance and alienate themselves from White friends and colleagues. These individuals often become caricatures of what they believe it means to be Black. That is, they adopt stereotypical representations of Blackness through their dress, language, and other aspects of appearance. As at the earlier stages of identity development, immersion individuals are relying upon external definitions of Blackness that are provided by the media and modeled by other Blacks.

At the second part of this stage, emersion, the individual continues to learn about Black and African culture, but she may become more critical of the information she's fed. Her search involves not only seeing Blacks in a positive

Diversity Case 11.1	Tim Gill and the Gill Foundation[1]

Tim Gill is the founder of the Denver, Colorado, desktop publishing company Quark. Gill started Quark with a $2,000 loan from his parents when he was laid off from a Denver software company in 1981 at the age of 27. In 2000, Gill retired from Quark as its chairman and chief technical officer leaving Quark with $600 million in yearly sales and 1,000 employees. Gill retired from Quark in order to be more involved in his foundation (Lopez, 2003–2004). The Gill Foundation supports gay and lesbian causes.

In addition to funding and supporting the gay and lesbian movement for civil rights, hundreds of social justice organizations and educational institutions have benefited from this foundation. The foundation now gets involved in the training and strategy development of the organizations it funds in order to help them continue to raise money to support their causes (Lopez, 2003-2004). More information about Tim Gill and the Gill foundation can be found at www.gillfoundation.org.

[1]Lopez, E. M. (2003–2004, Dec/Jan). The art of giving it all away: Tim Gill, from entrepreneur to philanthropist. *DiversityInc*, 67–68.

light but also understanding the strengths and weaknesses of her culture in order to form a realistic impression of her Black identity.

Internalization   Individuals reach a stage of internalization when they are able to merge their fully evolved racial (e.g., Black or Asian) identity with other aspects of their self, such as their gender or economic class. They are critical thinkers who are able to evaluate the racial stimuli in their environment and not be defined by them. Internalization stage individuals define for themselves what it means to be a member of their ethnic minority group. These individuals work toward the elimination of racism and other forms of oppression while maintaining a healthy commitment to their racial group.

Racial Identity Development: Whites

Like Blacks and people of color, Whites also have a unique challenge to developing their racial identity. In fact, many Whites (as we discussed when reviewing privilege) have never quite considered themselves as having a race. Race is something that is possessed by "others." For many, to be White is just simply to be "normal." For Whites who do engage in the process of developing a racial identity, the challenge is twofold. The first challenge is developing an antiracist identity. How can Whites do this if they've never considered privilege nor connected privilege with racism and White supremacy? The second challenge is developing a positive White identity that is not dependent upon the subordination of others; that is, feeling good about oneself and committed to one's White identity without feeling superior to other ethnic groups. As is the case with all of the racial identity models, White identity occurs over a number of stages.

Contact   White individuals at this stage of development have contact with members of other racial groups and perceive them to be different; to be the Other (Pharr, 1988). There is no consideration of one's own identity, only that "others" are different or diverse. "To be White is simply, to be" (Thompson & Carter, 1997, p. 23,). Individuals at the contact stage are not yet aware of the reality of racial inequality and they are blind to oppression and their participation in it.

Disintegration   Contact individuals move into disintegration often by increased exposure to discrimination or by taking a course or some type of training that is focused on diversity issues (Thompson & Carter, 1997). According to Helms (1990), disintegration is indicated by "conscious, though conflicted, acknowledgment of one's Whiteness" (p. 58). As these individuals begin to comprehend the reality of inequality based upon race (and other aspects of identity) they are forced to deal with the suppression of that reality that maintains dominant group privilege and they may become alienated by other Whites who prefer not to take on the difficult and complex challenge of inequality and racism. These individuals may become so conflicted and anxious about their new understanding of the world that they distance themselves from other Whites, and hope and attempt to form closer linkages with Blacks. However, many Blacks may be distrusting and suspicious of Whites who seem overly interested in their culture and experience.

Reintegration   Disintegration individuals may later realize that there are benefits to being White. In order to deal with this realization, these individuals come to accept their "White" identity and begin to interpret society's racial inequality as earned. That is, they believe that Whites hold major government offices and run almost all of the *Fortune* 500 companies because they *deserve* to. White individuals at this stage may avoid Blacks or only choose to have relationships with people of color who hold similar (likely preencounter) mindsets. When they choose to engage in discussions concerning diversity or race, they often do so in same-race groups and among individuals who have similar mindsets. More active expressions of reintegration may include denigrating people of color, behaving negatively toward Blacks, or even engaging in harassment or violence (Thompson & Carter, 1997).

Pseudoindependence   Moving beyond the reintegration stage is difficult but possible through a powerful and personal "identity-shattering" event that leads to abandonment of a racist identity (Thompson & Carter, 1997). Individuals at the next stage, pseudoindependence, have come to recognize the reality of racism and of having a non-White identity. These individuals seek to form

| Diversity Case 11.2 | White Identity and White Allies |

Dick Nash is a powerful White ally in the struggle to end oppression in and outside of the workplace. Dick Nash was a team leader and member of the diversity council of Westhollow Technology Center (WTC) in Houston, Texas. Nash wrote an article on privilege for the company's diversity newsletter and it was also posted on easels around the center. In this article, he described his own struggles with diversity and his journey toward identity development.

> I must confess that I am a member of all of the dominant groups listed above, and then some. I also struggled to understand my "groupness" and I took two sessions at Diversity Awareness Training to truly understand these concepts. Now, when I react to a situation as an "individual," I stop and review how my group memberships are influencing how I respond to the situation. I work at hearing everyone in my workgroup and recognizing him or her for their valuable contributions. I am far from perfect and continue to miss many of the dynamics, which affect the dominant/subordinate relationships, but this is a journey of learning and I am dedicated to finishing it.

From "Understanding Dominance and Subordination: One White Man's Experience," *The Diversity Factor* (Spring 2000), pp. 8–12. Reprinted with permission.

healthy relationships with people of color and to fight oppression; however, the way in which pseudoindependents accomplish this is by trying to make Blacks and other people of color more like Whites. White people at this stage understand racism in the abstract but have not yet come to grips with it in their own lives or how they may perpetuate racism and White privilege.

Immersion–Emersion White people who begin to consider their own participation in racism reach the immersion–emersion stage. The basic question at this stage is, What does it mean to be a White person? (Thompson & Carter, 1997, p. 25). As these individuals seek positive White identities they may choose to read biographies of White allies in the fight for civil rights or join consciousness-raising groups (Thompson & Carter, 1997). Rather than changing people of color, the challenge is to understand Whites and challenge other Whites to abandon racism.

Autonomy These individuals, after a process of learning and reflection, have a positive White identity in which they are comfortable. These individuals take personal responsibility for identifying and understanding the ways in which oppression shapes reality and they actively engage in the fight against oppression.

COMMONALITIES

Although these identity models describe different racial groups with their own unique challenges to developing positive identities, there are some commonalities between these models. Some of these commonalities are apparent while others are less so. As is very evident, the identity researchers like Cross, Helms, Thompson and Carter, and others talk about identity development as occurring in stages or statuses. However, Helms (1990) cautions us not to think of individuals as solely being fully in a particular stage. Instead it is more likely that we each represent a particular profile of identity development. Where we are in our identity development is then shaped by how highly we manifest the attitudes and behaviors that are representative of several stages.

Another commonality between the Black and White models of identity development has to do with the importance of experiences or encounters in order for exploration to occur. For Blacks and people of color the encounter is an encounter with racism. For Whites the encounter may also be with racism or with a "racial–moral dilemma," in which one has to choose to confront inherent and simultaneous feelings of racial superiority and feelings of egalitarianism and commitment to equality. Within the workplace these dilemmas may be related to the extent to which one supports a new diversity effort that may be perceived as disadvantaging White workers.

Both models also deal with the issue of the source of one's identity. In both models individuals move from an external to an internal definition of self (Helms & Piper, 1994). Within the Black model we see individuals initially being defined by society and later seeking a definition that resembles those of other Blacks (likely a stereotype). At the final stage we see individuals defining for themselves what it means to be Black through a process of education, critique, and integration with other aspects of oneself like gender or class. For White identity a similar process unfolds. Initially Whites do not even consider their own identity; they are allowed to walk through life in a racial fog in which racial identity is only something possessed by others. Later they seek positive (although dangerous) definitions of Whiteness built upon supremacy. Finally a search for a positive and nonracist identity ensues.

It is also important to realize that for any of the identity models described, as one works through these stages, reaching the internalization stage may not be the end of one's identity development. In fact most identity researchers believe that we recycle through these stages, especially if we are living and working within an environment that is not supportive of having a highly developed identity. Under these circumstances individuals may regress in their identity stage.

These models and those examining gender, sexual identity, and other aspects of identity are important in that they help us understand attitudes about diversity and diversity efforts in organizations and the resistance that organizations often encounter when starting to engage in diversity work (Cokley, Dreher, & Stockdale, 2004). Cokley et al. assert that for Blacks, as one example, racial identity has consequences for how one negotiates the demands of the workplace and how one advances in a career as well as one's level of productivity, state of well-being, and overall happiness. Block, Roberson, and Neuger (1995) found that Whites at a higher level of identity had more favorable responses to diverse situations at work than did Whites at lower levels of identity. Watts and Carter (1991) found that higher identity level Blacks were less positive about their organization's racial climate as compared to lower level Blacks. My own research on undergraduate students' attitudes regarding affirmative action revealed that low identity Whites and Blacks both had negative attitudes. Only those with moderate and high levels of identity differed by race. Both White and Black students had positive attitudes toward affirmative action, but Black students' attitudes were significantly more positive than Whites'. Button's (2001) research indicated that the sexual identity development of gay and lesbian employees was related to their satisfaction and commitment to their organization.

IDENTITY INTERACTIONS

Understanding identity development is useful for understanding diversity resistance and interracial relationships within the workplace. If we also consider, as was presented in chapter 10, that organizations are also at different stages of development in their diversity identities, understanding this literature has implications for comprehending reactions of minority workers to their employers.

Let's begin by considering the issues of the intersection of racial identity at work. If we refer back to the basic issue that identity development deals with the extent to which individuals have explored what their race means for them and have become committed to that group through a process of education and learning, then it is easy to understand that minority group members are often at higher stages of racial identity development than are Whites. In general, minority group members are more likely to have considered issues like race or ethnicity (do they have a choice?) as compared to dominant group members. In fact the literature supports this. Blacks and Latinos, for example, are often evaluated as being more advanced in their identity development as compared to Whites.

We have considered time and time again that the workplace is composed of an increasingly diverse workforce. In addition, the workforce is diverse in regard to racial identity development. Within any group of workers, for example, Latinos, there will be some individuals who are very low in their racial identity, others who are grappling with the middle stages of identity development, and those who are highly developed in regard to their identity. Likewise for other groups including dominant group members. However, given the literature, it is expected that on average minority group members will have more advanced racial identities than will Whites.

How does this diversity in identity development affect workplace relationships, especially those between leaders and their subordinates? Helms (1990) argues that, although the racial diversity within the relationship is important, the identity stages of those within the relationship may be even more important.

The identity stage of the person holding power within the relationship relative to a subordinate has very important implications for how the relationship will progress. Helms discusses three relationship types: **regressive, parallel,** and **progressive** to describe identity dynamics with counselor–client relationships. However, the relationship types apply to the workplace as well.

Regressive relationships are likely when leaders or managers are lower in their identity development as compared to their subordinates. When subordinates have issues they want to discuss with their manager related to race, for example, the leader may not yet have developed the knowledge and skills to deal with race as a business- or work-related issue. If that manager or leader is at a preencounter stage, it may leave the subordinate person feeling unheard and dissatisfied. It is likely that within this context issues of race and diversity are silenced and taboo. Subordinates working within this type of relationship may be seeking closure.

Parallel relationships occur when both a leader and a subordinate are at comparable levels of identity development. These relationships are only positive when both parties have reached high levels of identity development. In fact, this kind of dyad (especially if cross-race) can be a powerful force in exemplifying the benefits of diverse relationships for a work team or for the organization. Yet relationships between individuals who are both relatively low in identity development, albeit comfortable for those involved, do little to benefit the individuals, their work team, or their organization.

Finally, progressive relationships benefit subordinate individuals, their work environment, and their overall organizations. When leaders are at higher levels of identity as compared to subordinates, they are able to serve as powerful mentors and models of identity development. These leaders can communicate with workers at a lower level of individual identity in ways that promote their further exploration and commitment. These leaders also model important multicultural skills that their subordinates can learn.

Not much research has delved into the interaction of leader and subordinate identity development and its effect on the quality of those relationships. However, Chrobot-Mason (2004) found that identity development of both a majority group manager and the minority subordinate had significant effects on employees perceptions of manager support.

INTERSECTION OF INDIVIDUAL IDENTITY AND ORGANIZATIONAL MULTICULTURAL DEVELOPMENT

Chrobot-Mason and Thomas (2002) reviewed Helms's (1990) early work on the intersection of counselor–client identity and applied it to the issue of minority reactions to majority organizations. These authors used Helms's framework on the intersection of identities to describe the potential relationships that minority workers may have with their organization. Recall from chapter 10 that

Figure 11.1 | Interactive Model of Individual and Organizational Racial Identity Development

Organizational racial identity		Individual racial identity	
		Low identity ⟵————⟶ High identity	
		• Limited exploration of the meaning and significance of one's racial membership	• Radical self-actualization (internalized sense of self)
Low identity ↑	• Racial differences are ignored or devalued (monocultural workplace)	Negative parallel interaction	Regressive interaction
↓ High identity	• Diversity is part of the overall business strategy (multicultural workplace)	Progressive interaction	Positive parallel interaction

From T. Chrobot-Mason and K. M. Thomas, "Minority Employees in Majority Organizations: The Intersection of Individual and Organizational Racial Identity in the Workplace," *Human Resource Development Review* 1 (2001), p. 325. Reprinted by permission.

organizations may be low in their multicultural development (e.g., Cox's monolithic) or very high (e.g., Cox's multicultural). (See Diversity Figure 11.1.)

In those situations where minority workers are at higher levels of identity development as compared to their organizations (regressive), workers may be dissatisfied with their plight and inability to authentically contribute to their workplace. Attempts to alter the organizational landscape will likely fail due to overwhelming resistance from other employees and management, thus making the employee at risk for turnover (Chrobot-Mason & Thomas, 2002).

When both minority workers and their organizations are at comparable and high levels of identity development (positive-parallel), minority workers will feel able to contribute in meaningful ways to the organization without feeling confined to a "one best way" mentality or way of working. Employees are engaged and committed and embrace the learning that diversity offers them (Chrobot-Mason & Thomas, 2002). In contrast, when both individuals and their organization are comparably low in identity development (negative-parallel), minority individuals are complacent with their situation and experience little organizational pressure to learn and embrace diversity or diverse relationships. Instead minority workers are expected and rewarded for their assimilation.

<table>
<tr><td>

**Diversity
in Practice 11.1**

</td><td>

Negotiating Identity
at Work[1]

</td></tr>
</table>

How should organizations handle the dress and other visual expressions of one's identity at work? There is no easy answer. Title VII of the Civil Rights Act of 1964 protects employees against discrimination due to race, color, religion, gender, or national origin. Under Title VII religious dress is protected as long as it does not pose a safety hazard. For example, the following question and answer are posted on the Equal Employment Opportunity Commission's Web site:

> **"I am a Sikh man and the turban that I wear is a religiously-mandated article of clothing. My supervisor tells me that my turban makes my co-workers "uncomfortable," and has asked me to remove it. What should I do?**
>
> If a turban is religiously-mandated, you should ask your employer for a religious accommodation to wear it at work. Your employer has a legal obligation to grant your request if it does not impose a burden, or an "undue hardship," under Title VII. Claiming that your coworkers might be "upset" or "uncomfortable" when they see your turban is not an undue hardship.
>
> If you or your employer has questions about employer obligations to accommodate religious practices, feel free to <u>contact EEOC</u> for more detailed information. If your employer continues to insist that you remove your turban, or takes adverse action against you for refusing to remove it, you may want to contact EEOC to file a charge."
>
> *http://www.eeoc.gov/facts/backlash-employee.html*

How do organizations address the expression of ethnicity and culture in the workplace? There are no hard and fast rules. Johnson (2003–2004) provides several examples of how organizations are coping with increasing visual expressions of diversity in the workplace. For example, over time Safeco (the insurance company) has become more liberal in what it considers professional appearance in order to help promote a more hospitable climate for diversity. Once a conservative organization, Safeco relaxed its dress code in the 1990s to promote diversity. Employees now dress in a variety of manners, and corporate standards are accepting of tattoos and dreadlocks (Johnson, 2003–2004).

For more information see, Johnson, A. D. (2003–2004, Dec/Jan). Can you wear your diversity at work? Or could cornrows and saris sabotage your career? *Diversity Inc*, 48-52. Also visit the website of the EEOC for more information on Title VII and religious dress (http://www.eeoc.gov/facts/backlash-employee.html).

Progressive relationships between minority workers and their majority organizations are ideal but not without their friction. Initially, very low identity level minority workers may feel uncomfortable engaging in conversations related to diversity and may be a source of resistance. Low level minority workers will likely just want to fit in and be like everyone else. However, according to Chrobot-Mason and Thomas (2002), "The availability of successful diverse role models and mentors encourages low identity individuals to confront their stereotypes (including those of their own group) and replace them with more positive images" (p. 336). Eventually, as workers continue to grow they see the diversity of their organization as an asset and a tool for their career success and the effectiveness of their organization (Chrobot-Mason & Thomas).

Kirkland and Regan (1997) and Cooper and Thompson (1997) both demonstrate how an understanding of identity development models can be used within a professional context, especially in regard to assessing **racial climate.** Helms (1990) defined racial climate as a group's atmosphere for resolving racial conflict and the extent to which an environment encourages the development and positive racial identity development of group members regardless of their group membership. The extent to which those in positions of power are able to resolve racial dilemmas and promote racial identity development is therefore related to their ability to promote an inclusive and positive climate for diversity.

Kirkland and Regan (1997) use racial identity instruments to evaluate the climate for racial diversity within organizations as well as the identity development of future diversity training participants. The data provide these consultants with information about potential sources of diversity resistance as well as diversity attitudes within client organizations. Such instruments also provide good data regarding how to initiate training with participants. Cooper and Thompson (1997) also conduct racial identity assessment as part of their efforts to diagnose the climate for diversity within organizations.

CONCLUSION

Individuals create and direct organizations. Ultimately the ability of any organization to use diversity as a strategic and learning advantage is incumbent upon the diversity readiness and competence of its leaders and members. Individuals who have not progressed in their own identity development are unable to create work contexts in which diverse workers are engaged in their work and feel open to contribute in novel ways. Much of identity development is based upon self-awareness, exploration, and learning. Organizations must therefore create climates in which these three processes can occur. According to Thompson and Carter (1997), "Importantly, the racial identities of those in positions of influence contribute to the racial climate of a particular group or organization" (p. 29). Certainly diversity training can initiate this process. In addition, leaders and managers must take the initiative in modeling multicultural competencies and skills so that other employees can learn from their example. In addition, diverse decision-making teams that work under guidelines and conditions which promote openness, creativity, and nonjudgment can facilitate creating positive climates for diversity. Helms and Piper (1994) suggest that coalitions of workers with similar levels of identity development can perpetuate a specific organizational climate. It is therefore incumbent upon organizations to make sure that they provide the training and opportunities so that coalitions of workers with highly developed identities can create and support positive climates for diversity.

Discussion Items

1. Examine attitudes about the provision of same-sex employee benefits from the perspective of a lesbian worker at each of the three different levels of identity development described in Diversity Learning Point 11.3.
2. What kinds of encounters promote White identity development in organizations?
3. In what ways do you demonstrate your identity at school or in your workplace?

 InfoTrac College Edition

Be sure to log on to InfoTrac College Edition and search for additional readings on topics of interest to you.

Conclusion

Strategies for Success

My mission in writing this book has been to highlight the unique experiences of minority group members; namely, racial and ethnic minorities, women, and sexual minorities, in the workplace. We began this journey by exploring organizational strategies used to recruit a diverse applicant pool and how organizations' regulatory and public policy environments impact organizational decisions like selection.

We then sought to understand the unique experience of diverse workers as organizational insiders. We covered socialization and newcomer experience, barriers to and strategies for career development, diverse work group dynamics and conflict, diversity-related work stress, and leadership's role in creating positive and inclusive climates for diversity. We've ended this journey by stepping back from the minority individual's experience within organizations and analyzing the variety of organizational strategies used to address diversity. Finally, we concluded our journey by delving into the psyche of leaders and employees in order to understand how identity development shapes individual choices related to diversity and diversity resistance.

My hope is that, along the way, you have learned some important lessons that will facilitate your own career and its development, as well as lessons that will help you successfully lead, direct, and build organizations that are inclusive. Throughout the text, I have offered strategies for making diversity an asset to organizations. I would therefore like to use this last chapter in our journey to highlight a few of the recurring themes that can help you on your own passage as part of a diverse workforce and as a diversity leader.

INDIVIDUALS

The literature reviewed and examples provided in this text offer many lessons, especially for those at the beginning of their career.

• *Be proactive.* There are a number of ways in which the literature reviewed encourage readers to be proactive throughout all aspects of their career. Certainly success in the job-seeking process is incumbent upon going beyond the strategic diversity advertisements of organizations that blanket the Internet and business magazines. Organizations are trying to sell themselves while you as an applicant are attempting to sell yourself and your credentials. Look carefully at their Web sites and other materials to see if the messages they are sending are representative of what their organization is actually like. If the organizations *says* it values diversity, look for evidence of diversity in its leadership, its managerial workforce, its suppliers, and its retention rates.

• *Embrace developmental opportunities.* All workers should consider taking on challenging and visible opportunities and assignments in order to stretch themselves professionally and personally. Developmental opportunities that provide line management experience and budget accountability and which expand one's network and visibility are critical for future promotions. However, we must also begin to think about stretching ourselves in regard to diversity. Doing so may provide us with effective tools for gaining greater self-awareness and understanding as well as for enhancing interpersonal skills. This may mean forming diverse relationships and working in diverse groups and teams that you may not have considered previously.

• *Mentors and networks.* All workers need access to mentors and to networks that can provide them with valuable information about their job, their workplace, and the resources that are available within their organization. Mentors and networks also provide much needed psychosocial support. Having a diverse network of mentors and access to a diverse network are both important for dominant and minority group members alike. Minority group members need diverse mentors and networks so that they can gain insight into what it means to be employed by a particular organization or in a particular field or profession. Majority workers benefit by having a network of diverse mentors and access to a diverse network because it increases their understanding and sensitivity to the unique realities of diverse workers and their own identity and perhaps even their own forms of privilege. The ultimate goal of these mentoring and networking opportunities is to have individuals be more informed, identified, and engaged in their work and in their organization.

ORGANIZATIONAL

According to the literature reviewed for this book, there are several lessons for organizations that want to create inclusive climates and opportunities.

• *Leadership and diversity perspective.* The message that seemed to come up most frequently in our exploration of workplace diversity is the importance of leadership. Almost every organizational strategy or recommendation that was identified started with committed leadership. Without effective leadership diversity goals and mission statements lead nowhere. Like Dick Nash (presented in Diversity Case 11.2), these leaders must at least have begun their own identity development journey and be willing to put into *action* those practices that will eliminate barriers, like the glass ceiling, to the recruitment and retention of a diverse workforce. These leaders must work hard to create a work climate that is open and built upon trust so that all workers feel identified and engaged at work. Individuals who are diversity leaders in organizations seek out opportunities to reward workers who are successful diversity partners and to incorporate their diversity values throughout their organization's human resource system.

• *Support individual identity.* Organizations that are *least* successful in their diversity efforts are organizations that expect assimilation and have a "one right way" perspective regarding work. The benefit of diversity, from

---

Diversity Case 12.1	**The Xerox Model of Workplace Diversity**

In many ways the Xerox organization is a model of the recommendations offered throughout this text. It has repeatedly been recognized for its outstanding diversity efforts including *Fortune, Hispanic, DiversityInc,* magazines and organizations such as the Human Rights Campaign, the U.S. Department of Labor, the U.S. Small Business Administration, and the American Association for Single People. These awards come from having a diverse and appreciated workforce and its efforts to extend its value for diversity to the community overall.

Why is Xerox so successful?

Diversity Understanding

Clearly Xerox has a sophisticated understanding of diversity. According to their Web site, they view diversity as a hierarchy that involves the following points:

• *Creating diversity.* Making sure that people of different groups are represented in the organization.
• *Managing diversity.* Retaining and treating workers fairly regardless of gender, race, age, cultural background, sexual orientation, and physical ability.
• *Valuing diversity.* Creating an environment where diversity and varying perspectives are genuinely valued.
• *Leveraging diversity.* Making diversity critical to the organization's business strategy in order to strengthen and grow the business through a diverse customer base.

continued

Diversity Case 12.1	Continued

Diversity Programs

Xerox has instituted the following comprehensive set of diversity programs to support its diversity goals:

- *The balanced workforce strategy.* Ensures equal representation throughout the company
- *Employee roundtables.* Facilitate communication between senior managers and employees and provide numerous affinity groups to support workers
- *Minority/female vendor programs.* Support the organization's commitment to purchase supplies from qualified female- and minority-owned businesses
- *Work life programs.* Provide employees with resources for their personal and family lives
- *Training, development, and succession planning.* Improves the retention and development of diverse talent throughout all management levels

Diversity Role Model Behaviors

Xerox expects employees to practice and role model these behaviors to ensure that all individuals are treated with dignity and respect and are valued for their unique contributions.

- Know yourself and seek information
- Acknowledge and value the contribution of each employee
- Create a supportive work environment
- Ignite team spirit
- Use your personal leadership to enact fair practices
- Create and enforce human resource practices that value diversity

Xerox also encourages employees to get involved in their community. For example, the Xerox Community Involvement Program (XCIP) provides employees with the opportunity to volunteer to help solve community problems. Xerox's Social Service Leave Program provides selected employees with a one-year paid sabbatical to work in a social service program. More information about diversity at this model organization can be found at www.xerox.com.

Thomas and Ely's perspective, is the opportunity to think and work in different ways. Assimilation and expectations of conformity stifle the creativity, innovation, and decision-making benefits that diversity can offer. Leaders must ensure that explicit rules and implicit norms provide all workers with the opportunity to be authentic in the workplace. Support for employee identity also comes through supporting the formation of affinity groups and using the feedback from these groups as valuable data for organizational diversity efforts. Affinity groups can also be helpful in identifying individuals for decision-making teams and task forces.

- *Create learning opportunities.* Diversity training is an important tool for moving organizations from being monolithic to being multicultural. However, diversity learning opportunities should occur frequently and not just be delivered by a formal trainer. Organizations must encourage employees to learn from their superiors, from their subordinates, and from one another. Companies must also value the learning that takes place outside of organizational boundaries. For example, organizations that encourage volunteerism among their employees not only spread good will within their community, they also provide their employees with the opportunities to work alongside or under individuals who may be different from themselves. Volunteer and community-oriented opportunities can also create valuable opportunities for self-exploration.

Diversity requires individuals and organizations to think differently and to challenge old assumptions, norms, and behaviors. I hope the lessons in this journey will enable you to challenge old assumptions and beliefs that resist diversity in your workplace so that you can be a diversity leader.

 InfoTrac College Edition

Be sure to log on to InfoTrac College Edition and search for additional readings on topics of interest to you.

References

Abdel-Halim, A. A. (1981). Effects of job stress–job design–technology interaction on employee work satisfaction. *Academy of Management Journal, 24,* 260–273.

Age Discrimination in Employment Act of 1967 (29 U.S.C. 631).

Allport, G. W. (1954). *The Nature of Prejudice.* Reading, MA: Addison-Wesley.

American Association of University Professors, Committee on the Status of Women in the Academic Professions. (2002). Faculty salary and faculty distribution fact sheet 2000–2001. www.aaup.org.

American Council on Education (ACE), Higher Education and National Affairs Office. (2000). More women serve as college presidents, ACE survey shows. www.acenet.edu.

American Psychological Association. (1996). Affirmative action: Who benefits? *American Psychologist, 45,* 200–207.

Americans with Disabilities Act of 1990 (42 U.S.C. 12101).

Anfuso, D. (1995). Diversity keeps newspaper up with the times. *Personnel Journal, 74,* 30–41.

Anonymous. (2000, Spring). Understanding dominance and subordination: One White man's experience. *Diversity Factor,* 8–12.

Arana, M. (2001). The elusive Hispanic/Latino(a) identity. *Nieman Reports, 55,* 8–10.

Ashford, S. J., & Black, J. S. (1996). Proactivity during organizational entry. *Journal of Applied Psychology, 81*(2), 199–214.

Avery, D. R. (2003). Reactions to diversity in recruitment advertising: Are differences Black and White? *Journal of Applied Psychology, 88*(4), 672–679.

Avery, D. R., Hernandez, M., & Hebl, M. R. (2004). Who's watching the race? Racial salience in recruitment advertising. *Journal of Applied Social Psychology, 34*(1), 146–161.

Backhaus, K. B., Stone, B. A., & Heiner, K. (2002). Exploring the relationship between corporate social performance and employer attractiveness. *Business and Society, 41,* 292–318.

Bandura, A. (1982). Self-efficacy mechanism in human agency. *American Psychologist, 37,* 122–147.

Barber, A. E. (1998). *Recruiting employees: Individual and organizational perspectives.* Thousand Oaks, CA: Sage.

Barnett, R. C., & Hyde, J. S. (2001). Women, men, work, and family. *American Psychologist, 56,* 781–796.

Bassman, E., & London, M. (1993). Abusive managerial behaviour. *Leadership & Organizational Development Journal, 14*(2), 18–24.

Beehr, T. A., & Newman, J. E. (1978). Job stress, employee health, and organizational effectiveness: A facet analysis, model, and literature review. *Personnel Psychology, 31*(4), 665–699.

Bell, E. L. (1990). The bicultural life experience of career-oriented black women. *Journal of Organizational Behavior, 11,* 459–477.

Bell, E., & Nkomo, S. M. (2001). *Our separate ways: Black and white women and the struggle for professional identity.* Cambridge, MA: Harvard Business School Press.

Bell, M. P., Mclaughlin, M. E., & Sequeira, J. M. (2002). Discrimination, harassment, and the glass ceiling: Women executives as change agents. *Journal of Business Ethics, 37,* 65–76.

Berry, J. W. (1984). Cultural relations in plural society: Alternatives to segregation and their sociopsychological implications. In N. Miller & M. Brewer (Eds.), *Groups in contact.* New York: Academic Press.

Bhagat, R. S. (1983). The effects of stressful life events on individual performance effectiveness and work adjustment processes within organization settings: A research model. *Academy of Managemen Review, 8,* 660–671.

Blake, S. D. (1999). At the crossroads of race and gender: Lessons from the mentoring experiences of professional Black women. In A. J. Murrell, F. J. Crosby, & R. J. Ely (Eds.), *Mentoring dilemmas: Developmental relationships within multicultural organizations,* 83–104. Mahwah, NJ: Lawrence Erlbaum.

Blake-Beard, S. D. (2001). Taking a hard look at formal mentoring programs: A consideration of potential challenges facing women. *Journal of Management Development, 20,* 331–346.

Block, C. J., Roberson, L., & Neuger, D. A. (1995). White racial identity theory: A framework for understanding reactions toward interracial situations in organizations. *Journal of Vocational Behavior, 46,* 71–88.

Bowers, C. A., Pharmer, J. A., & Salas, E. (2000). When member homogeneity is needed in work teams. *Small Group Research, 31*(3), 305-327.

Bowman, P. J. (1991). Organizational psychology: African-American perspectives. In R. L. Jones (Ed.) *Black psychology,* 509–531. Berkeley, CA: Cobb and Henry.

Breaugh, J. A., & Starke, M. (2000). Research on employee recruitment: So many studies, so many remaining questions. *Journal of Management, 26,* 405–434.

Brewer, M. B., & Miller, N. (1996). *Intergroup relations.* Pacific Grove, CA: Brooks/Cole.

Brickson, S. (2000). The impact of identity orientation individual and organizational outcomes in demographically diverse settings. *Academy of Management Review, 25,* 82–101.

Brown, C. S. (2003). U.S. Labor Department launches Latino safety program. www.diversityinc.com [accessed on August 27, 2003].

Business–Higher Education Forum. (2002). Investing in People: Developing all of American's talent on campus and in the workplace. Washington, DC: Business-Higher Education Forum.

Butler, D., & Geis, F. L. (1990). Nonverbal affect responses to male and female leader: Implications for leadership evaluations. *Journal of Personality and Social Psychology, 58,* 48–59.

Button, S. B. (2001). Organizational efforts to affirm sexual diversity: A cross-level examination. *Journal of Applied Psychology, 86,* 17–28.

Cahoon, A., & Rowney, J. (1984). Sex differences in occupational stress among managers. R. J. Burke (Ed.), *Current issues in occupational stress: Research and intervention.* Downsview, ON: Faculty of Administrative Studies, York University.

Caldwell, D. F., & Spivey, W. A. (1983). The relationship between recruiting source and employee success: An analysis by race. *Personnel Psychology, 36,* 67–72.

Capowski, G. (1997). Dealing with the labor shortage from the inside out. *HR Focus, 74,* 2.

Carter, R. T., & Parks, E. E. (1996). Womanist identity and mental health. *Journal of Counseling and Development, 74,* 484–489.

Cascio, W. F. (2003) *Managing human resources: Productivity, quality of work life, profits* (6th ed.) Boston: McGraw-Hill Irwin.

Chambers, V. (2003). *Having it all? Black women and success.* New York: Doubleday.

Chao, G. G., O'Leary-Kelly, A. M., Wolf, S., Klein, H. J., & Gardner, P. D. (1994). Organizational socialization: Its content and consequences. *Journal of Applied Psychology, 79,* 730–743.

Chemers, M. M., & Murphy, S. E. (1995). Leadership and diversity in groups and organizations. In M. M. Chemers, S. Oskamp, & M. A. Costanzo (Eds.), *Diversity in organizations: New perspectives for a changing workplace,* 157–190. Thousand Oaks, CA: Sage.

Chrobot-Mason, D. (In press). Developing multicultural competence for managers: Same old leadership skills or something new? *Psychologist–Manager Journal.*

Chrobot-Mason, D. L., & Ruderman, M. (2004). Leadership in a diverse workplace. In M. Stockdale & F. Crosby (Eds.), *The psychology and management of workplace diversity,* 100–121. Oxford, UK: Blackwell.

Chrobot-Mason, D. L., & Thomas, K. M. (2002). Minority employees in majority organizations: The intersection of individual and organizational racial identity in the workplace. *Human Resource Development Review, 1,* 323–344.

Chrobot-Mason, D. L. (2004). Managing racial differences: The role of majority managers' ethnic identity development on minority employee perceptions of support. *Group and Organization Management, 29,* 5–31.

Church, A. H. (1995). Diversity in workgroup settings: A case study. *Leadership and Organization Development Journal, 1,* 3–9.

Civil Rights Act of 1991 (42 U.S.C. 1981A).

Clark, R., Anderson, N. B., Clark, V. R., & Williams, D. R. (1999). Racism as a stressor for African Americans. *American Psychologist, 54*(10), 805–816.

Cokley, K., Dreher, G. F., & Stockdale, M. S. (2004). Toward the inclusiveness and career success of African Americans in the workplace. In M. Stockdale & F. Crosby (Eds.), *The psychology and management of workplace diversity,* 168–190. Malden, MA: Blackwell.

Cole, Y. (2002). How to market yourself as a diversity-conscious professional. www.diversityinc. com.

Collins, P. M., Kamya, H. A., & Tourse, R. W. (1997). Questions of racial diversity and mentorship: An empirical exploration. *Social Work, 42,* 145–152.

Colquitt, J. A., Conlon, D. E., Wesson, M. J., Porter, C. O., & Ng, K. Y. (2001). Justice at the millennium: A meta-analytic review of 25 years of organizational justice research. *Journal of Applied Psychology, 85,* 678–707.

Connecticut v. Teal. (1982). 457 US 440.

Cooper, C., & Thompson, C. E. (1997). Managing corporate racial diversity. In Carter & Thompson (Eds.), *Racial identity theory: Implications for individuals, groups, and organizations.* New York: LEA.

Corson, D. (2000). Emancipatory leadership. *International Journal of Leadership in Education, 3,* 93–120.

Cox, T. (1991). The multicultural organization. *Academy of Management Executive, 5,* 34–48.

Cox, T. (1994). *Cultural diversity in organizations: Theory, research, and practice.* San Francisco: Berrett-Kohler.

Cox, T. (2002). Taking diversity to the next level. *Executive Excellence, 19,* 19.

Cox, T., & Beale, R. L. (1997). *Developing competency to manage diversity: Readings, cases, and activities.* San Francisco: Berrett-Kohler.

Cox, T., & Nkomo, S. M. (1991). A race and gender-group analysis of the early career experience of MBAs. *Work and Occupations, 18,* 431–446.

Crant, J. M. (2000). Proactive behavior in organizations. *Journal of Management, 26*(3), 435–462.

Crosby, F. J., Iyer, A., Clayton, S., & Downing, R. A. (2003). Affirmative action: Psychological data and the policy debates. *American Psychologist, 58,* 93–115.

Cross, E. Y., & Jenkins, B. (1999). Developing leadership for diversity. *Diversity Factor, 8*(1), 12–14.

Cross, W. E., Jr. (1991). *Shades of black: Diversity in African-American identity*. Philadelphia: Temple University Press.

Dass, P., & Parker, B. (1999). Strategies for managing human resource diversity: From resistance to learning. *Academy of Management Executive, 13,* 68–80.

Davidson, M., & Cooper, C. (1983). *Stress and the woman manager.* New York: St. Martin's.

Davidson, M. N. (2002). Know thine adversary: The impact of race on styles of dealing with conflict. *Sex Roles, 45,* 259–276.

Day, D. V. (2000). Leadership development: A review in context. *Leadership Quarterly, 11,* 581–613.

Day, L. E. (1995). The pitfalls of diversity training. *Training & Development, 49,* 24–29.

Day, N. E. & Schoenrade, P. (2000). The relationship among reported disclosure of sexual orientation, anti-discrimination policies, top management support and work attitudes of gay and lesbian employees. *Personnel Review, 29,* 346–363.

Deal, T. E., & Kennedy, A. A. (2000). *Corporate cultures.* New York: Perseus.

DeCarlo, D. T., & Gruenfield, D. H. (1989). *Stress in the American workplace: Alternatives for the working wounded.* Fort Washington: LRP.

DeFrank, R. S., & Ivancevich, J. M. (1998). Stress on the job: An executive update. *Academy of Management Executive, 12(3),* 55–66.

Delaney, J. T., & Huselid, M. A. (1996). The impact of human resource management practices on perceptions of organizational performance. *Academy of Management Journal, 39,* 949–969.

Den Hartog, D. N., & Koopman, P. L. (2001). Leadership in organizations. In N. Anderson, D. S. Ones, H. K. Sinangil, & C. Viswesvaran (Eds.), *Handbook of industrial, work, and organizational psychology,* 166–187. Thousand Oaks, CA: Sage.

Dipboye, R. L., Smith, C. S., & Howell, W. C. (1994). *Understanding industrial and organizational psychology: An integrated approach.* Fort Worth, TX: Harcourt Brace and Company.

Doverspike, D., Taylor, M. A., Shultz, K. S., & McKay, P. F. (2000). Responding to the challenge of a changing workforce: Recruiting nontraditional demographic groups. *Public Personnel Management, 29,* 445–459.

Dovidio, J. F., & Gaertner, S. L. (2000). Aversive racism and selection decisions: 1989–1999. *Psychological Science, 11,* 315–319.

Dreher, G. F., & Ash, R. A. (1990). A comparative study of mentoring among men and women in managerial, professional, and technical positions. *Journal of Applied Psychology, 75,* 539–546.

Eagly, A. H., & Carli, L. L. (2003). The female leadership advantage: An evaluation of the evidence. *Leadership Quarterly, 14,* 807–834.

Edmondson, E. L. J., & Nkomo, S. M. (2001). *Our separate ways: Black and white women and the struggle for professional identity.* Boston: Harvard Business School Press.

Elmes, M., & Connelley, D. L. (1997). Dreams of diversity and the realities of intergroup relations in organizations. In P. Prasad, A. J. Mills, M. Elmes, & A. Prasad (Eds.), *Managing the organizational melting pot: Dilemmas of workplace diversity,* 148–170. Thousand Oaks, CA: Sage

Ely, R. J., & Thomas, D. A. (2001). Cultural diversity at work: The effects of diversity perspectives on work group processes and outcomes. *Administrative Science Quarterly, 46,* 229–273.

Equal Employment Opportunity Commission: Uniform Guidelines on Employee Selection Procedures (29 C.F.R. 1607).

Ernst, S., & Degroat, T. J. (2000). Altered photo creates diverse illusion at U. of Wisconsin. www.diversityinc.com, accessed Jan. 9, 2001.

Executive Order 11246 of 1965 (3 C.F.R Section 167).

Eyring, A., & Stead, B. A. (1998). Shattering the glass ceiling: Some successful corporate practices. *Journal of Business Ethics, 17,* 245–251.

Feldman, D. C. (1991). Socialization, resocialization, and training: Reframing the research agenda. In I. L. Goldstein & Associates (Eds.), *Training and development in organizations,* 376–416. San Francisco: Jossey-Bass.

Ferdman, B. M., & Brody, S. E. (1996). Models of diversity training. In D. Landis & R. S. Bhagat (Eds.), *Handbook of intercultural training,* 282–303. Thousand Oaks, CA: Sage.

Ferdman, B. M. (1995). Cultural diversity and identity in organizations: Bridging the gap between group differences and individual uniqueness. In M. M. Chemers, S. Oskamp, & M. A. Costanzo (Eds.), *Diversity in organizations: New perspectives for a changing workplace,* 37–61. Thousand Oaks, CA: Sage.

Fernald, J. L. (1995). Interpersonal heterosexism. In B. Lott & D. Maluso (Eds.), *The social psychology of interpersonal discrimination,* 80–117. New York: The Guilford Press.

Fitzgerald, L. F., Hulin, C. L., & Drasgow, F. (1994). The antecedents and consequences of sexual harassment in organizations: An integrated model. In G. P. Keita & J. J. Hurrell (Eds.). *Job stress in a changing workforce,* 55–74. Washington, DC: APA.

Fletcher, S., & Kaplan, M. (2000, fall). The diversity change process: Integrating sexual orientation. *Diversity Factor,* 34–38.

Fontana, D. (1989). *Managing stress.* London: British Psychological Society.

Francois, V. G. (March 20, 2000). Employee input key to Mercedes-Benz diversity training. www.diversityinc.com.

French, W. L., & Bell, C. H. (1999). *Organization development: Behavioral science interventions for organization improvement.* Upper Saddle River, NJ: Prentice-Hall.

Friedman, R. A., & Davidson, M. N. (2001). Managing diversity and second-order conflict. *International Journal of Conflict Management, 12,* 132–153.

Frost, D. D. (1999). Review worst diversity practices to learn from others' mistakes. *HR Focus, 76,* 11–12.

Gatewood, R. D., & Feild, H. S. (2001). *Human resource selection.* Orlando, FL: Harcourt.

Giscombe, K., & Mattis, M. C. (2002). Leveling the playing field for women of color in corporate management: Is the business case enough? *Journal of Business Ethics, 37*(1), 103–119.

Glick, P., & Fiske, S. T. (2001). An ambivalent alliance: Hostile and benevolent sexism as complementary justifications for gender inequality. *American Psychologist, 6,* 109–118.

Glowinski, S. P., & Cooper, C. L. (1987). Managers and professionals in business/industrial settings: The research evidence. In J. M. Ivancevich & D. C. Ganster (Eds.), *Job stress: From theory to suggestion,* 177–193. New York. Hawthorne Press.

Gold, M. E. (2001). *An introduction to the law of employment discrimination.* Ithaca, NY: IRL Press/Cornell University Press.

Goldstein, I. L., & Ford, J. K. (2002). *Training in organizations* (4th ed.). Belmont, CA: Wadsworth Group.

Goldstein, I. L., & Gilliam, P. (1990). Training system issues in the year 2000. *American Psychologist, 45,* 134–143.

Gomez-Mejia, L. R., Balkin, D. B., & Cardy, R. (1994). *Managing human resources.* New York: Simon & Schuster Trade.

Griggs v. Duke Power Company. (1971). 401 US 424.

Gupta, N., & Beehr, T. A. (1979). Job stress and employee behaviors. *Organizational Behavior and Human Performance, 23,* 373–387.

Gutierres, S. E., Saenz, D. S., & Green, B. L. (1994). Job stress and health outcomes among White and Hispanic employees: A test of the person–environment fit model. In G. P. Keita & J. J. Hurrell (Eds.), *Job stress in a changing workforce,* 107–126. Washington, DC: APA

Gutman, A. (2000). *EEO law and personnel practices.* Thousand Oaks, CA: Sage.

Gutman, A. (2003). On the legal front: The *Grutter, Gratz,* & *Costa* Rulings. *Industrial-Organizational Psychologist, 41*(2), 117–127.

Guzzo, R. A., & Shea, G. P. (1992) Group performance and intergroup relations in organizations. In M. D. Dunnette & L. Hough (Eds.), *Handbook of industrial and organizational psychology* (2nd ed., Vol. 3, 269–313). Palo Alto, CA: Consulting Psychologists Press.

Hall, D. T. (1986). Individual and organizational career development in changing times. In D. T. Hall (Eds.), *Career development in organizations.* San Francisco: Jossey-Bass.

Hammonds, K. H. (2000, July). Difference is power. http://www.fastcompany.com/online/36/power.html, accessed March 24, 2004.

Hansen, N. D., Pepitone-Arreola-Rockwell, F., & Green, A. F. (2000). Multicultural competence: Criteria and case examples. *Professional Psychology: Research and Practice, 31, 652–660.*

Harquil, C. V., & Cox, T. (1994). Organizational culture and acculturation. In T. Cox (Ed.), *Cultural diversity in organizations: Theory, research, and practice,* 161–176. San Francisco: Berrett Kohler.

Harris, M. M., & Fink, L. S. (1987). A field study of applicant reactions to employment opportunities: Does the recruiter make a difference? *Personnel Psychology, 40, 765–783.*

Harrison, D. A., Price, K. H., & Bell, M. P. (1998). Beyond relational demography: Time and the effects of surface- and deep-level diversity on work group cohesion. *Academy of Management Journal, 41, 96–107.*

Hays-Thomas, R. (2004). Why now? The contemporary focus on managing diversity. In M. Stockdale & F. Crosby (Eds.), *The psychology and management of workplace diversity,* 3–30. Oxford, UK: Blackwell.

Heilman, M., & Block, C. (1992). Presumed incompetent? Stigmatization affirmative action efforts. *Journal of Applied Psychology, 77, 536–544.*

Helms, J. E. (1990). *Black and white racial identity.* New York: Greenwood.

Helms, J. E., & Piper, R. E. (1994). Implications of racial identity theory for vocational psychology. *Journal of Vocational Psychology, 44, 124–138.*

Hewlett, S. A. (2002). Executive women and the myth of having it all. *Harvard Business Review, 80(4), 66–73.*

Higgins, M. C., & Kram, K. E. (2001). Reconceptualizing mentoring at work: A developmental network perspective. *Academy of Management Review, 26, 264–288.*

Highhouse, S., Stierwalt, S. L., Bachiochi, P., Elder, A. E., & Fisher, G. (1999). Effects of advertised human resource management practices on attraction of African American applicants. *Personnel Psychology, 52, 425–442.*

Hinton, E. L. (2002) CEOs must take diversity seriously or suffer the consequences. www.diversityinc.com.

Holvino, E., Ferdman, B., & Merrill-Sands, D. (2004). Creating and sustaining diversity and inclusion in organizations: Strategies and approaches. In M. Stockdale & F. Crosby (Eds.), *The psychology and management of workplace diversity,* 245–276. Malden, MA.: Blackwell.

Honeycutt, T. L., & Rosen, B. (1997). Family-friendly human resource policies, salary levels, and salient identity as predictors of organizational attraction. *Journal of Vocational Behavior, 50, 271–290.*

House, J. S. (1974). Occupational stress and coronary heart disease: A review and theoretical integration. *Journal of Health and Social Behavior, 15(1), 12–27.*

Hurrell, J. J., Jr., Murphy, L. R., Sauter, S. L., & Cooper, C. L. (Eds.). (1988). *Occupational stress: Issues and developments in research.* New York: Taylor & Francis.

Ibarra, H. (1992). Homophily and differential returns: Sex differences in network structure and access in an advertising firm. *Administrative Science Quarterly, 37, 422–447.*

Ibarra, H. (1995). Race, opportunity, and diversity of social circles in managerial networks. *Academy of Management Journal, 38, 673–701.*

Ibarra, H. (1999). Provisional selves: Experimenting with image and identity in professional adaptation. *Administrative Science Quarterly, 44, 764–791.*

Immigration Reform and Control Act of 1986 (8 U.S.C. 1324).

Ivancevich, J. M., & Matteson, M. T. (1980*). Stress and work.* Glenview, IL: Scott, Foresman, and Co.

Jackson, S. E., & Ruderman, M. N. (1995). Introduction: Perspectives for understanding diverse work teams. In S. E. Jackson, M. N. Ruderman (Eds.), *Diversity in work teams: Research paradigms for a changing workplace.* Washington, DC: American Psychological Association.

Jackson, S. E., & Joshi, A. (2001). Research on domestic and international diversity in organizations: A merger that works? In N. Anderson, D. S. Ones, H. K. Sinangil, & C. Viswesvaran (Eds.), *Handbook of industrial work, and organizational psychology,* Vol. 2, 206–222. London, UK: Sage.

Jackson, S. E., Stone, V. K., & Alvarez, E. B. (1993). Socialization amidst diversity: Impact of demographics on work team oldtimers and newcomers. In L. L. Cummings & B. M. Staw (Eds.), *Research in organizational behavior.* Greenwich, CT: JAI Press.

Jacobson, J. (2001). In brochures, what you see isn't necessarily what you get. *Chronicle of Higher Education, 47,* A41–A42.

Jacques, R. (1997). The unbearable whiteness of being: Reflections of a pale, stale male. In P. Prasad, A. Mills, M. Elmes, & A. Prasad (Eds.). *Managing the organizational melting pot: Dilemmas of workplace diversity,* 80–106. Thousand Oaks, CA: Sage.

James, K. (1994). Social identity: Work stress, and minority workers' health. In G. P. Keita & J. J. Hurrell (Eds.), *Job stress in a changing workforce,* 127–146. Washington, DC: APA.

James, S. (1994). John Henryism and the health of African-Americans. *Culture, Medicine, and Psychiatry, 6,* 259–278.

Jehn, K. A. (1995). A multimethod examination of the benefits and detriments of intragroup conflict. *Administrative Science Quarterly, 42*(2), 256–282.

Jehn, K. A., Northcraft, G. B., & Neale, M. A. (1999). Why differences make a difference: A field study of diversity, conflict, and performance in workgroups. *Administrative Science Quarterly, 44*(4), 741–763.

Jex, S. M. (2002). *Organizational psychology: A scientist–practitioner approach.* New York: John Wiley & Sons.

Jick, T. D., & Micz, L. F. (1985). Sex differences in work stress. *Academy of Management Review, 10,* 408–420.

Johnson, A. D. (2003–2004, Dec/Jan). Can you wear your diversity at work? Or could cornrows and saris sabotage your career? *Diversity Inc, 2,* 48–52.

Johnston, W., & Packer, A. (1987). *Workforce 2000: Work and workers for the twenty-first century.* Indianapolis: Hudson Institute.

Jones, M. (2002). *Social psychology of prejudice.* Upper Saddle River, NJ: Prentice-Hall.

Kanter, R. (1977). *Men and women of the corporation.* New York: Basic Books.

Kanter, R. B. (1993). *Men and women of the corporation.* New York: Basic Books.

Keita, G. P., & Jones, J. J. (Eds.). (1994). *Job stress in a changing workforce.* Washington, DC: American Psychological Association.

Kelly, K., & Streeter, D. (1992). The roles of gender in organizations. *Issues, Theory and Practice in Industrial Organizational Psychology, 13,* 285–337.

Kirkland, S. E., & Regan, A. M. (1997). Organizational racial identity training. In R. T. Carter & C. E. Thompson (Eds.), *Racial identity theory: Implications for individuals, groups, and organizations,* 159–176. New York: Lawrence Erlbaum & Associates.

Knouse, S. B., & Webb, S. C. (2001). Virtual networking for women and minorities. *Career Development International, 6,* 226–228.

Kram, K. (1985). *Mentoring at work: Developmental relationships in Glenview: Organizational life.* Glenview, IL: Scott, Foresman.

Kram, K. E., & Hall, D. T. (1996). Mentoring in a context of diversity and turbulence. In E. E. Kossek & S. A. Lobel (Eds.), *Managing diversity: Human resource strategies for transforming the workplace,* 108–136. Cambridge, MA: Blackwell.

Krumm, D. (2001). *Psychology at work: An introduction to industrial/organizational psychology.* Fort Worth, TX: Worth Publishers.

Laabs, J. (1999). Overload. *Workforce, 78*(1), 30–37.

Lau, D. C., & Murnighan, J. K. (1998). Demographic diversity and faultlines: The compositional dynamics of organizational groups. *Academy of Management Review, 22,* 325–340.

Liden, R. C., & Parsons, C. K. (1986). A field study of job applicant interview perceptions, alternative opportunities, and demographic characteristics. *Personnel Psychology, 39,* 109–123.

Lopez, E. M. (2003–2004, Dec/Jan). The art of giving it all away: Tim Gill, from entrepreneur to philanthropist. *DiversityInc, 2,* 67–68.

Lott, B., & Maluso, D. (1995). Introduction: Framing the questions. In B. Lott & D. Maluso (Eds.), *The social psychology of interpersonal discrimination,* 1–11. New York: The Guilford Press.

Louis, M. R. (1980). Surprise and sense making: What newcomers experience in entering unfamiliar organizational settings. *Administrative Science Quarterly, 25,* 226–251.

Lubensky, M. E., Holland, S. L., Wiethoff, C., & Crosby, F. J. (2004). Diversity and sexual orientation: Including and valuing sexual minorities in the workplace. In M. Stockdale & F. Crosby (Eds.), *The Psychology and Management of Workplace Diversity,* 206–223. Malden, MA: Blackwell.

Luce, R. A., Barber, A. E., & Hillman, A. J. (2001). Good deeds and misdeeds: A mediated model of the effect of corporate social performance on organizational attractiveness. *Business and Society,* 40, 397–415.

Lyness, K. S., & Thompson, D. E. (2000). Climbing the corporate ladder: Do female and male executives follow the same route? *Journal of Applied Psychology, 85* (1), 86–101.

Maier, M. (1997, Summer). Invisible privilege: What White men don't see. *Diversity Factor,* 28–33.

Marsella, A. J. (1994). Women and well-being in an ethnoculturally pluralistic society: Conceptual and methodological issues. In G. P. Keita & J. J. Hurrell (Eds.), *Job stress in a changing workforce,* 147–160. Washington, DC: APA.

Matteson, M. T., & Ivancevich, J. M. (1987). *Controlling work stress.* San Francisco: Jossey-Bass.

Mauer, S. D., Howe, V., & Lee, T. W. (1992). Organizational recruiting as marketing management: An interdisciplinary study of engineering graduates. *Personnel Psychology, 45,* 807–833.

Maume, D. J. (1999). Glass ceilings and glass escalators: Occupational segregation and race and sex differences in managerial promotions. *Work and Occupations, 26,* 483–509.

McLeod, P. L., Lobel, S. A., & Cox, T., Jr. (1996). Ethnic diversity and creativity in small groups. *Small Group Research,* 27(2), 248–264.

McDaniel, R. R., & Walls, M. E. (1997). Diversity as a management strategy for organizations: A view through the lenses of chaos and quantum theories. *Journal of Management Inquiry, 6,* 363–375.

McDonald, L. M., & Korabik, K. (1991). Sources of stress and ways of coping among male and female managers. *Journal of Social Behavior and Personality, 6,* 185–198.

McDonnell Douglas Corp. v. Green. (1973). 411 US 792.

McGuire, G. M. (1999). Do race and sex affect employees' access to and help from mentors? Insights from the study of a large corporation. In A. J. Murrell, F. J. Crosby & R. J. Ely (Eds.), *Mentoring dilemmas: Developmental relationships within multicultural organizations,* 105–120. Mahwah, NJ: Lawrence Erlbaum.

McIntosh, P. (1993). White privilege and male privilege: A personal account of coming to see correspondences through work in women's studies. In A. Minas (Ed.), *Gender basics.* San Francisco: Wadsworth.

Mendez-Russell, A. (2001). Diversity leadership. *Executive Excellence, 18,* 28.

Milliken, F. J., & Martins, L. L. (1996). Searching for common threads: Understanding the multiple effects of diversity in organizational groups. *Academy of Management Review, 21,* 402–433.

Moran, J. J. (1998). *Employment law: New challenges in the business environment.* Upper Saddle River, NJ: Prentice-Hall.

Moreland, R. L., & Levine, J. M. (2002). Socialization and trust in work groups. *Group Processes & Intergroup Relations,* 5(3), 185–202.

Morrison, A. M. (1992). *The new leaders: Guidelines on leadership diversity in America*. San Francisco: Jossey-Bass.

Morrison, A. M., White, R. P., Van Velsor, E., & The Center for Creative Leadership. (1992). *Breaking the glass ceiling: Can women reach the top of America's largest corporations?* (2nd ed.). Reading, MA: Addison-Wesley Publishing.

Morrison, E. W. (1993). Longitudinal study of the effects of information seeking on newcomer socialization. *Journal of Applied Psychology, 78,* 173–183.

Morrison, E. W. (2002). Newcomers' relationships: The role of social network ties during socialization. *Academy of Management Journal, 45*(6), 1149–1160.

Mueller, N. L. (1996). Wisconsin Power and Light's model diversity program. *Training & Development, 50,* 57–60.

Murphy, B. C. (2001). Anti-gay/lesbian violence in the United States. In D. J. Christie, R. V. Wagner, & D. D. Winter (Eds.). *Peace, conflict, and violence: Peace psychology for the 21st century,* 28–38. Upper Saddle River, NJ: Prentice-Hall.

National Institute of Occupational Safety and Health (NIOSH) (1999). *Stresss . . . At Work.* Cincinnati, OH: National Institute of Occupational Safety and Health.

Nelson, D. L., & Burke, R. J. (2000). Women executives: Health, stress, and success. *Academy of Management Executive, 14,* 107–121.

Nelson, D. L., & Hitt, M. A. (1992). Employed women and stress. In J. C. Quick, L. R. Murphy, & J. J. Hurrell, Jr. (Eds.). *Stress & well-being at work: Assessments and interventions for occupational mental-health.* Washington, DC: American Psychological Association.

Nelson, D. L., & Quick, J. C. (1985). Professional women: Are distress and disease inevitable? *Academy of Management Review, 10*(2), 206–218.

Nelson, D. L., Quick, J. C., & Hitt, J. C. (1989). Men and women of the personnel profession: Some differences and similarities in their stress. *Stress Medicine, 5,* 145–152.

Nieva, V. F., & Gutek, B. A (1981). *Women and work: A psychological perspective.* New York: Praeger.

Nkomo, S. M., & Cox, T., Jr. (1996). Diverse identities in organizations. In S. R. Clegg, C. Hardy, & W. R. Nord (Eds.), *Handbook of organization studies,* 338–356. London: Sage.

Northwestern National Life (1991). *Employee burnout: American's newest epidemic.* Minneapolis, MN: Northwestern National Life Insurance Company.

Offermann, L. R., & Phan, L. U. (2002). Cultural intelligent leadership for a diverse world. In R. Riggio, S. E. Murphy, F. J. Pirozzolo (Eds.). *Multiple intelligences and leadership,* 187–214. Mahwah, NJ: LEA.

Ohlott, P. J., Chrobot-Mason, D., Dalton, M., Deal, J. J., & Hoppe, M. (2003). When identity groups collide: Leadership strategy as a moderator of identity-based conflict at work. Paper presented at the Annual Meeting of the Academy of Management, Seattle, WA.

Ohlott, P. J., Ruderman, M. N., & McCauley, C. D. (1994). Gender differences in managers' developmental job experiences. *Academy of Management Journal, 37,* 46–67.

Parker, P. S., & Ogilvie, D. (1996). Gender, culture, and leadership: Toward a culturally distinct model of African-American women executives' leadership strategies. *Leadership Quarterly, 7,* 189–214.

Pelled, L. H., Eisenhardt, K. M., & Xin, K. R. (1999). Exploring the black box: An analysis of work group diversity, conflict, and performance. *Administrative Science Quarterly, 44,* 1–28.

Perkins, L. A., & Thomas, K. M (2002). The spillover effects of demography on organizational efforts to recruit. Presentation delivered at the Society for Industrial-Organizational Psychology, Toronto, Canada.

Perkins, L. A., Thomas, K. M., & Taylor, G. A. (2000). Advertising and recruitment: Marketing to minorities. *Psychology and Marketing, 17,* 235–255.

Pettigrew, T. F. (1979). The ultimate attribution error: Extending Allport's cognitive analysis of prejudice. *Personality and Social Psychology Bulletin, 5*(4), 461–476.

Pettigrew, T. F., & Martin, J. (1987). Shaping the organizational context for Black American inclusion. *Journal of Social Issues, 43,* 41–78.

Pharr, S. (1988). The common elements of oppressions. *Homophobia: A weapon of sexism*, 53–64. Little Rock, AR: Chardon.

Phinney, J. (1996). When we talk about American ethnic groups, what do we mean? *American Psychologist, 51*, 918–927.

Pittenger, K. (1996). Networking strategies for minority managers. *Academy of Management Executive, 10*, 62–63.

Powell, G. N. (1984). Effects of job attributes and recruiting practices on applicant decisions: A comparison. *Personnel Psychology, 37*, 721–732.

Powell, G. N. (1998). The simultaneous pursuit of Person–Organization fit and diversity. *Organizational dynamics, 26*, 50–61.

Powell, G. N., & Butterfield, D. A. (1994). Investigating the "glass ceiling" phenomenon: An empirical study of actual promotions to top management. *Academy of Management Journal, 37*, 68–86.

Powell, G. N., & Butterfield, D. A. (1997). Effect of race on promotions to top management in a federal department. *Academy of Management Journal, 40*, 112–128.

Powell-Kiran, J., Farley, J. A., & Geisinger, K. F. (1989). The relationship between recruiting source, applicant quality, and hire performance: An analysis by sex, ethnicity, and age. *Personnel Psychology, 42*, 293–308.

Proudford, K. L., & Smith, K. K. (2003). Group membership salience and the movement of conflict: Reconceptualizing the interaction among race, gender, and hierarchy. *Group and Organization Management, 28*, 18–44.

Proudford, K. L., & Thomas, K. M. (1999). Organizational outsiders within. *Journal of Career Development, 26*, 1–6.

Quick, J. C., & Quick, J. D. (1984). *Organizational stress and preventive management*. New York: McGraw-Hill.

Ragins, B. R., & Cornwell, J. M. (2001). Pink triangles: Antecedents and consequences of perceived workplace discrimination against gay and lesbian employees. *Journal of Applied Psychology, 86*, 1244–1266.

Ragins, B. R., & Cotton, J. L. (1991). Easier said than done: Gender differences in perceived barriers to gaining a mentor. *Academy of Management Journal, 34*, 939–951.

Ragins, B. R. (1997). Diversified mentoring relationships in organizations: A power perspective. *Academy of Management Review, 22*, 482–521.

Ragins, B. R., Townsend, B., & Mattis, M. (1998). Gender gap in the executive suite: CEOs and female executives report on breaking the glass ceiling. *Academy of Management Executive, 12*, 28–42.

Rahim, M. A., & Buntzman, G. F. (1991). Impression management and organizational conflict. In R. A. Giacalone & P. Rosenfeld (Eds.), *Applied impression management*, 157–176. Newbury Park, CA: Sage.

Regents of University of California v. Bakke. (1978). 438 US 265.

Rehabilitation Act of 1973 (29 U.S.C. 701).

Reid, B. A. (1994). Mentorship ensures equal opportunity. *Personnel Journal, 73*, 122–123.

Richeson, J. A., & Shelton, J. N. (2003). When prejudice does not pay: Effects of interracial contact on executive function. *Psychological Science, 14*, 287–290.

Riordan, C. M., & Shore, L. M. (1997). Demographic diversity and employee attitudes: An empirical examination of relational demography within work units. *Journal of Applied Psychology, 82*, 342–358.

Robbins, S. P. (1998). *Organizational behavior: Concepts, controversies, application*. Upper Saddle River, NJ: Prentice-Hall.

Roberson, L., Deitch, E. A., Brief, A. P., & Block, C. J. (2003). Stereotype threat and feedback seeking in the workplace. *Journal of Vocational Behavior, 62*, 176–188.

Roberson, L., Kulik, C. T., & Pepper, M. B. (2001). Designing effective diversity training: Influence of group composition and trainee experience. *Journal of Organizational Behavior, 22*, 871–885.

Rosenthal, R. (2002). Covert communication in classrooms, clinics, courtrooms, and cubicles. *American Psychologist, 57,* 839–849.

Rosin, H. M., & Korabik, K. (1991). Work place factors and female managers' attrition from organizations. *Journal of Occupational Psychology, 64,* 317–330.

Ross, L. (1977). The intuitive psychologist and his shortcomings: Distortions in the attrbibution process. In L. Berkowitz (ed.) *Advances in experimental social psychology,* vol. 10, 173–219. New York: Academic Press.

Rousseau, D. M. (1996). Changing the deal while keeping the people. *Academy of Management Executive, 10,* 50–61.

Rynes, S. L., & Miller, H. E. (1983). Recruiter and job influences on candidates for employment. *Journal of Applied Psychology, 68,* 146–154.

Rynes, S., & Rosen, B. (1995). A field survey of factors affecting the adoption and perceived success of diversity training. *Personnel Psychology, 48,* 247–270.

Sagrestano, L. M. (2004). Health implications of workplace diversity. In M. S. Stockdale & F. J. Crosby (Eds.), *The psychology and management of workplace diversity,* 122–144. UK: Blackwell.

Saks, A. M., & Ashforth, B. E. (1997). Organizational socialization: Making sense of the past and present as a prologue for the future. *Journal of Vocational Behavior, 51,* 234–279.

Sampson, E. E. (1999). *Dealing with difference: An introduction to the social psychology of prejudice.* Fort Worth, TX: Harcourt.

Schneider, B. (1983). An interactionist perspective on organizational effectiveness. In K. S. Cameron & D. A. Whetten (Eds.), *Organizational effectiveness: A comparison of multiple models,* 27–54. San Diego, CA: Academic.

Schneider, B. (1987). The people make the place. *Personnel Psychology, 40*(3), 437–456

Schneider, B., Goldstein, H. W., & Smith, D. B. (1995). The ASA framework: An update. *Personnel Psychology, 48,* 747–833.

Schneider, S. K., & Northcraft, G. B. (1999). Three social dilemmas of workforce diversity in organizations: A social identity perspective. *Human Relations, 52,* 1445–1467.

Schneider, B., Smith, D. B., Taylor, S., & Fleenor, J. (1998). Personality and organizations: A test of the homogeneity of personality hypothesis. *Journal of Applied Psychology, 83*(3), 462–470.

Schofield, J. W. (1986). Causes and consequences of the colorblind perspective. In J. Dovidio & S. Gaertner (Eds.), *Prejudice, discrimination, and racism,* 231–253. NY: Academic.

Schuler, R. S. (1980). Definition and conceptualization of stress in organizations. *Organizational Behavior and Human Performance, 25*(2), 184–215.

Selig Center for Economic Growth, Terry College of Business, University of Georgia (2002). *Georgia business and economic conditions, 62*(2), 1–27.

Sherif, M., Harvey, O. J., White, B. J., Hood, W. R., & Sherif, C. W. (1988). *The robbers cave experiment.* Middletown, CT: Wesleyan University Press.

Sims, R. R. (2002). *Organizational success through effective human resources management.* Westport, CT: Quorum Books.

Smith, E. M. (1985). Ethnic minorities: Life stress, social support, and mental health issues. *Counseling Psychologist, 13*(4), 537–579.

Stavraka, C. (2000, Oct. 11). Coke mandates diversity training for all U.S. workers. www.diversityinc.com.

Steele, C. M. (1997). A threat in the air: How stereotypes shape intellectual identity and performance. *American Psychologist, 52,* 613–629.

Steele, C. M., & Aronson, J. (1995). Stereotype threat and the intellectual test performance of African Americans. *Journal of Personality and Social Psychology, 69,* 797–811.

Stephan, W. G., & Stephan, C. W. (1985). Intergroup anxiety. *Journal of Social Issues, 41*(3), 157–175.

Sue, D. W. (1995). Multicultural organizational development: Implications for the counseling profession. In J. G. Ponterotto, J. M. Casas, L. A. Suzuki, & C. M. Alexander (Eds.), *Handbook of multicultural counseling*, 474–492. Thousand Oaks, CA: Sage.

Sue, D. W., Arredondo, P., & McDavis, R. J. (1992). Multicultural counseling competencies and standards: A call to the profession. *Journal of Multicultural Counseling and Development, 20*, 64–88.

Sue, D. W., Parham, T. A., & Santiago, G. B. (1998). The changing face of work in the United States: Implications for individual, institutional, and societal survival. *Cultural diversity and mental health, 4*, 153–164.

Tannen, D. (1990). *You just don't understand: Women and men in conversation.* New York: William Morrow.

Tajfel, H. (1981). *Human Groups and Social Categories: Studies in Social Psychology.* Cambridge: Cambridge University Press.

Tajfel, H., & Turner, J. C. (1979). An integrative theory of intergroup conflict. In W. G. Austin & S. Worchel (Eds.), *The social psychology of intergroup relations*, 33–47. Monterey, CA: Brooks/Cole.

Tajfel, H., & Turner, J. C. (1986). The social identity theory of intergroup behavior. In S. Worchel & W. G. Austin (Eds.), *Psychology of intergroup relations*, 7–24. Chicago: Nelson-Hall.

Tatum, B. D. (1999). *Why are all the Black kids sitting together in the cafeteria?* New York: Basic Books.

Taylor, M. S., & Bergmann, T. J. (1987). Organizational recruitment activities and applicants' reactions at different stages of the recruitment process. *Personnel Psychology, 40*, 261–285.

Thaler-Carter, R. E. (2001, June). Diversify your recruitment advertising. *HR Magazine*, 92–100.

Thomas, D. A. (1990). Racial dynamics in cross-race developmental relationships. *Journal of Organizational Behavior, 2*, 479–492.

Thomas, D. A. (2001). The truth about mentoring minorities: Race matters. *Harvard Business Review*, April, 98–107.

Thomas, D. A., & Ely, R. J. (1996, Sept.–Oct.). Making differences matter: A new paradigm for managing diversity. *Harvard Business Review*, 79–90.

Thomas. D. A., & Gabarro, J. J. (1999). *Breaking through: The making of minority executives in corporate America.* Boston, MA: Harvard Business School Press.

Thomas, K. M. (1998). Psychological readiness for multicultural leadership. *Management Development Forum, 1*, 99–112.

Thomas, K. M., & Chrobot-Mason, D. (In press). Group level explanations of workplace discrimination. In R. Diboye & A. Colella (Eds.), *The psychological and organizational bases of discrimination at work.* San Francisco: Jossey-Bass.

Thomas, K. M., & Landau, H. I. (2002). Fairness and justice from an I/O perspective. [ERIC Clearinghouse ACVE, CEO85498]

Thomas, K. M., Mack, D. A., & Montagliani, A. (2004). The arguments against diversity: Are they valid? In M. Stockdale & F. Crosby (Eds.), *The psychology and management of workplace diversity*, 100–121. Oxford, UK: Blackwell.

Thomas, K. M., Phillips, L. D., & Brown, S. (1998). Redefining race in the workplace: Insights from ethnic identity theory. *Journal of Black Psychology, 24*, 76–92.

Thomas, K. M., Proudford, K. L., & Cader, J. (1999). Global outsiders within: Informal roles of women of colour. *International Review of Women and Leadership, 5*(2), 14–25.

Thomas, K. M., & Wise, P. G. (1999). Organizational attractiveness and individual differences: Are diverse applicants attracted by different factors? *Journal of Business and Psychology, 13*, 375–390.

Thompson, C. E., & Carter, R. T. (1997). An overview and elaboration of Helm's racial identity development theory. In C. E. Thompson & R. T. Carter (Eds.), *Racial identity theory: Applications to individual, group, and organizational interventions* (pp. 15–32). Mahwah, NJ: LEA.

Thompson, D. E., & Gooler, L. E. (1996). Capitalizing on the benefits of diversity through work-teams. In E. E. Kossek & S. A. Lobel (Eds.), *Managing diversity: Human resource strategies for transforming the workplace,* 392–437. Oxford, UK: Blackwell.

Title VII of the Civil Rights Act of 1964 (42 U.S.C. 2000e).

Tom, V. R. (1971). The role of personality and organizational images in the recruiting process. *Organizational Behavior and Human Performance, 6,* 573–592.

Triandis, H. C. (1995). A theoretical framework for the study of diversity. In M. M. Chemers, S. Oskamp, & M. A. Costanzo (Eds.), *Diversity in organizations: New perspectives for a changing workplace,* 11–36. Thousand Oaks, CA: Sage.

Tsui, A. S., & Gutek, B. A. (1999). *Demographic differences in organizations: Current research and future directions.* Lanham, MD: Lexington Books.

Tsui, A. S., & O'Reilly, C. A., III. (1989). Beyond simple demographic effects: The importance of relational demography in supervisor–subordinate dyads. *Academy of Management Journal, 32,* 402–423.

Tsui, A. S., Egan, T. D., & O'Reilly, C. A., III. (1992). Being different: Relational demography and organizational attachment. *Administrative Science Quarterly, 37,* 549–579.

Turban, D. B., & Dougherty, T. W. (1992). Influences of campus recruiting on applicant attraction to firms. *Academy of Management Journal, 35,* 739–765.

Turban, D. B., Forret, M. L., & Hendrickson, C. L. (1998). Applicant attraction to firms: Influences of organization reputation, job and organizational attributes, and recruiter behaviors. *Journal of Vocational Behavior, 52,* 24–44.

Turner, J. C. (1985). Social categorization and the self-concept: A self-cognitive theory of group behavior. In E. J. Lawler (Ed.), *Advances in group processes: Theory and research,* vol. 2, 77–121. Greenwich, CT: JAI.

Twomey, D. P. (2002). *Employment discrimination law: A manager's guide: Text and cases.* Cincinnati OH: West/Thomson Learning.

Van Maanen, J., & Schein, E. H. (1979). Toward a theory of organizational socialization. *Research in Organizational Behavior, 1,* 209–264.

Vietnam Era Veterans' Readjustment Assistance Act of 1974 (38 U.S.C. 2011).

Walters, K. L., & Simoni, J. M. (1993). Lesbian and gay male group identity attitudes and self-esteem: Implications for counseling. *Journal of Counseling Psychology, 40,* 94–99.

Wanberg, C. R., & Kammeyer-Mueller, J. D. (2000). Predictors and outcomes of proactivity in the socialization process. *Journal of Applied Psychology, 85,* 373–385.

Wards Cove Packing Co. v. Antonio. (1989). 490 US 642.

Watson v. Ft. Worth Bank & Trust. (1988). 487 US 977.

Watts, R. J., & Carter, R. T. (1991). Psychological aspects of racism in organizations. *Group and Organization Studies, 16,* 328–344.

Weiten, W. (2001). *Psychology: Themes and variations* (5th ed.). Belmont, CA: Wadsworth/Thomson Learning.

White, M. B. (1999). Organization 2005: New strategies at P & G. *Diversity Factor, 18,* 16–20.

Wildman, S. A., & Davis, A. D. (1996). Making systems of privilege visible. In S. M. Wildman (Ed.). *Privilege revealed: How invisible preference undermines America.* New York: NYU Press.

Williams, M., & Bauer, T. N. (1994). The effect of a managing diversity policy on organizational attractiveness. *Group and Organization Management, 19*(3), 295–308.

Williams, K. Y., & O'Reilly, C. A., III. (1998). Demography and diversity in organizations. *Research in Organizational Behavior, 20,* 77–140.

Winter, R. *Executive stress.* New York: McGraw-Hill.

Winters, M. (2002). Sustaining inclusion. *Executive Excellence, 19,* 11.

Word, C. O., Zanna, M. P., & Cooper, J. (1974). The nonverbal mediation of self-fulfilling prophecies in interracial interaction. *Journal of Experimental Social Psychology, 10,* 109–120.

Zachary, M. K. (1999). Discrimination laws provide protection to job applicants. *Supervision, 60*, 21–23.

Zeilberger, R. (2002). Deaths of Latino workers soar. www.diversityinc.com, accessed August 27, 2003.

Zimmer, M. J., Sullivan, C. A., Richards, R. F., & Calloway, D. A. (1997). *Cases and materials on employment discrimination*. New York: Aspen Law and Business.

Zunker, V. G. (1990). *Career counseling: Applied concepts of life planning* (3rd ed.). Pacific Grove, CA: Brooks/Cole.

Name Index

Subject Index

Note: page numbers in *italics* refer to figures and tables

Photo Credits